PROGRESS IN BEHAVIOR MODIFICATION

Volume 27

CONTRIBUTORS TO THIS VOLUME

Martin Agran

Maralyn Billings

Edward R. Christophersen

Michael H. Epstein

Michael D. Franzen

Carolyn Hughes

Matthew E. Lambert

Ronald C. Martella

Ellen Olinger

Patricia C. Purvis

PROGRESS IN BEHAVIOR

MODIFICATION

EDITED BY

Michel Hersen

University of Pittsburgh School of Medicine
Pittsburgh, Pennsylvania

Richard M. Eisler

Department of Psychology
Virginia Polytechnic Institute and State University
Blacksburg, Virginia

Peter M. Miller

Hilton Head Health Institute
Hilton Head Island, South Carolina

Volume 27

1991

SAGE PUBLICATIONS
The International Professional Publishers
Newbury Park   London   New Delhi

For information address:

 SAGE Publications, Inc.
2455 Teller Road
Newbury Park, California 91320

SAGE Publications Ltd.
6 Bonhill Street
London EC2A 4PU
United Kingdom

SAGE Publications India Pvt. Ltd.
M-32 Market
Greater Kailash I
New Delhi 110 048 India

Printed in the United States of America

Library of Congress: 75-646720

ISBN 0-8039-4196-X

FIRST PRINTING, 1991

Sage Production Editor: Judith L. Hunter

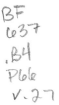

CONTENTS

Behavioral Assessment and Treatment of Brain-Impaired Individuals

Michael D. Franzen

Harnessing Computer Technology for Behavioral Therapy Training and Research

Matthew E. Lambert and Maralyn Billings

Injury Control in Children

Edward R. Christophersen and Patricia C. Purvis

The Behavioral Model and Adolescents with Behavior Disorders: A Review of Selected Treatment Studies

Ellen Olinger and Michael H. Epstein

CONTRIBUTORS

MARTIN AGRAN (Ph.D.) is Associate Professor in the Department of Special Education, Utah State University, Logan. His research interests include self-management, transition, and the education of students with severe disabilities.

MARALYN BILLINGS (B.S.W., B.A.) is a doctoral student in counseling psychology, Department of Psychology, Texas Tech University, Lubbock. Her clinical and research interests are in the areas of behavior therapy and assessment, professional development, and computer-based training.

EDWARD R. CHRISTOPHERSEN (Ph.D.) is Professor of Pediatrics at the University of Missouri at Kansas City, School of Medicine, and Chief, Behavioral Pediatrics Section, Children's Mercy Hospital, Kansas City, Missouri. He is a Fellow (Clinical Division) of the American Psychological Association. His clinical and research interests are in behavioral pediatrics.

MICHAEL H. EPSTEIN received his bachelor's and master's degrees from American University and his doctoral degree in special education from the University of Virginia. He is currently Professor of Special Education at Northern Illinois University and a Research Scientist at Educational Research and Services Center in DeKalb, Illinois. He has taught seriously emotionally disturbed students, has served as a director of special education programs, and has trained teachers to work with students with learning and behavior disorders. His research interests involve studying the status of adolescents with behavior disorders and developing educational programs.

MICHAEL D. FRANZEN (Ph.D.) received his doctorate from Southern Illinois University in 1983. Currently, he is Director of Neuropsychology at West Virginia University Health Sciences Center, where he is Associate Professor of Behavioral Medicine and Psychiatry. He is also Associate Professor of Psychology at West Virginia University. His research interests include the application of behavioral methodology and assessment strategies to neuropsychological assessment and treatment as well as the application of psychometric evaluation methods to clinical neuropsychology. His other research interests include medical neuropsychology and the effect of psychiatric conditions on cognitive functions.

CAROLYN HUGHES (Ph.D.) is Assistant Professor, Special Education Program, College of Education, Arizona State University, Tempe. Her research interests include self-management and problem solving among individuals with mental retardation, support services for employees with disabilities, and interactions among employees with and without disabilities.

MATTHEW E. LAMBERT (Ph.D.) is Assistant Professor of Psychology in the Department of Psychology, Texas Tech University, Lubbock. His clinical and research interests are in the areas of computer use for therapist training and evaluation, computer-based decision support systems, and behaviorally oriented practice guidelines for clinical practice.

RONALD C. MARTELLA (M.S.) is a doctoral candidate in the Department of Special Education, Utah State University, Logan. His research interests are in the areas of independent living skills and behavior disorders.

ELLEN OLINGER (Ed.D.) is Assistant Professor in Special Education at Northeastern Illinois University of Chicago. She teaches courses in a variety of areas, including methods for teaching children and adolescents with behavior disorders and/or learning disabilities, assessment, and consultation skills. She is the Coordinator of the master's program in learning disabilities. She previously taught for several years in a self-contained behavior disorders program. She earned her doctorate at Northern Illinois University in 1987.

PATRICIA C. PURVIS (M.S.Ed., Ph.D.) is currently a Post-Doctoral Fellow in the Behavioral Pediatrics Department at Children's Mercy Hospital, Kansas City, Missouri. Her interests include working with youngsters with school problems, attention deficit hyperactivity disorder and anxiety disorders, and injury control.

INDEPENDENT PERFORMANCE AMONG INDIVIDUALS WITH MENTAL RETARDATION: PROMOTING GENERALIZATION THROUGH SELF-INSTRUCTION

CAROLYN HUGHES

Arizona State University

I. INTRODUCTION

The recent thrust toward integrating individuals with mental retardation into the community requires the independent performance of socially valued behaviors under conditions not associated with training situations. However, programming for generalization of newly acquired skills rarely is incorporated into instructional goals for people with mental retardation (Haring, 1988). Berg, Wacker, and Flynn (1990) identified self-instruction as an effective instructional strategy for promoting independent performance among persons with mental retardation. When self-instruction is used, individuals are taught to verbalize a sequence of statements when performing a task. The statements serve to direct task performance or appropriate responses to a situation. For example, Agran, Fodor-David, and Moore

7

(1986) taught four hospital employees with mental retardation to self-instruct while completing job tasks in sequence. Self-instructional training resulted in increased job-task sequencing for all employees that was maintained for up to three months.

Applications of self-instruction typically are based upon a training sequence developed by Meichenbaum and Goodman (1971) comprising combinations of components that include a rationale for instruction, modeling, rehearsal, corrective feedback, and reinforcement presented during several brief training periods (e.g., one or two 2-hour sessions or four or five 30-minute sessions). The original (1971) training sequence consisted of five steps, including (a) trainer performs task, instructing aloud while subject observes; (b) subject performs task while trainer instructs aloud; (c) subject performs task while self-instructing aloud; (d) subject performs task while whispering; and (e) subject performs task while self-instructing covertly.

Contemporary applications of self-instruction typically omit the final two steps of Meichenbaum and Goodman's training sequence because of research requirements for measuring self-instructions verbalized by subjects during performance. Self-instructional statements that individuals are taught to verbalize while performing a task typically are the same as those taught in the 1971 training sequence and include (a) stating the problem, (b) stating the response, (c) self-evaluating, and (d) self-reinforcing. This chapter (a) reviews studies investigating the use of self-instruction among individuals with mental retardation in community settings with generalization of skills as the primary focus, (b) presents a model for teaching self-instruction that promotes independent skill performance (generalization), and (c) discusses future areas of research.

II. REVIEW PROCEDURES

Studies were included in the review based upon four criteria: (a) that the study was conducted in a community setting, (b) that the main component of the independent variable was self-instruction (Meichenbaum & Goodman, 1971), (c) that the subjects were individuals with mental retardation, and (d) that the study was published in a refereed journal. The studies were evaluated in terms of methodological factors relating to (a) generalization across people, situations, and tasks; (b) generalization over time; and (c) acquisition, generalization, and maintenance of self-instruction.

III. FACTORS RELATING TO GENERALIZATION ACROSS PEOPLE, SITUATIONS, AND TASKS

Table 1 displays factors identified across studies relating to generalization across people, situations, and tasks. Characteristics evaluated include (a) level of disability; (b) type of generalization assessed; (c) type of response assessed (e.g., on-task behavior); (d) instructional strategies, identified by Stokes and Baer (1977), to program generalization (i.e., train and hope, sequential modification, introduce to natural maintaining contingencies, train sufficient exemplars, train loosely, use indiscriminable contingencies, program common stimuli, mediate generalization, train "to generalize"); and (e) additional assistance provided, if required. Findings indicated that none of the eight studies evaluated assessed generalization across people. Seven studies assessed generalization across situations (Agran et al., 1986; Agran, Salzberg, & Stowitschek, 1987; Hughes & Petersen, 1989; Hughes & Rusch, 1989; Rusch, McKee, Chadsey-Rusch, & Renzaglia, 1988; Rusch, Morgan, Martin, Riva, & Agran, 1985; Salend, Ellis, & Reynolds, 1989) and four studies assessed generalization across tasks (Agran et al., 1987; Hughes & Rusch, 1989; Rusch et al., 1988; Whitman, Spence, & Maxwell, 1987). A description of studies that assessed generalization across situations and tasks follows.

A.   Generalization Across Situations

All studies measured generalization of tasks from the training to the work situation, except Whitman et al. (1987), which assessed task performance in the training situation only. Generalization was produced in the remaining seven studies; however, additional intervention was required in three studies (Agran et al., 1986; Rusch et al., 1988; Salend et al., 1989), and performance varied in a fourth study (Agran et al., 1987). For example, Agran et al. (1986) introduced additional training sessions with two subjects whose job-task sequencing failed to generalize from the training to the work situation and introduced verbal prompting with three subjects when their job-task sequencing decreased during work performance. Rusch et al. (1988) introduced corrective feedback during performance when appropriate requesting failed to generalize from the training to the work situation.

Differential outcomes across studies appeared to relate only to instructional strategies used to program generalization. Level of disability and type of response assessed did not covary with outcomes. Specifically, generalization occurred in one study with individuals with severe mental retardation (Hughes & Rusch, 1989), but did not occur until additional intervention was introduced in three other studies (Agran et al., 1987; Rusch et al., 1988; Salend et al., 1989). Generalization occurred with individuals with mild to moderate mental retardation in two studies (Hughes & Petersen, 1989; Rusch et al., 1985), although additional intervention was required to produce generalization in another study (Agran et al., 1986). Type of response assessed varied across studies (i.e., sequencing job tasks, initiating contacts, maintaining on-task behavior, solving work-related problems, requesting materials, packaging items, and sorting and sequencing letters) and did not appear to relate to generalization.

Instructional strategies used to program generalization. Three instructional strategies used to program generalization across situations were found to be effective unequivocally across studies. These strategies include (a) train sufficient exemplars (i.e., teaching multiple examples of stimulus conditions or responses), (b) program common stimuli (i.e., introducing similar stimuli in the training and

TABLE 1
Factors Relating to Generalization Across People, Situations, and Tasks

Study	Level of Disability	Generalization Produced?	Response Assessed	Instructional Strategies Used to Program Generalization	Additional Assistance Required?
Agran et al. (1986)	3 mild MR 1 moderate MR	Yes	Job-task sequencing, task completion, and decreased task repetition generalized from training to work situation	1. Train and hope	Yes, additional training required with two subjects
		Not known	Generalization across people or tasks not assessed	None	
Agran et al. (1987)	behavior disordered 1 moderate MR 2 severe MR	Yes	Contacts initiated by subjects generalized from training to work situation	1. Train and hope	No, however, generalized responding was variable for two subjects (one with severe MR)
		No	Training contacts initiated when out of materials did not generalize to contacts initiated when needs assistance	1. Train and hope	
		Not known	Generalization across people not assessed	None	
Hughes & Petersen (1989)	1 mild MR 3 moderate MR	Yes	On-task behavior across varied tasks generalized from training to work situation	1. Train sufficient exemplars 2. Program common stimuli 3. Mediate generalization	No
		Not known	Generalization across people or tasks not assessed	None	

Study	Participants		Generalization assessed	Strategy	Maintenance
Hughes & Rusch (1989)	2 severe MR	Yes	Correct responses across trained problem situations generalized from training to work situation	1. Train sufficient exemplars 2. Program common stimuli 3. Mediate generalization	No
		Yes	Correct responses generalized from trained to untrained problem situations	1. Train sufficient exemplars	No
		Not known	Generalization across people not assessed	None	
Rusch et al. (1988)	1 severe MR	Yes	Appropriate requests generalized from training to work situation	1. Train and hope	Yes, instructional feedback provided in performance
		No	Training appropriate requests when materials missing did not generalize to appropriate requests when not enough materials	1. Train and hope	
		Not known	Generalization across people not assessed	None	
Rusch et al. (1985)	1 mild MR 1 moderate MR	Yes	Percentage of time spent working generalized from training to work situation	1. Train sufficient exemplars 2. Program common stimuli	No
		Not known	Generalization across people or tasks not assessed	None	

(continued)

11

TABLE 1 (Continued)

Study	Level of Disability	Generalization Produced?	Response Assessed	Instructional Strategies Used to Program Generalization	Additional Assistance Required?
Salend et al. (1989)	4 severe MR	Yes	Number of packages completed generalized from training to work situation	1. Train and hope	Yes, subjects prompted to self-instruct at beginning and end of each performance session and whenever they failed to self-instruct
		Not known	Generalization across people or tasks not assessed	None	
Whitman et al. (1987)	14 mild-moderate MR (between-group design)	Yes	Sorting and sequencing letters generalized to similar task (i.e., stimulus differed only in letters used and sequence for sorting letters)	1. Train and hope	No
		Not known	Generalization across people or situations not assessed	None	

generalization setting), and (c) mediate generalization (i.e., teaching a response, such as a self-generated verbal prompt, as a strategy to produce generalization across stimulus conditions; Stokes & Baer, 1977). Applications of these instructional strategies produced generalization without the need for additional intervention across studies (Hughes & Petersen, 1989; Hughes & Rusch, 1989; Rusch et al., 1985). Two instructional strategies consistently identified with generalized responding were (a) training sufficient exemplars and (b) program common stimuli, while the absence of these two strategies consistently resulted in a lack of generalization.

For example, Hughes and Petersen (1989) employed all three strategies for programming generalization by (a) teaching on-task behavior across varied tasks (train sufficient exemplars), (b) using a permanent picture cue to prompt self-instructing and telling subjects to respond in training as if in response to work demands (program common stimuli), and (c) reminding subjects in training to self-instruct when in the work situation (mediate generalization). Results indicated that on-task behavior for all four subjects generalized from training to the work situation.

Hughes and Rusch (1989) also used all three strategies by teaching problem-solving across five problem situations (train sufficient exemplars), telling subjects to respond in training as if in response to work demands (program common stimuli), and reminding subjects when in training to self-instruct when in the work situation (mediate generalization). Both subjects in the Hughes and Rusch (1989) study generalized their problem-solving skills across situations. Rusch et al. (1985) used two strategies to train two employees in their study that sought to teach subjects to generalize their time spent working from the training to the work situation. Time spent working was taught across three food service tasks (train sufficient exemplars) and subjects were told to respond in training as if in response to work demands (program common stimuli). Following training, both employees increased their time spent working during lunch and dinner to exceed performance standards set by coworkers.

The remaining studies that required additional intervention to produce generalization or that produced variability in performance used only a train and hope strategy (i.e., probing without programming for generalization following acquisition of a response; Stokes & Baer, 1977). For example, additional training sessions were required with two of four subjects and self-instructional statements taught had to be modified for one subject in the Agran et al. (1986) study before job-task sequencing generalized across situations. Agran et al. (1987) found that generalization across situations for initiating contact with supervisors was variable for two of four subjects. Instructional feedback was required during work performance before appropriate requests generalized across situations in Rusch et al. (1988), and trainer prompting to self-instruct in the work situation was employed in Salend et al. (1989). An important characteristic of these studies is that correct responding was taught with only one rather than with multiple examples of the response class; common stimuli were not introduced across situations; and subjects were not taught to mediate generalization across situations.

B.   Generalization Across Tasks

Four studies assessed generalization across tasks. Of these, two studies were successful in producing generalization (Hughes & Rusch, 1989; Whitman et al., 1987) and two were not (Agran et al., 1987; Rusch et al., 1988). Favorable outcomes appeared to relate to instructional strategies used to program generalization and level of disability rather than type of response assessed. Specifically, the teaching of self-instruction in combination with one example of a desired response appeared to produce generalization across tasks among subjects with mild to moderate mental retardation. However, the teaching of multiple examples of a response was required to produce generalization among subjects with severe mental retardation.

Instructional strategies used to program generalization. Both studies that produced unfavorable outcomes used only train and hope strategies to program generalization. Agran et al. (1987) found that teaching subjects to initiate contacts with supervisors when they were out of materials did not generalize to initiating contacts when in need of assistance. Similarly, the teaching of appropriate requesting when materials were missing did not generalize to appropriate requesting when not enough materials were available in the Rusch et al. (1988) study. Both studies taught only single instances of the desired response to subjects with severe mental retardation.

Whitman et al. (1987) also used only a train and hope strategy (i.e., single-instance teaching), yet, in their study, subjects with mild to moderate mental retardation were successful in generalizing across tasks. Employees of a sheltered workshop were taught to sort and sequence a set of alphabet letters. Following one assessment probe on the training task, the same task was modeled using a different set and sequence of letters. The employees then were asked to complete the second task once as a generalization probe. Limited generalization across tasks was demonstrated in this study, however, because training and generalization tasks were very similar with respect to stimulus dimensions and response requirements. Additionally, repeated measures of generalization were not taken, and only group means, rather than individual data, were reported. As a group, subjects in this study had fewer correct responses to the generalization than the training probe (i.e., approximately 15 versus 18 correct responses). Finally, trainer modeling of the generalization task cannot be separated from the effects of teaching self-instruction with only one example.

A more convincing demonstration of generalization was provided by Hughes and Rusch (1989), who employed a train sufficient exemplars strategy (i.e., teaching multiple exemplars) with individuals with severe mental retardation. In their study, two employees of a janitorial supply company learned to solve a variety of task-related problems typical of those that occurred throughout the workday. Correct responses to five problem situations were trained (i.e., multiple exemplars), and five problem situations served as generalization probes. Generalization was demonstrated when employees applied the problem-solving strategy across functionally dissimilar responses (e.g., moving obstacles in the way, finding missing materials, plugging in disconnected equipment). Therefore, compared with Whitman et al. (1987), in which only within-class generalized responding was demonstrated (i.e., sorting and sequencing letters), Hughes and Rusch (1989) demonstrated generalization across a broad response class (i.e., responding correctly to varied task-related problem situations). Furthermore, Hughes and Rusch (1989) were successful in producing generalization among individuals with more severe disabilities than the subjects in the Whitman et al. (1987) study (i.e., severe versus mild to moderate mental retardation).

To program generalization across tasks, Hughes and Rusch (1989) used a train sufficient exemplars strategy in combination with self-instruction. This method also was found to be successful at producing generalization across situations. Whereas teaching self-instruction with only one example of a response class may be sufficient to produce generalization across very similar tasks and with individuals with mild to moderate mental retardation, using multiple exemplars may be necessary to produce generalization across a broad response class (e.g., varied problems throughout the workday) among individuals with severe mental retardation.

IV. FACTORS RELATING TO GENERALIZATION
OVER TIME

Factors relating to generalization over time (maintenance) are shown in Table 2. Categories evaluated include (a) length of assessment, (b) type of response assessed, (c) instructional strategies used to program generalization (i.e., methods identified by Stokes and Baer, 1977; number of self-instruction statements taught, Meichenbaum & Goodman, 1971; length of self-instruction training); and (d) additional assistance provided, if required.

Findings indicated that all studies demonstrated generalization over time; however, length of assessment ranged from two days (Whitman et al., 1987) to six months after training was removed (Hughes & Rusch, 1989). A mediate generalization strategy was used across all studies as a method to program generalization by teaching subjects to self-instruct. Stokes and Baer (1977) argued that mediating generalization (i.e., self-instructing) provides a salient verbal stimulus that serves to maintain performance. However, despite applications of self-instruction across studies, additional assistance was required to maintain performance in four studies. Specifically, additional intervention was needed in two studies (Agran et al., 1986, 1987), training was only partially withdrawn in one study (Salend et al., 1989), and one study employed additional intervention and maintained partial application of training components (Rusch et al., 1988).

Generalization over time appeared to relate to a combination of three factors, including (a) length of self-instruction training, (b) number of self-instruction statements taught, and (c) level of disability. Individual training sessions typically were 30 minutes in length across studies. Three to four training sessions were

TABLE 2
Factors Relating to Generalization Across Time

Study	Length of Assessment	Type of Response Assessed	Instructional Strategies Used to Program Generalization	Additional Assistance Required?
Agran et al. (1986)	Assessments taken for 31, 29, 20, and 4 consecutive sessions across subjects	Job-task sequencing, task completion, and decreased task repetition maintained following withdrawal of training	1. Mediate generalization (teach self-instruction) 2. Statements 1 and 2 taught in five 30- to 40-minute sessions	Yes, additional training for one subject with moderate MR and verbal prompting for three subjects required to maintain performance
Agran et al. (1987)	Intermittent probes taken for contacts initiated when out of materials across 80, 65, 64, and 40 sessions across four subjects. Intermittent probes taken for contacts initiated when needs assistance across 30 and 25 sessions across two subjects	Contacts initiated by subjects maintained following withdrawal of training	1. Mediate generalization (teach self-instruction) 2. Statements 1 and 2 taught in four 20- to 30-minute sessions	Yes, two subjects required verbal prompting to maintain performance
Hughes & Petersen (1989)	Assessments taken for 20, 16, 13, and 10 consecutive sessions across subjects and 1 follow-up probe two weeks after termination of consecutive sessions	On-task behavior for all subjects maintained following withdrawal of training	1. Mediate generalization (teach self-instruction) 2. Program common stimuli 3. Statements 1-4 taught in 3-4 30-minute sessions	No
Hughes & Rusch (1989)	Assessments taken for 14 and 9 consecutive sessions across subjects, then monthly probes for 6 months after termination of consecutive sessions	Correct responses to trained and untrained problem situations maintained following withdrawal of training	1. Mediate generalization (teach self-instruction) 2. Program common stimuli 3. Statements 1-4 taught in 15-16 30-minute sessions	No

Study			
Rusch et al. (1988)	Self-instruction training in effect throughout study, although decreased in intensity, therefore, response maintenance following total withdrawal of training not assessed; assessments were taken for 27 and 17 consecutive sessions across behaviors during which training was gradually lessened but never completely eliminated	Appropriate requests when materials missing and when not enough materials maintained when training was partially (never completely) withdrawn	1. Mediate generalization (teach self-instruction) 2. Statements 1-2 taught in four sessions of unstated length — Yes, 28-42 additional training sessions with partial training components provided as well as corrective feedback in performance
Rusch et al. (1985)	Assessments taken for 24 and 18 consecutive sessions across subjects	Percentage of time spent working for both subjects maintained following withdrawal of training	1. Mediate generalization (teach self-instruction) 2. Program common stimuli 3. Statements 1-4 taught in four 30-minute sessions — No
Salend et al. (1989)	Response maintenance following total withdrawal of training not assessed because verbal prompts continued to be delivered after remainder of self-instruction training withdrawn; Assessments were taken for 5 consecutive sessions across subjects after remainder of self-instruction training withdrawn	Number of packages completed maintained following partial (not complete) withdrawal of training	1. Mediate generalization (teach self-instruction) 2. State 2 taught in 15-30 sessions of unstated length — Yes, verbal prompting provided during performance
Whitman et al. (1987)	One assessment only taken 2 days after training withdrawn	Only training task (sorting and sequencing letters) assessed during maintenance, not generalization task	1. Mediate generalization (teach self-instruction) 2. Statements 1-4 taught in one session of a maximum of 70 minutes — No

sufficient to produce generalization without additional assistance for subjects with mild to moderate mental retardation only when all four verbal statements of the Meichenbaum and Goodman training sequence were taught, that is (a) stating the problem, (b) stating the response, (c) self-evaluating, and (d) self-reinforcing (Hughes & Petersen, 1989; Rusch et al., 1985; Whitman et al., 1987). The use of only the first two statements (i.e., stating the problem, stating the correct response) for people with mild to moderate mental retardation required additional training, verbal prompting, or both to maintain performance (Agran et al., 1986, 1987).

With individuals with severe mental retardation, 15 to 42 training sessions were required to produce generalization over time. However, performance was maintained without additional assistance only when all self-instruction statements were taught (Hughes & Rusch, 1989). Simply teaching the individual to state the problem (step 1) and state the response (step 2) required both performance feedback and continuous partial application of training components to maintain performance (Rusch et al., 1988). When stating the response (step 2) was taught exclusively, performance was maintained by externally delivered verbal prompting (Salend et al., 1989).

The use of all four statements of the Meichenbaum and Goodman self-instruction training sequence appears to correspond unequivocally to generalization over time without additional assistance across all levels of disability (Hughes & Petersen, 1989; Hughes & Rusch, 1989; Rusch et al., 1985; Whitman et al., 1987). Length of self-instruction training appears to relate to level of disability. Specifically, 3 to 4 training sessions in combination with teaching 4 self-instruction statements were sufficient to produce maintenance with subjects with mild to moderate mental retardation (Hughes & Petersen, 1989; Rusch et al., 1985; Whitman et al., 1987), while at least 15 training sessions were required with individuals with severe mental retardation (Hughes & Rusch, 1989).

V. FACTORS RELATING TO ACQUISITION, GENERALIZATION, AND MAINTENANCE OF SELF-INSTRUCTION

Table 3 displays factors relating to acquisition, generalization, and maintenance of self-instruction. Characteristics evaluated included (a) assessment of acquisition of self-instruction during training and (b) assessment of generalization and maintenance of self-instruction across people, situations, and tasks. Although level of communication skills of subjects is likely to be a factor relating to self-instructing, lack of information across studies precluded evaluating the contribution of this factor. Findings indicated that five studies assessed the acquisition of self-instruction (Agran et al., 1987; Hughes & Rusch, 1989; Rusch et al., 1988; Salend et al., 1989; Whitman et al., 1987). No study assessed generalization and maintenance of self-instruction across people, four studies provided assessments across situations (Agran et al., 1986, 1987; Hughes & Rusch, 1989; Rusch et al., 1988), and two studies provided assessments across tasks (Hughes & Rusch, 1989; Whitman et al.,

1987). The following sections overview factors relating to acquisition, generalization, and maintenance of self-instruction.

A. Acquisition of Self-Instruction During Training

Because data collection methods differed, varying amounts of information are available across the five studies that assessed acquisition of self-instruction during training. Studies that reported only mean percentages (versus repeated measures) of self-instructions verbalized across training did not provide information on the acquisition of individual self-instruction statements over time (Agran et al., 1987; Salend et al., 1989; Whitman et al., 1987). Furthermore, only studies that reported repeated measures assessed the correspondence of frequency of self-instructing and frequency of correct motor responses (Hughes & Rusch, 1989; Rusch et al., 1988). This information is necessary for establishing a functional relationship between self-instructing and correct responding during training.

Subjects self-instructed with varying frequency across studies. Frequency of self-instructing appeared to relate to a combination of factors, including level of disability, length of self-instruction training, and number of self-instruction steps taught (see Table 2). A maximum of 70 minutes of training time in combination with teaching all four self-instruction statements (Meichenbaum & Goodman, 1971) resulted in 90% self-instruction statements verbalized with subjects with mild to moderate mental retardation (Whitman et al., 1987). Similar levels of self-instructing were produced with subjects with severe mental retardation only when a minimum of 15 training sessions were provided in combination with teaching all four self-instruction steps (Hughes & Rusch, 1989).

B. Generalization and Maintenance of Self-Instruction
Across Situations

Three of four studies that assessed generalization and maintenance of self-instruction across situations reported repeated measures (Agran et al., 1986; Hughes & Rusch, 1989; Rusch et al., 1988). These studies indicated correspondence between frequency of self-instructing and correct responding; however, additional assistance was provided in two studies, thus confounding the establishment of a functional relationship between self-instructing and correct responding (Agran et al., 1986; Rusch et al., 1988). Agran et al. (1987) provided only mean percentages of self-instructions verbalized; however, they narratively described a low occurrence of self-instruction that did not correlate with frequency of correct responses. Only Hughes and Rusch (1989) reported a high frequency of self-instructing that correlated with correct responding without the need for additional assistance, perhaps as a result of providing extensive training sessions in combination with teaching all four steps of the Meichenbaum and Goodman self-instruction sequence (i.e., stating the problem, stating the response, self-evaluating, self-reinforcing). Additionally, self-instruction was taught in combination with multiple exemplars of the response class (see Tables 1 and 2).

TABLE 3

Factors Relating to Acquisition, Generalization, and Maintenance of Self-instruction

Study	Acquisition Assessed During Training?	Generalization and Maintenance Assessed Across People?	Generalization and Maintenance Assessed Across Situations?	Generalization and Maintenance Assessed Across Tasks?
Agran et al. (1986)	No	No	Yes, self-instructing did generalize to and maintain in work situation; however, additional training required with two subjects (one with moderate MR) to maintain performance	No
Agran et al. (1987)	Yes, however, subjects generally did not verbalize self-instructions to training	No	Yes, however, few self-instructions verbalized across subjects in work situation	No
Hughes & Petersen (1989)	No	No	No	No
Hughes & Rusch (1989)	Yes, 92% and 81% self-instruction steps verbalized across subjects during training, requiring verbal prompting on 28% of steps	No	Yes, frequency of self-instructing corresponded with correct responses after self-instructing probed in work situation	Yes, frequency of self-instructing corresponded with correct responses after self-instructing probed across untrained tasks
Rusch et al. (1988)	Yes, however, all four self-instruction statements not acquired in training until instructional feedback was provided during performance	No	Yes, however, self-instructing did not generalize to work situation until corrective feedback in performance was provided	No

Rusch et al. (1985)	No	No	No	No
Salend et al. (1989)	Yes, however, not known if frequency of self-instructing corresponded with frequency of correct responses	No	No	No
Whitman et al. (1987)	Yes, mean of 90% self-instruction statements verbalized across subjects on one probe	No	No	Yes, subjects verbalized an approximate mean of 60% of the self-instruction statements on one generalization task probe and 80% on one maintenance probe

C. Generalization and Maintenance of Self-Instruction Across Tasks

Hughes and Rusch (1989) and Whitman et al. (1987) assessed generalization and maintenance of self-instruction across tasks. However, because only one generalization and one maintenance probe were taken in the Whitman et al. (1987) study, there is no information on self-instructing across performance sessions. Furthermore, data were reported as group means; therefore, frequency of self-instructing cannot be correlated with frequency of correct responding across individual subjects. Fairly high occurrences of self-instructing were reported for generalization (60%) and maintenance (80%) probes following a maximum of 70 minutes total training time in combination with teaching all four self-instruction statements.

Hughes and Rusch (1989) also reported a high rate of occurrence for self-instruction across tasks. Because their data were reported as repeated measures for individual subjects, we are able to establish that frequency of self-instructing corresponded to frequency of correct responding across tasks. More extensive training sessions (i.e., 15 or 16) combined with teaching all four self-instruction statements were required in this study to produce generalization and maintenance of self-instruction, perhaps relating to subject disability level (i.e., severe versus mild to moderate mental retardation).

VI. TEACHING SELF-INSTRUCTION UTILIZING MULTIPLE EXEMPLARS

As can be seen in Tables 1-3, limited generalization across people, situations, tasks, and over time has been demonstrated across investigations of self-instruction in community settings. In response to such a lack of generalization, this chapter proposes a model for teaching self-instruction (utilizing multiple exemplars) that is based upon a combination of factors found in the current review to be effective in producing generalization. First, factors found to be effective to produce generalization are discussed. Next, individual steps of the proposed model are described.

A. Factors Found to Be Effective in Producing Generalization

Instructional strategies found to produce generalization across situations and tasks include (a) train sufficient exemplars, (b) program common stimuli, and (c) mediate generalization (Stokes & Baer, 1977; see Table 1). For example, Hughes and Rusch (1989) elicited generalized responding by teaching problem-solving across five situations (train sufficient exemplars), telling employees to respond in training as if they were actually working (program common stimuli), and telling employees while being trained to remember to self-instruct when working (mediate generalization). No factor other than instructional strategies used was found to relate consistently to generalization across situations and tasks.

The strategy of mediating generalization (Stokes & Baer, 1977) by teaching self-instruction was found to produce generalization over time. Additionally, a combination of three factors appears to account for the effectiveness of self-instruction training in maintaining performance (see Table 2). These factors include (a) length of self-instruction training, (b) number of self-instruction statements taught, and (c) level of disability. The use of all four steps of the Meichenbaum and Goodman self-instruction training sequence (i.e., stating the problem, stating the correct response, self-evaluating, self-reinforcing) appears to maintain performance without additional assistance across all levels of disability (Hughes & Petersen, 1989; Hughes & Rusch, 1989; Rusch et al., 1985; Whitman et al., 1987). Length of training required appears to relate to disability level. Specifically, 3 to 4 training sessions in combination with teaching four self-instruction statements have been shown to be sufficient to maintain performance with subjects with mild to moderate mental retardation (Hughes & Petersen, 1989; Rusch et al., 1985; Whitman et al., 1987), while at least 15 training sessions have been required with individuals with severe mental retardation (Hughes & Rusch, 1989).

Level of disability, length of self-instruction training, and number of self-instruction statements taught relate to acquisition, generalization, and maintenance of self-instruction (see Table 3). Teaching all four steps of the Meichenbaum and Goodman training sequence and adjusting number of training sessions to disability level appear to enhance acquisition, generalization, and maintenance of self-instruction (Hughes & Rusch, 1989; Whitman et al., 1987). Additionally, obtaining repeated measures of self-instructions verbalized across tasks and situations provides information on the acquisition of self-instructing over time as well as the means for establishing a functional relationship between self-instructing and correct responding (Hughes & Rusch, 1989; Rusch et al., 1988).

B. Proposed Model for Promoting Generalization

The above factors found to be effective in producing generalization have been incorporated into a model for teaching self-instruction utilizing multiple exemplars. The *multiple exemplar* component of the model requires teaching more than one example of a desired response to produce a generalized response. For example, Horner, Jones, and Williams (1985) taught three individuals with mental retardation to cross streets independently. Initially, these individuals were taught to cross 8 different types of intersections. Following the initial training condition, ongoing training and assessment were conducted during which generalization occurred across 20 untrained street intersections. The proposed model combines the multiple exemplar approach with teaching self-instruction to produce generalization across people, situations, tasks, and over time. A description of the model follows.

Step 1: Select an array of examples. Living and working in the community require that individuals with mental retardation respond independently to varying stimulus conditions in their environment. To determine the range (typically referred to as the "universe") of conditions that an individual is likely to encounter in a particular work setting, the setting must be surveyed (Horner, Sprague, & Wilcox,

1982). Because it is impractical to attempt to teach singular responses to each of the myriad stimuli in an environment, representative examples of the universe of stimulus conditions and required responses are selected as teaching examples, based upon setting surveys.

Hughes and Rusch (1989) asked a work supervisor in a company that packaged liquid soap to identify work-related problem situations that supported employees were likely to encounter throughout the workday as well as correct responses to these problems. The array of problem situations identified by the supervisor (the survey) served as the universe of stimuli to which employees were expected to respond. Based upon the supervisor's survey of the work setting, 10 examples representative of the universe of identified responses were selected to serve as teaching examples (see Table 4).

Step 2. Classify responses into teaching sets. After teaching several examples of related responses, one would expect generalized responding to occur across functionally related situations (Engelmann & Carnine, 1982; Haring & Laitinen, in press). For example, after teaching someone to plug in a fan and a lamp, one would expect the individual to be able to plug in a radio (i.e., to generalize). Therefore, when generalized responding is the goal of the instruction, an instructional program should focus upon teaching similar responses to similar stimulus situations concurrently rather than in isolation.

To determine relatedness among responses (i.e., classifying responses into teaching sets), a functional analysis should be conducted to determine the response operations required to produce an effect on the environment (Haring & Laitinen, in press). Related responses, then, should be classified into teaching sets to enhance skill acquisition and generalized responding across functionally related skills. For example, Rusch et al. (1985) observed food service employees who worked in a university cafeteria to determine the range of task-related responses required throughout the workday. Observation revealed that specific responsibilities while working on the food serving line included keeping the counter and other surfaces clean; checking supplies of plates, silverware, and glasses; replenishing condiments; and restocking bread, butter, and desserts. Based on the response requirements needed to perform these tasks, Rusch et al. (1985) classified responses into three teaching sets: wiping surfaces, checking supplies, and restocking supplies. The employees then were taught to self-instruct when performing responses representative of each of the teaching sets. Following training, the percentage of time spent working was found to increase across all assigned tasks throughout the workday.

Step 3. Divide items of sets into trained responses and generalization probes. Because the goal of this model is to produce generalization, we must determine if similar responses that are acquired under similar stimulus conditions will occur in the presence of nontrained stimuli. To provide an assessment of an individual's generalized responding across related but novel situations not encountered during training, items of teaching sets should be divided equally and assigned at random either to a group of responses to be trained or to a group of responses to serve as generalization probes (untrained) (Haring & Laitinen, in press). After teaching

TABLE 4
Work-related Problem Situations and Correct Responses

Problem Situation	Instruction	Correct Response
1. Paper towel in drain of sink; sink full of water[a]	Instructed by trainer to wring out rag in sink	Remove paper towel; drain sink (move obstacle)
2. 5 pieces of trash on table[b]	Instructed by trainer to go to table to begin work	Throw trash in basket located within 2m of table (move obstacle)
3. Radio is unplugged	Instructed by trainer to turn on radio	Plug in radio and turn on (plug in appliance)
4. Box is on table next to soap-dispensing machine	Instructed by trainer to put tray on table	Put box in proper place or seek assistance (move obstacle)
5. Bundle on table where work is to be conducted	Instructed by trainer to begin working	Put bundle in proper place (move obstacle)
6. Tape dispenser is empty	Instructed by trainer to get tape dispenser	Find tape and fill tape dispenser (find missing item)
7. Cardboard pad is in box with chip board	Instructed by trainer to get more chip boards	Find pad and put in proper place (find missing item)
8. Chair is in center of work room	Instructed by trainer to hang rag by sink	Put chair next to table (move obstacle)
9. Puddle of soap on table where work is to be conducted	Instructed by trainer to begin working	Wipe up soap with rag (move obstacle)
10. Box containing hair nets is in wrong place	Instructed by trainer to get hair net	Find box and put in proper place (find missing item)

SOURCE: From "Teaching Supported Employees with Severe Mental Retardation to Solve Problems" by C. Hughes and F. R. Rusch, 1989, *Journal of Applied Behavior Analysis;* adapted by permission.

a. Trained responses for Myra; generalization probes for Les: 1, 3, 5, 7, 9.

b. Trained responses for Les; generalization probes for Myra: 2, 4, 6, 8, 10.

several trained responses, we expect individuals to respond correctly to generalization probes (i.e., untrained but similar stimuli).

Hughes and Rusch (1989) selected 10 problem situations that employees were likely to encounter throughout their workday. Responses to these situations then were assigned to one of three functionally related teaching sets, including plugging in appliances, finding missing items, and moving obstacles. Members of each set then were assigned randomly either to a group of five trained responses or to a group of five generalization probes (see Table 4). For example, because Problem Situation 1 (paper towel in drain of sink) and Problem Situation 2 (5 pieces of trash on table) both required moving an obstacle, these two responses were assigned to different groups. As indicated in Table 4, trained responses for one employee, Myra, served as generalization probes for the other employee, Les. Conversely, trained responses for Les served as generalization probes for Myra.

Observation of the employees' performance during baseline revealed that Myra made no correct responses to either trained or untrained problem situations, and Les made only four correct responses out of a total of 50 problem presentations (see the two upper panels of Figure 1). Correct responses to trained and untrained problems continued to be assessed after self-instruction training was introduced with the group of trained responses. Data indicated that self-instruction with multiple exemplars resulted in increased correct responding to trained problem situations for both employees as well as increased generalized responding to untrained problems (generalization probes). Additionally, correct responding to both trained and untrained problems was maintained for six months following daily, repeated observation and recording (see follow-up data in Figure 1).

Step 4: Teach trained responses using self-instruction. Teaching self-instruction in combination with multiple exemplars has been shown to produce generalization and maintenance of performance without the need for additional external assistance. The success of procedures used to teach self-instruction appears to relate to three factors. These factors include (a) training sequence used, (b) self-instruction statements taught, and (c) length of training time. Hughes and Petersen (1989), Hughes and Rusch (1989), and Rusch et al. (1985) taught self-instruction using a variation of Meichenbaum and Goodman's training sequence (see Table 5). These investigators incorporated components designed to program for generalization, including train sufficient exemplars, program common stimuli, and mediate generalization strategies (Strokes & Baer, 1977). Use of the training sequence resulted in generalization of target behaviors (Hughes & Petersen, 1989; Hughes & Rusch, 1989; Rusch et al., 1985). For example, Hughes and Rusch (1989) taught two employees with severe mental retardation to self-instruct in response to five problem situations using the above steps. Both employees were observed to generalize their use of the self-instructions to the work situation and in response to untrained problem situations. Additionally, the employees continued to self-instruct after trainer assistance was withdrawn.

The use of all four steps of Meichenbaum and Goodman's self-instruction sequence (i.e., stating the problem, stating the response, self-evaluating, self-reinforcing) has produced generalization without the need for additional intervention (Hughes & Petersen, 1989; Hughes & Rusch, 1989; Rusch et al., 1985; Whitman et al., 1987; see Table 2). Studies that taught only step 1 (state problem) and/or step 2 (state response) required additional assistance to produce generalization (Agran et al., 1986, 1987; Rusch et al., 1988; Salend et al., 1989).

For example, Hughes and Rusch (1989) taught two supported employees to verbalize the following statements in response to five problem situations: (a) stating the problem (e.g., "No soap"); (b) stating the response (e.g., "Find it"); (c) self-evaluating (e.g., "Fixed it"); and (d) self-reinforcing (e.g., "Good"). Myra and Les, the two employees, verbalized 92% and 81% of the self-instruction statements across

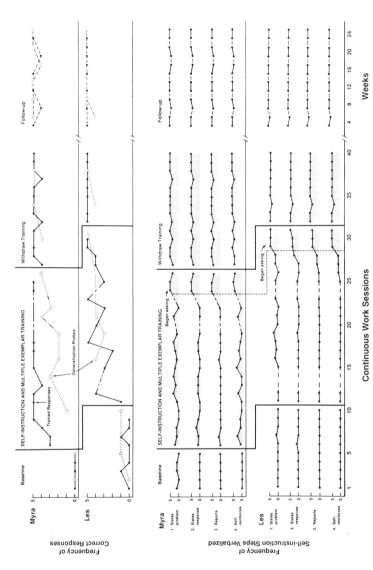

Figure 1. Frequency of Correct Responses to Trained and Untrained Problem Situations (generalization probes) and Frequency of Self-Instruction Steps Verbalized During Performance

SOURCE: From "Teaching Supported Employees with Severe Mental Retardation to Solve Problems" by C. Hughes and F. R. Rusch, *Journal of Applied Behavior Analysis* (1989, p. 369); reprinted by permission.

NOTE: Broken lines indicate data missing due to employee absence.

TABLE 5

Comparison Between Current Model and
Meichenbaum and Goodman's (1971) Training Sequence

Current Model	*Meichenbaum and Goodman (1971)*	*Comparison*
1. Trainer provides rationale for self-instruction training and tells subjects to respond as if in response to work demands (program common stimuli)	1. Trainer does not provide rationale or tell subjects to respond as if in response to work demands	Different
2. Trainer models multiple examples of tasks while self-instructing aloud (teach sufficient exemplars and mediate generalization)	2. Trainer models multiple examples of tasks while self-instructing aloud (teach sufficient exemplars and mediate generalization)	Same
3. Subject performs tasks while trainer instructs	3. Subject performs tasks while trainer instructs	Same
4. Subject performs tasks while self-instructing aloud	4. Subject performs tasks while self-instructing aloud	Same
5. Subject does not perform tasks while whispering	5. Subject performs tasks while whispering	Different
6. Subject does not perform tasks while self-instructing covertly	6. Subject performs tasks while self-instructing covertly	Different
7. Trainer provides corrective feedback and prompting, if needed	7. Trainer provides corrective feedback and prompting, if needed	Same
8. Trainer reminds subject in training to self-instruct when working (mediate generalization)	8. Trainer does not remind subject to self-instruct when working	Different

all training sessions, respectively. The lower two panels of Figure 1 display the generalized use of the four trained self-instructional statements during work performance. Few verbalizations of self-instructions occurred for the employees during either baseline or self-instruction with the multiple exemplar training strategy until requests for verbalizations were initiated during session 24 for Myra and session 29 for Les. When asked, "What are you doing?" after the initiation of a correct response, the frequency of verbalization of all four self-instruction steps corresponded, with few exceptions, to the frequency of correct responses for both Myra and Les. On only 2 occasions out of 85 did Myra fail to verbalize a self-reinforcement statement. Les failed to state the correct response 2 times and to self-evaluate 3 times out of 60 opportunities. On all other occasions, frequency of self-instruction steps corresponded identically to frequency of correct responses. This correspondence was maintained throughout the six months of follow-up assessment.

Adjusting length of training time to subject disability level in combination with teaching four self-instruction statements has produced generalization without the need for further training (see Table 2). For example, a minimum of 15 30-minute training sessions was needed to produce generalization with individuals with severe mental retardation (Hughes & Rusch, 1989). In contrast, a minimum of 70 minutes of training time was required to produce similar results with individuals with mild to moderate mental retardation (Whitman et al., 1987).

Based on the above information, guidelines can be established for teaching self-instruction, which include (a) using a training sequence that programs for generalization, (b) teaching all four self-instruction steps of the Meichenbaum and Goodman training sequence regardless of level of disability, and (c) adapting number of training sessions according to subject disability level.

Step 5: Evaluate the effect of training. To isolate the point at which individuals learn to self-instruct, repeated measures of their self-instructing while responding to multiple exemplars must be taken during training. Additionally, to assess generalization across people, situations, and tasks, repeated measures of generalized use of the self-instructional strategy with both trained and untrained responses must be taken during performance.

For example, Rusch et al. (1988) collected data from repeated measures of frequency of correct responding and self-instructing across all performance and training sessions. Data revealed that self-instructing was being learned gradually during training; it is interesting that no self-instruction statements were acquired in training until corrective feedback was provided during performance. Thereafter, frequency of self-instructions and frequency of correct responses corresponded throughout the remainder of the study. Repeated measures obtained by Hughes and Rusch (1989) revealed that generalization of correct responding to untrained problem situations during performance occurred simultaneously with the acquisition of self-instruction during training. Their data also demonstrated that frequency of self-instructing corresponded with frequency of correct responding during performance.

Step 6: Withdraw training and evaluate the effect of withdrawal. The decision about when to withdraw training should be based upon frequency of correct responses during performance, because the ultimate test of a teaching strategy is whether an individual can perform desired responses in settings where training did not occur and in circumstances that are novel. Criterion performance is determined by establishing a range of acceptable behavior as determined by significant others within a setting (e.g., supervisors, employers, teachers) (Rusch, Chadsey-Rusch, & Lagomarcino, 1987). When an individual is performing at criterion level during performance observation sessions, an assessment of response maintenance can be obtained by using a partial withdrawal of training (Rusch & Kazdin, 1981). Individual training components can be withdrawn or an entire training package can be withdrawn across one baseline of a multiple-baseline design while performance measures continue to be taken. In Hughes and Rusch (1989), a performance criterion of four or five correct responses across three consecutive sessions (the total possible was five responses per session) was established. Withdrawal of training sequentially across subjects resulted in maintenance of training gains throughout six months of follow-up evaluation without the need for direct instruction.

VII. FUTURE AREAS OF RESEARCH

Several suggestions for future research are posed by this review and the proposed model for teaching self-instruction using multiple exemplars. First, no attempt was made to separate the effects of the two components of the proposed strategy (i.e., self-instructing and responding to multiple examples; see Hughes & Rusch, 1989). It is not known whether teaching either component exclusively would result in generalization.

Teaching multiple examples has been effective in producing generalization without using self-instruction (e.g., general case programming). However, investigations employing general case programming typically have focused only upon within-class generalization, for example, generalized use of vending machines or crossing similar intersections (see Horner et al., 1985; Sprague & Horner, 1984). In contrast, subjects in the Hughes and Rusch (1989) study learned to use the combined self-instruction and multiple-exemplar strategy to solve a broad range of problems requiring a variety of functionally dissimilar responses. For example, employees learned to remove obstacles that were in the way, get more materials that were missing, and plug in equipment that was disconnected from a power source.

When multiple exemplars are taught without self-instruction as an additional component, researchers have been ineffective in producing generalized responding across a broad range of responses, such as that reported by Hughes and Rusch (1989) (Doyle, Goldstein, Bourgeois, & Nakles, 1989; Secan, Egel, & Tilley, 1989). On the other hand, teaching self-instruction exclusively without multiple examples has been ineffective in producing generalization (Agran et al., 1986, 1987; Rusch et al., 1988; Salend et al., 1989). Teaching self-instruction with multiple examples, however, has resulted in generalized responding across a wide range of stimulus conditions (Hughes & Petersen, 1989; Hughes & Rusch, 1989; Rusch et al., 1985). It may be that teaching self-instruction in combination with multiple exemplars provides individuals with a strategy that produces generalization across a broad range of responses. As theorized by Engelmann and Carnine (1982), there is no sharp line between initial learning and subsequent generalization; both responses require an awareness of "sameness" of characteristics among stimuli. Teaching self-instruction with multiple exemplars may provide individuals with a cognitive strategy that allows them to attend to similarities among stimuli and, subsequently, to generalize their responses across similar stimuli.

Furthermore, it may be that the unique contribution of the self-instructional component of the combined strategy is the role that language serves in prompting generalization. Stokes and Baer (1977) suggested that language may serve as a salient common stimulus that prompts nonverbal behavior across varying conditions. Whitman (1990) argued that language serves as a vehicle for directing behavior and that language, as a behavior itself, is unique in its ability to influence the acquisition of other behaviors, both verbal and nonverbal. Catania, Matthews, and Shimoff (1982) suggested that, by verbally describing their environment, individuals formulate "rules" and learn to act in accordance with these rules. In other words, nonverbal (motor) behavior comes under the control of verbal behavior. Finally, Whitman (1990) claimed that, at a minimum, language is an important tool for labeling, monitoring, analyzing, and controlling one's behavior. Language may serve as an antecedent control technique for an individual by providing a self-delivered prompt that initiates a response and as a reinforcer by providing a consequence for the response.

Because persons with mental retardation typically experience language delays, traditional direct instruction methods (i.e., control of behavior via verbal directions delivered by change agents such as teachers or parents) may not be the most appropriate method for teaching these people (Whitman, 1987). Direct instruction methods assume a certain degree of linguistic skill on the part of the learner; in addition, they tend to foster dependence upon prompts and consequences delivered by the change agent (Whitman, 1990).

Whitman (1987) suggested that teaching persons with mental retardation to self-instruct remediates language deficits by teaching production of relevant verbal cues and use of these cues as an attention-focusing device and also by providing a vehicle for processing information and a means for regulating behavior. In other words, self-instructional training provides the linguistic skills necessary to regulate behavior and teaches active use of these skills (Whitman, 1990).

Self-instruction may serve as a problem-solving strategy because individuals, through the use of verbal behavior, actively process information. Verbal behavior may provide the tools for individuals to examine a problem situation, examine their strategic repertoires, formulate a plan of action, enact that plan, evaluate the plan as implemented, and revise that plan if necessary. Verbal behavior may allow persons in problem (novel) situations to identify strategies that have worked in similar task situations. Skinner (1953) suggests that the difficulty of "solving a problem" relates to the availability of the response that constitutes the solution; that is, the similarity of the problem-solving response to earlier responses made by an individual makes solving the problem "easier."

Similarly, Carnine (1990) claims that the process of solving a problem requires finding "sameness" across situations or stimulus conditions. Verbal behavior may facilitate this process by helping people to verbally identify similarities across tasks and solutions (responses). Keogh, Whitman, and Maxwell (1988) indicate that, when individuals are taught to self-instruct, they improve their ability to verbalize appropriate problem-solving strategies and to perform on academic tasks. It may be that the ability to self-instruct facilitates problem solving by providing the linguistic tools necessary to identify relevant similarities.

Studies have compared the effects of instructional programs that contain a verbal strategy with programs that do not. Typically, addition of the verbal strategy has produced more effective results among people with mental retardation (see Leon & Pepe, 1983; Park & Gaylord-Ross, 1989; Whitman et al., 1987). Teaching individuals with limited verbal skills (e.g., persons with mental retardation) to use a verbal strategy may be effective because doing so provides the linguistic skills needed to perform independently in novel situations (i.e., to identify similarities across situations). Teaching with multiple exemplars may provide sufficient opportunity to use the strategy to produce generalization across novel stimulus conditions. Future research should attempt to isolate the separate effects of the two components of the combined strategy.

A second suggestion for future research is that self-instructing initially may interfere with subjects' generalized responding. For example, Hughes and Rusch (1989) taught subjects to verbalize four statements in response to five problem situations, requiring at least 15 30-minute sessions to achieve criterion performance (i.e., 80% correct responses across three consecutive performance sessions). Engelmann and Carnine (1982) suggest that, in teaching a cognitive strategy consisting of multiple steps, considerable interference may occur before an individual receives a second example of a stimulus condition to which generalization is expected. An individual's performance of the multiple steps of the cognitive strategy precludes juxtaposition of examples of the stimulus class, preventing massed practice on the generalization concept. Therefore, the individual's "memory requirements" are increased substantially, and the total amount of time needed to teach generalization is increased. Engelmann and Carnine (1982) recommend that the components of a strategy should be pretaught with one example before individuals are expected to apply the entire strategy to multiple examples of stimulus conditions. Learning a strategy would then occur prior to, and not interfere with, presentation of multiple examples of a stimulus condition across which an individual is expected to generalize. Future research should examine the effects of preteaching on the total training time needed to produce generalized responding.

Third, although two examples frequently are considered to be sufficient in producing stimulus generalization, research has not yet established the minimum number of examples required to produce generalized responding (Haring, 1985; Stokes & Baer, 1977). Five training examples were effective in producing generalization in Hughes and Rusch (1989); previous studies have used as many as eight examples (Horner et al., 1985) and as few as two (Pancsofar & Bates, 1985). Stokes and Baer (1977) argue that the number of examples required to produce generalized responding may vary, depending upon characteristics of the task to be learned and an individual's skill repertoire in relation to the task. Further, if generalization is desired across a wide range of topographically dissimilar responses, more examples may need to be trained to represent the diversity of required responses to assure generalized responding.

To further refine the model for teaching self-instruction with multiple exemplars proposed in this chapter, rules for determining the optimum number and diversity of teaching examples required to produce generalized responding should be established based upon relevant factors (e.g., type of responses, diversity of responses, subjects's skill repertoire). Future research should seek to determine the most efficient method for teaching multiple exemplars in combination with self-instruction.

VIII. SUMMARY

The full participation of individuals with mental retardation in the community requires performance of newly acquired skills in novel circumstances and across the varying demands characteristic of life in the everyday world. For example, a person who has learned how to ride a bus may have to adapt to changes in scheduling, bus routes, or fares. Or an employee who has been taught by a coworker to make salads in a fast-food restaurant will need to continue to complete orders when the coworker no longer is present. Although skill generalization is an implicit educational goal, instructional strategies rarely are employed to influence the attainment of this goal (Haring & Laitinen, in press). Self-instruction is a strategy that has been effective in promoting the independent performance of people with mental retardation. Self-instruction provides individuals with the means for guiding their own behavior in novel situations not associated with training and after assistance has been withdrawn. For example, by using self-instruction, people with mental retardation have learned, among other skills, to sequence their tasks, increase their rate of production, and solve work-related problems.

This chapter evaluated studies that investigated use of self-instruction among individuals with mental retardation in community settings. The focus of the review was on identification of factors relating to generalization across people, situations, tasks, and time. The combination of these factors suggests a model for promoting independent performance among individuals with mental retardation. This model combines self-instruction with teaching multiple exemplars and comprises the following six steps: (a) Select an array of examples (responses) an individual is likely to be required to perform in an environment (step 1); (b) classify responses into teaching sets based upon a functional analysis (step 2); (c) divide items of each set into responses that will serve as training examples and those that will serve as generalization probes (step 3); (d) teach trained examples using self-instruction (step 4); (e) evaluate effect of training on trained and untrained examples (i.e., generalization probes) as well as verbalized self-instructional statements (step 5); and (f) withdraw training based upon performance criteria while evaluating the effect of withdrawal (step 6). These steps represent the best practices for promoting independent performance of individuals with mental retardation in the community.

REFERENCES

Agran, M., Fodor-Davis, J., & Moore, S. (1986). The effects of self-instructional training on job-task sequencing: Suggesting a problem-solving strategy. *Education and Training of the Mentally Retarded, 21,* 273-281.

Agran, M., Salzberg, C. L., & Stowitschek, J. J. (1987). An analysis of the effects of a social skills training program using self-instructions on the acquisition and generalization of two social behaviors in a work setting. *The Journal of the Association for Persons with Severe Handicaps, 12,* 131-139.

Berg, W. K., Wacker, D. P., & Flynn, T. H. (1990). Teaching generalization and maintenance of work behavior. In F. R. Rusch (Ed.), *Supported employment: Models, methods, and issues* (pp. 145-160). Sycamore, IL: Sycamore.

Carnine, D. (1900). New research on the brain: Implications for instruction. *Phi Delta Kappan, 71,* 372-377.

Catania, A. C., Matthews, B. A., & Shimoff, E. (1982). Instructed versus shaped human verbal behavior interaction with nonverbal responding. *Journal of the Experimental Analysis of Behavior, 38,* 233-248.

Doyle, P. J., Goldstein, H., Bourgeois, M. S., & Nakles, K. O. (1989). Facilitating generalized requesting behavior in Broca's aphasia: An experimental analysis of a generalization training procedure. *Journal of Applied Behavior Analysis, 22,* 157-170.

Engelmann, S., & Carnine, D. W. (1982). *Theory of instruction: Principles and applications.* New York: Irvington.

Haring, N. G. (Ed.). (1988). *Generalization for students with severe handicaps: Strategies and solutions.* Seattle: University of Washington Press.

Haring, T. G. (1985). Teaching between-class generalization of toy play behavior to handicapped children. *Journal of Applied Behavior Analysis, 18,* 127-139.

Haring, T. G., & Laitinen, R. E. (in press). Extending complex repertoires of critical skills. In R. J. Gaylord-Ross (Ed.), *Issues and research in special education* (Vol. 2). New York: Teachers College Press.

Horner, R. H., Jones, D. N., & Williams, J. A. (1985). A functional approach to training generalized street crossing. *The Journal of the Association for the Severely Handicapped, 10,* 71-78.

Horner, R. H., Sprague, J., & Wilcox, B. (1982). General case programming for community activities. In B. Wilcox & G. T. Bellamy (Eds.), *Design of high school programs for severely handicapped students* (pp. 61-98). Baltimore: Paul H. Brookes.

Hughes, C., & Petersen, D. L. (1989). Utilizing a self-instructional training package to increase on-task behavior and work performance. *Education and Training in Mental Retardation, 24,* 114-120.

Hughes, C., & Rusch, F. R. (1989). Teaching supported employees with severe mental retardation to solve problems. *Journal of Applied Behavior Analysis, 22,* 365-372.

Keogh, D. A., Whitman, T. L., & Maxwell, S. E. (1988). Self-instruction versus external instruction: Individual differences and training effectiveness. *Cognitive Therapy and Researcher, 12,* 591-610.

Leon, J. A., & Pepe, H. J. (1983). Self-instructional training: Cognitive behavior modification for remediating arithmetic deficits. *Exceptional Children, 50,* 54-60.

Meichenbaum, D., & Goodman, J. (1971). Training impulsive children to talk to themselves: A means of developing self-control. *Journal of Abnormal Psychology, 77,* 116-126.

Pancsofar, E., & Bates, P. (1985). The impact of the acquisition of successive exemplars on generalization. *The Journal of the Association for Persons with Severe Handicaps, 10,* 3-11.

Park, H., & Gaylord-Ross, R. (1989). A problem-solving approach to social skills training in employment settings with mentally retarded youth. *Journal of Applied Behavior Analysis, 22,* 373-380.

Rusch, F. R., Chadsey-Rusch, J., & Lagomarcino, T. (1987). Preparing students for employment. In M. E. Snell (Ed.), *Systematic instruction for persons with severe handicaps* (3rd ed., pp. 471-490). Columbus, OH: Charles E. Merrill.

Rusch, F. R., & Kazdin, A. E. (1981). Toward a methodology of withdrawal designs for the assessment of response maintenance. *Journal of Applied Behavior Analysis, 14,* 131-140.

Rusch, F. R., McKee, M., Chadsey-Rusch, J., & Renzaglia, A. (1988). Teaching a student with severe handicaps to self-instruct: A brief report. *Education and Training in Mental Retardation, 23,* 51-58.

Rusch, F. R., Morgan, T. K., Martin, J. E., Riva, M., & Agran, M. (1985). Competitive employment: Teaching mentally retarded adults self-instructional strategies. *Applied Research in Mental Retardation, 6,* 389-407.

Salend, S. J., Ellis, L. L., & Reynolds, C. J. (1989). Using self-instruction to teach vocational skills to individuals who are severely retarded. *Education and Training in Mental Retardation, 24,* 248-254.

Secan, K. E., Egel, A. L., & Tilley, C. S. (1989). Acquisition, generalization, and maintenance of question-answering skills in autistic children. *Journal of Applied Behavior Analysis, 22,* 181-196.

Skinner, B. F. (1953). *Science and human behavior.* New York: Macmillan.

Sprague, J., & Horner, R. (1984). The effects of single instance, multiple instance, and general case training on generalized vending machine use by moderately and severely handicapped students. *Journal of Applied Behavior Analysis, 17,* 273-278.

Stokes, T., & Baer, D. (1977). An implicit technology of generalization. *Journal of Applied Behavior Analysis, 10,* 349-367.

Whitman, T. L. (1987). Self-instruction, individual differences, and mental retardation. *American Journal of Mental Deficiency, 92,* 213-223.

Whitman, T. L. (1990). Self-regulation and mental retardation. *American Journal on Mental Retardation, 94,* 347-362.

Whitman, T. L., Spence, B. H., & Maxwell, S. E. (1987). A comparison of external and self-instructional teaching formats with mentally retarded adults in a vocational training setting. *Research in Developmental Disabilities, 8,* 371-388.

TEACHING SELF-INSTRUCTIONAL SKILLS TO PERSONS WITH MENTAL RETARDATION: A DESCRIPTIVE AND EXPERIMENTAL ANALYSIS

MARTIN AGRAN
RONALD C. MARTELLA
Utah State University

I. INTRODUCTION

Use of self-control procedures involves either alterations in the consequences following a response or in the antecedents that precede a response (Mahoney & Mahoney, 1976; Thoresen & Coates, 1977). To alter the antecedents involves limiting the range of discriminative stimuli that exert control over behavior (Rusch, Morgan, Martin, Riva, & Agran, 1985). That is, individuals are trained to perform desired behavior in the presence of discriminative stimuli. These stimuli become associated with the behavior and thus increase the likelihood of that behavior occurring again (Wehman, 1975). Among the procedures that have been used to manipulate antecedents have been self-instructions (Agran & Martin, 1987), which represent verbalizations that are used to cue or direct behavior (Friedling & O'Leary, 1979). Israel (1978) suggests that such self-generated verbal behavior may have a regulatory or directive function. That is, self-instructions may acquire discriminative stimulus control over succeeding responses. Thereby, emitting self-instructions may provide persons with mental retardation with opportunities to manage their own behavior rather than being managed by others. As a result, they may become more independent and less dependent on others.

Although the number of self-instructional training studies involving persons with mental retardation remain limited, several studies on the effects of self-instructional training have recently been reported in the research literature. In all, these studies support the feasibility of teaching persons with mental retardation to use self-instructions to facilitate the acquisition of new skills and to generalize and maintain these newly acquired skills across a variety of settings and conditions, despite previous assertions that the cognitive or verbal limitations characteristic of persons with mental retardation preclude such training (Luria, 1961). Because of the linguistic deficiencies of participants, modifications in the verbalizations taught may need to be made (Agran, Fodor-Davis, & Moore, 1986); nevertheless, the use of self-instructions by persons with mental retardation appears to be an efficient procedure to promote independent functioning.

The purpose of this chapter is to review the effects of self-instructional training on the adaptive functioning of persons with mild to severe mental retardation. First, a behavioral definition of self-instructional training is suggested. Next, different types of self-instructions are presented. Following, applications across school, community, and work environments are described. Last, an experimental analysis of self-instructional training is provided and unexamined issues in self-instructional training are discussed. Overall, the chapter suggests that self-instructional training for persons with mental retardation represents an efficient intervention to facilitate their acquisition, generalization, and maintenance of a variety of adaptive skills across school, community, and work environments.

A. Suggesting a Behavioral Definition

A difficulty in understanding the operative variables associated with reported behavior changes and self-instructions has been speculation by researchers that self-control procedures represent strategies that function on hypothesized cognitive processes or structures, that is, inferred events. Indeed, self-instruction procedures are particularly susceptible to the interpretation of reported results being a function of internal causes (Brigham, 1989). Consequently, self-instructions are often regarded as covert mediators, which function as silent verbalizations that control voluntary behavior (Langer, 1969). For example, Luria (1961) suggests that internalization of speech provides the child a basis of self-regulation of behavior and increased control over the environment. This happens in the following way. First, the speech of parents or guardians controls children's overt behavior. Then, when children are older, their own speech internally controls their overt behavior. Such internalized or covert speech becomes the means by which subsequent behavior will be regulated. Although such self-directed speech is emitted mostly by children, Meichenbaum (1977) suggests that older children or adults can use self-directed verbalizations to mediate their behavior.

There is no question that the human environment is in many ways a language environment, and our behavior is controlled largely through language (Watson & Tharp, 1989). Needless to say, language often has a strong and immediate effect on our behavior. Because covert behavior is subject to the same principles as overt behavior (Homme, 1965), it is clear that a great deal of our behavior may be controlled by subvocal speech. Nevertheless, ascribing observed behavior change to inferred or private events, however appealing conceptually, has only obscured behavioral analysis. Failure to understand instructional interactions in terms of observed, public events provides no way to identify the role or contributions of intervention components. Further, without empirical scrutiny, there is no way in which functional relationships can be suggested. As Brigham (1989) noted, our focus should be on understanding behavior-environment interactions and not trying to influence internal events.

Needless to say, an assumption of applied behavior analysis is that the factors responsible for behavior change involve the individual's history and the environment. Following this assumption, it may be helpful to assess the effects produced by self-instructions in terms of stimulus control.

When there is a high probability that an individual will perform a particular response when a specific stimulus is present, it is suggested that this response is under stimulus control. Teaching persons with mental retardation to perform target behaviors when specific stimuli are present is, in part, predicated on the assumption that they will be able to discriminate that the cue is present, that is, the stimuli are sufficiently discernible. However, when the antecedent stimuli are not as apparent, it is imperative that the saliency of the stimulus is promoted. In effect, self-instructional training represents the application of stimulus control to skill development by providing additional verbal cues.

Because persons with mental retardation often have difficulties problem solving or remembering what to do next, they may benefit from self-generated verbal prompts that provide additional or redundant cues for desired behavior. Use of self-instructions increases the opportunities for persons with mental retardation to attend to important cues. With increased opportunities to repeat and hear their own instructions, their recall of task instructions may increase.

Malott (1984) suggests that self-managed behavior represents an example of rule-governed behavior. As such, self-instructions serve as rules or cues designed to establish direct-acting contingencies. These contingencies are in contrast to contingencies that may be weak or delayed and serve to reinforce or punish the causal response class. As with other types of rules or cues, they are designed to provide stimulus control. By using self-instructions, individuals can put their behavior under appropriate stimulus control. This will allow them to complete a desired response and access a desired reinforcer or avoid an undesired outcome or condition.

B. Types of Self-Instructions

An obvious advantage of self-instructions is their portability; they can be tailored to a variety of situations or tasks. Although the self-instructional format typically used is one that follows a problem-solving format, there are several types of self-instructional formats that have been investigated. A description of each follows.

1. PROBLEM SOLVING

This format involves teaching a set of verbalizations to help the individuals determine an appropriate response to a problematic situation. First, the individual is taught to verbalize that he or she does have a problem or that a problem exists in the environment. Second, a solution to the problem is verbalized. Next, a self-directed instruction to perform the planned response is emitted. For example, Agran, Salzberg, and Stowitschek (1987) taught five employees with moderate or severe handicaps to emit a set of self-instructions when they ran out of work materials or needed assistance. The self-instructions included the following: "I ran out of work materials. I need to get more. I'll get up and ask for more." This procedure allowed participants to apply a basic problem-solving strategy to a common work problem.

2. DID-NEXT-NOW

Self-instructions can be used to help an individual complete a task sequence. Such self-instructions help the individual to state what response was just completed and what response(s) needs to be done next. This format provides the individual with a review of the response performed and an opportunity to rehearse verbally what needs to be done next. Thus the completion of each task (i.e., the verbal statement) becomes the stimulus condition for the next task. Agran et al. (1986) reported that this strategy increased job-task sequencing for four students with mental retardation.

3. WHAT/WHERE

This format is appropriate for responses that the individual can perform but that are not under stimulus control. Participants are instructed to emit verbal prompts to guide their performance on a task. Specifically, they are taught to select key words from an instruction or from written information so they can ascertain *what* to do and *where* to do it. Agran, Fodor-Davis, Moore, and Deer (1989) taught five students with moderate to severe intellectual disabilities to use such a strategy to promote their instruction-following skills. This training produced strong and immediate changes for participants in following instructions.

4. INTERACTIVE

Meichenbaum and Goodman (1971) recommend that self-instructions be taught using a sequence in which the individual is first instructed to repeat the self-instructions aloud, then to whisper them, and, last, to repeat them silently. However, a limitation of this approach is that, when an individual is either whispering or quietly repeating the verbalization, it is difficult, if not impossible, to determine whether he or she is indeed self-instructing. Without accurate information on the frequency of occurrence of self-instructions, there is no way to suggest that a functional relationship exists. Thus self-instructions need to be emitted at a sufficient volume so their occurrence may be reported. Such responding may, however, produce another problem. Overtly emitting self-instructions aloud may produce negative perceptions in others in the setting. Although desired changes may be reported, such verbalizations may be socially inappropriate.

To ameliorate such a problem, Agran, Fodor-Davis, Moore, and Martella (1990) investigated the effects of an interactive self-instructional format on the food preparation skills of students with mental retardation. The self-instructions were approached as questions. They reminded the participants what to do when performing the task while they were interacting with customers. Three verbalizations were taught. The first verbalization reminded the individual of the step completed (e.g., "Here's the rye bread"). The second directed the participant to the next step (e.g., "Spreads are next"). The last verbalization was a question addressed to the person with whom the participant was interacting (e.g., "What type of spreads would you like?"). The strategy promoted the students' work performance and allowed them to self-instruct overtly in a socially acceptable manner.

In summary, several types of self-instructional formats have been investigated. These formats were designed to provide appropriate verbal regulatory or problem-solving structures to aid task performance.

II. DEMONSTRATIONS IN SCHOOL ENVIRONMENTS

To assess the effects of self-instructions in school environments, researchers have utilized both group (see Table 1) and single-subject designs. Descriptions of these applications are presented below for the following domains: behavior management, academic instruction, and prevocational training.

A. Behavior Management

Burgio, Whitman, and Johnson (1980) used a self-instructional package to increase the attending behavior of two individuals. The self-instructional package involved an experimenter who modeled the task (math or printing) while verbalizing the self-instructions. After the experimenter modeled the behaviors, the participants were asked to verbalize the self-instructions while performing the tasks. During this time, the experimenter whispered the self-instructions along with the participant, faded himself from the self-instructional prompts, and, finally, remained silent. The percentage of intervals of off-task behavior during math, printing, and phonics was recorded. After training, a decrease in off-task behavior was observed in transfer and classroom settings. Also, the percentage of intervals of self-instructions increased for math and printing across both settings. Further, generalization across settings was reported. Maintenance was not assessed in the study.

B. Academic Instruction

Table 1 summarizes the group design studies reviewed.

1. GROUP DESIGN

Guralnick (1976) investigated the effects of self-instructional training on the matching-to-sample skills of 32 children with mental retardation. They were randomly assigned to one of four groups: self-instruction training, model alone, feedback alone, and control. The training for the self-instructional group consisted of modeling verbalizations and corresponding motor behavior, then fading from audible to covert self-instructions. Instructions were given to all groups to proceed slowly, look carefully, and self-reinforce. In addition, the self-instructional group was provided with a problem-solving strategy that involved training them to be familiar with a sample of forms, to differentiate between the critical dimensions of the stimuli, and to eliminate incorrect alternatives by checking with a standard. A modeling-only group observed the same modeling of verbalizations and behavior as the self-instructional group but did not receive self-instructional training. A feedback-only group did not receive modeling or self-instructional training but received feedback on their performance.

Guralnick reported a statistically significant difference at the .01 alpha level between the self-instructional group and the other three groups (i.e., modeling, feedback, control) on the posttest assessment. These results suggest that self-instructional training best facilitated the acquisition of the target behavior. Generalization across responses was also assessed. Statistically significant differences between the self-instructional group and the other groups were reported across different test forms but not on a different set of materials (i.e., Matching Familiar Figures Test). However, a problem with the generalization assessment was that no baseline or pretest measures of generalization were assessed. Also, no maintenance data were gathered.

Borkowski and Varnhagen (1984) trained one group of individuals with mental retardation to use self-instructions to facilitate their acquisition of picture labeling skills. A second group received traditional didactic training, and a training group received no instruction. Self-instructional and didactic training were divided into two sets. The first set involved anticipation training (i.e., being able to anticipate and remember the order of events within a passage). The second training set involved paraphrase training (i.e., being able to repeat what has been read in one's own words). Borkowski and Varnhagen reported no difference between the two experimental conditions when tested for statistical significance at the .05 alpha

TABLE 1

Descriptive Information of Reviewed Group Design Verbal Mediation Studies

Citation	Number of Subjects	(CA) Age	Label	Data on DV V NV		Design	Generalization (actual)	Maintenance
Borkowski & Varnhagen (1984)	18	$\bar{x}$ = 8	NS	No	Yes	MG/PP/C	Yes (No)	Yes

Effect size(s):
    Anticipation training—
        strategy self-instruction training/control = 1.82
        strategy self-instruction training/strategy training = −.42
        strategy training/control = 2.28
    Paraphrase training—
        strategy self-instruction training/control = 1.00
        strategy self-instruction training/strategy training = −.74
        strategy training/control = 1.51

Guralnick (1976)	32	6-14	Mild-Moderate	No	Yes	MD/PP/C	Yes (No)	No

Effect size(s): Not enough data reported (i.e., no sd's)

Leon & Pepe (1983)	37	9-12	LD/Mild	No	Yes	2G/PP/ Contrast	Yes (No)	No

Effect size(s):
    Remediation of errors—self-instruction/Contrast = 2.20

Peters & Davies (1981)	27	x = 16	NS	No	Yes	2G/PP/NC	Yes (Yes)	No

Effect size(s):
    Number of errors—self-instruction/modeling alone −1.76
    Latency—self-instruction/modeling alone = 1.47

NOTE: DV = dependent variable; V = verbal behavior; NV = nonverbal or overt behavior; NS = not specified; PP = pre-posttest; D = data taken during; P = posttest only; MG = multiple groups (three or more); 2G = two groups; C = control group used; NC = no control group; ND = not enough data.

level. The differences between the two experimental groups and the control group were, however, statistically significant at the .05 alpha level. Also, the responses to new stimuli were assessed. The authors report that the two training groups did not generalize the strategies until three weeks after training. No differences were observed between the two experimental groups at the three-week measure; however, the experimental groups were statistically significantly different from the control group at the .05 level. Baseline or pretest measures of generalization were not assessed. Maintenance data were presented three weeks after training with no statistically significant changes from a one-week posttraining assessment.

Peters and Davies (1981) taught matching-to-sample tasks to participants in two groups: self-instruction and modeling. A self-instructional group received instructions to observe the experimenter model the self-instructions and motor behavior. After modeling, the participants were instructed to perform the target behaviors by themselves while talking aloud. Later, they were instructed to self-instruct covertly. The participants in this group were required to do the following in their verbalizations: (a) ask what was required for the task, (b) remind themselves to go slowly and carefully, (c) prompt themselves to check each alternative and the standard before answering, and (d) self-reinforce each of the three previous verbalizations. Modeling of the self-instructions was provided to the modeling group, but its members were not asked to self-instruct. A statistically significant difference on performance between the self-instructional and modeling groups at the .05 alpha level on the Matching Familiar Figures Test was reported. Generalization across responses on the Matching Familiar Figures Test before and after training was also assessed. The results indicated that the participants in the self-instructional group generalized their responding to the Matching Familiar Figures Test. Maintenance was not assessed.

Finally, Leon and Pepe (1983) investigated the effects of self-instructions in remediating deficits in arithmetic computation for 24 children with mild mental retardation and 13 students with learning disabilities. These students were assigned to either a self-instructional group or a systematic instruction-only group. In all, 6 students with learning disabilities and 11 students with mild mental retardation were assigned to the self-instructional group, and 7 students with learning disabilities and 13 students with mild mental retardation were assigned to the contrast, instruction-only group. Both groups received the same curriculum for teaching the use of mathematics skills; however, the self-instructional group received training in the use of self-instructions. The self-instructional training sequence was modeled on the procedure reported by Meichenbaum and Goodman (1971). Leon and Pepe (1983) reported that the self-instructional training was statistically significantly more effective at the .05 alpha level in remediating deficits as compared with the systematic instruction-only group. Also, they indicated that self-instructional training appeared to enhance generalization across responses; however, response level on the generalization (i.e., untrained) problems before training was initiated was not assessed. The authors concluded that self-instructional training was appropriate to teach students problem-solving operations and facilitated the transfer of stimulus control from teacher to student. Maintenance was not assessed in this investigation.

2. SINGLE-SUBJECT DESIGN

Albion and Salzberg (1982) trained four students with mental retardation to use self-instructions to improve their math performance. First, the participants were told that, if they learned to say the "right things," it could improve their school performance. They were then trained in how to use self-instructions prior to working on sample math problems. A fifth participant remained in a protracted baseline condition. The self-instructions taught included (a) work slowly and carefully, (b) keep eyes on paper, (c) avoid useless talk with others, and (d) ignore others who attempt to bother me. Also, participants were taught to score their own math worksheets with the use of an answer sheet and were given gummed stars to place along vertical boxes on daily progress monitoring charts if they met the established criteria. Improvements in the completion rate of correctly performed math problems were reported for three of the four participants. Generalization was not assessed; however, maintenance data collected one week after training terminated were reported.

Johnston, Whitman, and Johnson (1980) trained three students with mental retardation to improve their math performance using self-instructions. The training package included having the trainer solve a problem that required regrouping while participants talked aloud (i.e., modeling of verbal and actual performance), performing a similar task while the trainer instructed them aloud, and rehearsing self-verbalizations while being frequently prompted by the trainer. After participants were able to independently perform the task while self-instructing aloud, they were requested to perform the task while whispering to themselves, followed by the use of private speech. An increase in the percentage of problems completed correctly was reported while the rate of completion decreased. However, self-instructions were faded to private speech, thus precluding the measurement of self-instructions emitted. Generalization across responses and settings were reported, although data were not gathered in the natural classroom. The authors indicate that, according to teachers' reports, there were improvements in the participants' math computational skills and their responses to similar math problems. Maintenance data were not gathered.

Last, Whitman and Johnson (1983) also investigated the effects of self-instructional training on the math performance of nine students with mental retardation. The self-instructions involved a series of questions and answers used in solving math problems that required regrouping. For example, questions included, (a) What kind of problem is this? and, (b) Now what do I do? The results indicated that the frequency of self-instructions displayed by the participants varied considerably (i.e., less than 25% for two participants, between 25% and 50% for five participants, and greater than 50% for two participants). The data reported suggest that either the self-instructions were not responsible for the participants' improvements on math problems or the self-instructions were silently emitted. Nevertheless, generalization was also observed from the training settings to the classroom and across math problems during the presentation of similar problems requiring regrouping. Maintenance was not assessed.

C. Prevocational Training

Four studies addressed the effects of teaching self-instructions on the acquisition of vocational tasks. Wacker, Carroll, and Moe (1980) taught four children with moderate mental retardation to use self-instructions to enhance their performance in an assembly task composed of three different colored paper circles. The students were taught in a five-step training program to verbalize the color of the circles before assembling paper snowmen. Praise, graduated guidance, and repeated demonstrations were also included within the training package. The training package enabled the students to generalize the learned task from the training setting to the regular classroom and to maintain the response for up to three weeks.

As a follow-up to the Wacker et al. (1980) study, Wacker and Greenebaum (1984) taught participants to appropriately sort cards using a "self-labeling" technique. Two groups were trained separately. Group 1 received nonverbal training that involved experimenter demonstration of correct sorting, contingent praise for correct sorting of cards, and correction of errors. Group 2 received verbal training that consisted of verbal instructions to label the cards before each trial, reinforcement and correction for the participant's response, and reinforcement and correction for card sorting. Both groups successfully acquired the card sorting behavior. However, the verbal training group's performance generalized to a novel shape and a novel dimension (i.e., colors), whereas the nonverbal training group's behavior did not generalize. Because the nonverbal training group did not show generalization, the experimenters trained the group in labeling and observed a subsequent improvement in generalization. Although generalization was achieved after training, it was not measured before training was started.

Agran et al. (1989) examined the effects of a multicomponent self-instructional program on the instruction-following skills of five students with moderate to severe intellectual disabilities who were receiving a required school-based training program in janitorial skills prior to their performance in a supported employment project. The students were instructed to state to themselves what they were supposed to do and where they were supposed to do it after being given an instruction. Data were collected on responses to both trained and untrained instructions. The findings demonstrated that the training program enhanced the instruction-following skills of all participants across both trained and untrained instructions. Further, the increases were maintained for up to three months.

Last, Agran et al. (1990) examined the effects of a peer-delivered self-instructional training program on the work performance of three participants involved in a supported employment project at a university cafeteria. Two students with mild mental retardation were trained to teach three students with moderate mental retardation to make sandwiches. To minimize potential negative perceptions by customers, an interactive self-instructional format was used in which verbalizations were treated as questions. The results demonstrated that the peer-delivered instruction was effective in teaching a relatively complex work task to two of the three participants; for the third participant, a combined picture cue and self-instructional training program, directed by a trainer, produced greater improvement. Additionally, all participants generalized their skills across novel customers.

III. DEMONSTRATIONS IN COMMUNITY ENVIRONMENTS

Although the utility of self-instructional programs has been demonstrated in school and work environments, the use of these strategies in residential environments has not been reported (Agran & Martin, 1987), except for one investigation. Keogh, Faw, Whitman, and Reid (1984) investigated the effects of self-instructional training on the development of social-leisure skills (i.e., game-playing skills) for two youths with severe mental retardation. The participants were taught to emit a number of verbalizations specific to six games. The multiple-probe design was used to assess the effects of the intervention. The results revealed an increase for both participants in game proficiency and level of verbalization. In particular, it was noted that the participants used the self-instructions not only to guide their performance but also to instruct one another.

IV. DEMONSTRATIONS IN WORK ENVIRONMENTS

Although the number of investigations is limited, the feasibility of teaching persons with mental retardation to use self-instructions to enhance their work performance has been demonstrated. The following section will review applications of self-instructional training in work environments. First, the effects of self-instructional training on facilitating social skill development will be described. Next, the effects of training on work productivity will be reviewed. Last, the effects of training on the development of problem-solving skills will be discussed.

A. Social Skills

To date, three studies on the effects of self-instructional training on social skills in work environments have been reported. Agran et al. (1987) investigated the effects of a social skills training programs with a self-instruction component on two social skills identified as critical to employment success: self-initiated contacts with a supervisor when an employee ran out of work materials and self-initiated contacts with a supervisor when an employee needed assistance. Five sheltered workshop employees with moderate to severe handicaps participated. Following a problem-solving format, the participants were instructed to emit several self-instructions pertaining to the nature of the problem (i.e., "I ran out of swing assemblies") and a means to resolve it (i.e., "I need to ask for more assemblies"). The results indicated that the training was effective in increasing the number of self-initiated contacts for all participants. Further, the findings revealed that the skills generalized across settings and were maintained for up to three months.

Rusch, McKee, Chadsey-Rusch, and Renzaglia (1988) conducted a systematic replication of Agran et al. (1987). A secondary-level student with severe handicaps, who worked at a film center, was trained to say that he needed more materials. The intervention involved preinstruction and corrective feedback in the performance setting. Although Rusch et al. (1985) and Agran et al. (1987) found that preinstruction was sufficient to change the target behavior, the current study did not support this finding. Nevertheless, the results indicated that the intervention produced rapid changes in the number of requests for materials.

Last, Gardner, Clees, and Cole (1983) examined a multicomponent self-management program, including self-instructions, on reducing the frequency of disruptive verbal ruminations by persons with moderate mental retardation in a sheltered training facility. Although decreases in verbalizations were reported, the number of self-instructions emitted was not reported.

B. Productivity

Several researchers have investigated the effects of self-instructional programs on promoting productivity. Rusch et al. (1985) investigated the effects of training on time spent working for two employees with mental retardation who were employed as food service employees. The training was provided in four 30-minute sessions. The results indicated that the training produced improvements for both participants. Further, targeted work behavior was maintained for four and six weeks, respectively.

Salend, Ellis, and Reynolds (1989) investigated the effects of a self-instructional program on the work performance of four persons with severe mental retardation in a vocational training program. The participants were engaged in packaging combs into plastic bags. Production rates and error rates were selected as dependent variables. The findings revealed that the training produced dramatic effects in increasing production levels with corollary decreases in error rates.

Moore, Agran, and Fodor-Davis (1989) examined the effects of a self-management program, involving self-instructions, goal setting, and self-reinforcement, on the production rates of four workers with severe mental retardation employed at a sheltered training facility. The participants were instructed to set performance goals for themselves (i.e., set timers to specified periods of time) and to reinforce themselves with coins when they met their criteria. Although a component analysis was not conducted, the findings revealed that all participants increased their production rates to criterion levels. Further, the increases were maintained for up to three months.

Hughes and Petersen (1989) examined the effects of a self-instructional program on increasing the on-task behavior and work accuracy and completion of three sheltered workshop employees with mild to moderate mental retardation. In addition to the self-instructions, the intervention included picture cues and a self-reinforcement procedure. The results indicated that all target behaviors improved.

Rusch, Martin, Lagomarcino, and White (1987) taught a woman with moderate mental retardation to sequence her job-related duties at a fast-food restaurant via the use of verbal mediation. She was instructed to verbally rehearse her job sequence prior to her work performance. The findings revealed that positive and consistent changes occurred. Although the strategy did not involve the use of self-instructions per se, the strategy employed demonstrated the efficacy of improving work performance through the use of self-generated verbal behavior.

Crouch, Karlan, and Rusch (1984) examined the effects of correspondence training on participants' start time, task duration, and supervisor ratings. The participants were mentally retarded and employed as kitchen workers. They were instructed to say when they would start and complete their work. First, they were reinforced for stating these times. Next, they were reinforced only for the positive correspondence between their stated times and their actual start and completion times. The results indicated that the correspondence training was effective in increasing the task speed of all participants, although one participant did not achieve the criterion level.

Last, Whitman, Spence, and Maxwell (1987) investigated the effects of self-instructions on the work performance of 19 sheltered workshop employees with mild to moderate mental retardation. The participants were divided randomly into two groups: one group received self-instructional training and the second group received externally directed instruction. Statistical analyses (i.e., ANCOVAs and MANCOVAs) were conducted to determine differences between the training procedures. The results revealed that there were no differences in training time between the two procedures; however, differences were noted in task performance and across generalization measures. In all, the self-instructional training permitted more participants to achieve criterion levels than had those who received the externally delivered instruction.

C. Problem Solving

Self-instructional training has been used effectively to enhance problem-solving for persons with mental retardation. Agran et al. (1987) examined the effects of a self-instructional training package on the job-task sequencing of four students with mild to moderate mental retardation enrolled in a hospital work skills training program. The students were instructed to say what they had just finished doing, what they needed to do next, and what they were going to do now. One student who was unable to consistently report the self-instructions was instructed to provide a verbal label prior to each task response. The results demonstrated that the package increased job-task sequencing for all participants. Additionally, the data revealed increases in task completion with corresponding decreases in unnecessary task repetition. Further, the behavior changes were maintained for up to three months.

Hughes and Rusch (1989) taught two employees with severe mental retardation, employed by a janitorial supply company, to solve work-related problems (e.g., materials in wrong place, work area littered). The participants were instructed to state the problem, provide a correct response, perform the stated response, report the action taken, and then reinforce themselves. The problematical situations presented included both trained and untrained situations. The results demonstrated that the skills acquired by the participants generalized across untrained problem situations. The authors suggest that combining self-instructional training with multiple learning strategies represents an effective procedure to solve unique problems in work environments.

In a systematic replication of Hughes and Rusch (1989), Hughes and Rusch (1990) incorporated two major changes. First, a precise monitoring of self-instructions emitted throughout the investigation was conducted. Second, participants' responses to both trained and untrained situations during each observation session were made. As in the previous study, the participants used self-instructions to respond appropriately to both trained and untrained situations. The data reported, however, revealed that high frequencies of correct responses did not occur until after the participants verbalized all of the self-instructions. Thus the self-instructions did not appear to have a problem-solving function until after the complete self-instructional sequence was acquired and consistently performed in response to multiple exemplars.

V. EXPERIMENTAL ANALYSIS

A review of the investigations on the effects of self-instructional training reveals several major methodological issues. First, self-instructional packages typically consist of several components such as modeling, verbal instruction, and reinforcement. Although the self-instructional component may be posited as the primary component in the package, this component is likely to interact with other components in the package. Consequently, it is imprudent to suggest that the self-instructions alone produced the reported behavior changes. For example, modeling may have been the critical component in producing change, rather than the self-instructions, or the two together may have been more effective than either alone.

Although some researchers may be tempted to make claims that the self-instructions alone may produce desired changes, other researchers have indicated that this claim cannot be made. For example, Burgio et al. (1980) suggest that self-instructions may be used to decrease hyperactivity but stated that a component analysis was not done to substantiate the argument. Other authors (i.e., Agran et al., 1986, 1987; Albion & Salzberg, 1982; Cole, Gardner, & Karan, 1985; Rusch et al., 1985) also indicate that a component analysis was not done in their investigations of the effects of self-instructional training and thus note that it was unclear which variables, singularly or in combination, were responsible for the treatment gains, generalization, or maintenance. According to Hughes and Petersen (1989, p. 114), "Self-instruction appears to be influenced by different arrangements of treatment components." The statement that self-instructional training is effective is not a problem if researchers conclude that the total training package led to the desired results (e.g., Agran et al., 1987; Burgio et al., 1980). If researchers fail to credit the total packages used, major threats to the validity of their investigations may be present.

Second, in several of the investigations using group designs, important information was missing. For example, Guralnick (1976) suggests that self-instructional training resulted in significantly greater improvements from pre- to posttest assessments than other types of training. Participants ranged in age from 6-14 years, and their IQs ranged from 45 to 83; however, no information was given on the standard deviation of the IQ, age, or group characteristics. Although random assignment reduces the possibility of having selection biases, it does not assure that selection bias will be eliminated. It is conceivable that the self-instructional group was older and/or higher functioning than the other groups. This explanation may account for some of the differences. In addition, standard deviations were not reported in the study; thus standardized mean differences between groups could not be calculated. Therefore, there is uncertainty as to whether or not the obtained results approached educational/psychological significance for group comparisons in terms of this particular effect size calculation.

Third, another potential problem may have been apparent in the study by Peters and Davies (1981). The researchers randomly assigned 14 individuals to two groups and presented information indicating that the groups did not differ in mental age or IQ. Upon examination of the means and standard deviations of the two groups before and after training, skewed distributions of IQ may have been present. For example, the mean latency for the self-instructional group was 18.1 after training and the standard deviation was 10.1. The pretest mean latency for the modeling groups was 8.9 and the standard deviation was 8.3. Finally, the posttest mean latency for the modeling group was 9.6 and the standard deviation was 5.8. Therefore, the distributions for both groups may not have been normal. This may make interpretation of the data difficult because the distributions seem to be highly skewed, even though the t-test is robust to violations to this assumption. It is apparent from Table 1, however, that large effect sizes were present in the investigation. For example, the effect size for self-instructions versus modeling alone on number of errors was −1.76; the latency was 1.47. From these results, it is apparent that the self-instructional group's performance was far superior to the modeling-alone group.

Fourth, other issues also warrant experimental analysis. Researchers have reported that one method of achieving generalization and maintenance of treatment gains is through the use of self-instructions. It is postulated that the self-instructions act as discriminative stimuli that are portable in any environment (Stokes, Osnes, & Guevremont, 1987). Thus generalization is achieved because the discriminative stimuli are always present. A question remains, however, as to whether the self-instructions are in and of themselves discriminative stimuli that control the emission of a target behavior. It is also possible that self-instructions are a separate set of responses that are performed concurrently with the target behavior. In the studies in which generalization across responses were reported, it remains unclear whether generalization occurred due to the self-instructions or due to other discriminative stimuli that were present in the generalization environment. This issue warrants further study.

VI. UNEXAMINED ISSUES

Self-instructional training has been viewed as a more robust training technique than more conventional, externally managed procedures (e.g., feedback, modeling) (Guralnick, 1976; Peters & Davies, 1981). As noted previously, a potential problem in suggesting the effectiveness of self-instructional procedures is uncertainty as to whether the self-instructions are controlling the behavior or the environmental consequences. An empirical demonstration that the self-instructions are the controlling variable requires an assessment of the frequency of occurrence of the verbalizations taught. According to Meichenbaum and Goodman (1971), self-instructions should be faded to covert verbalizations. However, if this is done, there is no way to determine objectively whether the participants are actually self-instructing. To ensure that there is indeed a relationship between the verbalizations emitted and the subsequent responses performed, a precise measurement of both the verbal behavior and the target behavior is required. Future research needs to address this issue more systematically.

A related problem involves the implementation of the independent variable. Assessing the accomplishments of participants without measuring program details does not provide sufficient information to evaluate programs (Voeltz & Evans, 1983). Therefore, it is critical for researchers to confirm the implementation of the independent variable through systematic observation (Shaver, 1983). This procedure seems especially important for self-instructional research because the self-instructions, in effect, serve as the independent variable. Verification of the correct delivery of self-instruction needs at least to involve measuring the emission of self-instructions until skill acquisition before the participant is requested to self-instruct covertly. These data may provide sufficient information to suggest a relationship between the self-instructions emitted and the corresponding responses.

One method that has been recommended to investigate the controlling properties of self-instructions is to calculate conditional probabilities (Matthews, Shimoff, & Catania, 1987; Patterson, 1979). The calculation of conditional probabilities allows an investigator to relate the probability of responses, given the presence of stimuli to responses in the absence of those stimuli. Thus conditional probabilities suggest a functional relation between a response and a controlling stimulus (Patterson, 1979). For example, if one wishes to measure the effects self-instructions have on a response and to determine whether the self-instruction (S) acts as a discriminative stimulus for a response (R), the conditional probability of a response, given a self-instruction emitted (i.e., p[R/S]), can be calculated. In addition, one can calculate the following: the probability that a self-instruction would occur, given a target response (i.e., p[S/R]); the probability that a response would not occur (NR), given a self-instruction (i.e., p[NR/S]); the probability that a response would occur, given no self-instruction (NS) (i.e., p[R/NS]); the probability that a response would not occur, given no self-instruction (i.e., p[NR/NS]); the probability that a self-instruction would occur, given no response (i.e., p[S/NR]); the probability that a

TABLE 2

Example of Calculating Conditional Probabilities

		(R) Response	(NR) No Response	Total
(S)	Self-Instruction	80	10	90
(NS)	No Self-Instruction	20	40	60
	Total	100	50	150

1. p (R/S) = 80/90 = .89
2. p (R/NS) = 20/60 = .33
3. p (R) = 100/150 = .67

Conclusion: The self-instructions affect the probability of a response; the response is not independent of self-instructions.

1. p (S/R) = 80/100 = .80
2. p (S/NR) = 10/50 = .20
3. p (S) = 90/150 = .60

Conclusion: There is a high probability that a self-instruction occurred given the response; there is a low probability that a self-instruction occurred given no response.

1. p (NR/S) = 10/90 = .11
2. p (NR/NS) = 40/60 = .67è3. p (NR) = 50/150 = .33

Conclusion: There is a high probability that when there is not self-instruction, there will be no response, and a low probability that, when there is a self-instruction, there is no response.

1. p (NS/R) = 20/100 = .20
2. p (NS/NR) = 40/50 = .80
3. p (NS) = 60/150 = .40

Conclusion: There is a high probability that, when a response did not occur, there was no self-instruction, and a low probability that, when there was a response, there was no self-instruction.

self-instruction would not occur, given a response (i.e., p[NS/R]); and the probability that a self-instruction would not occur, given no response (i.e., p[NS/NR]). Any or all of these conditional probabilities can be calculated depending on the information desired. After the appropriate conditional probabilities are calculated, they are then compared with the base rate of the event. For example, if one desired to calculate the conditional probability of a response, given a self-instruction (i.e., p[R/S]), the base rate of the event R (i.e., p[R]) would be used for comparison. If the results from the calculated probabilities differed, it would be then determined that the response was dependent on the self-instruction emitted. On the other hand, if the results were the same, the response could be said to be independent of the self-instruction. Sample calculations and conclusions are provided in Table 2. This information could be valuable when making claims on the importance of teaching self-instructions to individuals with mental retardation.

Although conditional probabilities can help determine the controlling effects of self-instructions, a caveat arises. If self-instructions are not discriminative stimuli for the target response, but are responses independent of target behaviors, which are shaped by the trainer, conclusions drawn about the controlling effects of the self-instructions must be made with caution. If the participants' self-instructions and target behaviors are emitted at similar rates, a conditional probability may falsely indicate that the behavior was dependent on the self-instructions. Thus it is important to make observations of a population of opportunities for self-instructional/response sequences in which the participant sometimes does not self-instruct (Matthews et al., 1987). Under these circumstances, it would be possible to determine whether a response occurs in the absence of the self-instruction or is dependent on the self-instruction.

Last, although demonstrations of the effectiveness of self-instructional training programs have been reported across a variety of school and work environments, applications across community environments are few. Browder and Shapiro (1985) indicate that most self-management research has been conducted in artificial or noncommunity settings. They recommended that demonstrations need to be extended across daily living skills and in the natural settings where these skills are performed. Self-instructional strategies represent a potentially useful technology to enhance the acquisition, maintenance, and generalization of community living skills, and further research is warranted.

Also, self-instructional training packages have been shown to be an effective training methodology for improving a variety of school, work, and community living skills. Clearly, it is important to use the most effective training methods available; thus it is important to use the most effective training methods to measure the effectiveness and/or contribution of critical components of training packages. In all, a closer look at self-instructions and their impact on overt target behaviors of participants is needed.

REFERENCES

Agran, M., Fodor-Davis, J., & Moore, S. (1986). The effects of self-instructional training on job-task sequencing: Suggesting a problem-solving strategy. *Education and Training of the Mentally Retarded, 21,* 273-281.

Agran, M., Fodor-Davis, J., Moore, S., & Deer, M. (1989). The application of a self-management program on instruction-following skills. *The Journal of the Association for Persons with Severe Handicaps, 14,* 147-154.

Agran, M., Fodor-Davis, J., Moore, S., & Martella, R. (1990). *Effects of peer-delivered self-instructional training on a lunch-making work task for students with severe handicaps.* Manuscript submitted for publication.

Agran, M., & Martin, J. E. (1987). Applying a technology of self-control in community environments for individuals who are mentally retarded. In M. Hersen, R. M. Eisler, & P. M. Miller (Eds.), *Progress in behavior modification* (pp. 108-149). Newbury Park, CA: Sage.

Agran, M., Salzberg, C. L., & Stowitschek, J. J. (1987). An analysis of the effects of a social skills training program using self-instructions on the acquisition and generalization of two social behaviors in a work setting. *The Journal of the Association for Persons with Severe Handicaps, 12*, 131-139.

Albion, F. M., & Salzberg, C. L. (1982). The effect of self-instructions on the rate of correct addition problems with mentally retarded children. *Education and Treatment of Children, 5*, 121-131.

Borkowski, J. G., & Varnhagen, C. K. (1984). Transfer of learning strategies: Contrast of self-instructional and traditional training formats with EMR children. *American Journal of Mental Deficiency, 88*, 369-379.

Brigham, T. A. (1989). *Self-management for adolescents: A skills training program.* New York: Guilford.

Browder, D. M., & Shapiro, E. S. (1985). Applications of self-management to individuals with severe handicaps. *The Journal of the Association for Persons with Severe Handicaps, 10*, 200-208.

Burgio, L. D., Whitman, T. L., & Johnson, M. R. (1980). A self-instructional package for increasing attending behavior in educable mentally retarded children. *Journal of Applied Behavior Analysis, 13*, 443-459.

Cole, C. L., Gardner, W. I., & Karan, O. C. (1985). Self-management training of mentally retarded adults presenting severe conduct difficulties. *Applied Research in Mental Retardation, 6*, 337-347.

Crouch, K. P., Karlan, G. R., & Rusch, F. R. (1984). Competitive employment: Utilizing the correspondence training paradigm to enhance productivity. *Education and Training of the Mentally Retarded, 19*, 268-275.

Friedling, C., & O'Leary, S. G. (1979). The effects of self-instructional training on second- and third-grade hyperactive children: A failure to replicate. *Journal of Applied Behavior Analysis, 12*, 211-219.

Gardner, W. I., Clees, T. J., & Cole, C. L. (1983). Self-management of disruptive verbal ruminations by a mentally retarded adult. *Applied Research in Mental Retardation, 4*, 41-58.

Guralnick, M. J. (1976). Solving complex perceptual discrimination problems: Techniques for the development of problem-solving strategies. *American Journal of Mental Deficiency, 81*, 18-25.

Homme, L. E. (1965). Perspectives in psychology: XXIV. Control of coverants, the operants of the mind. *Psychological Record, 15*, 501-511.

Hughes, C., & Petersen, D. L. (1989). Utilizing a self-instructional training package to increase on-task behavior and work performance. *Education and Training of the Mentally Retarded, 24*, 114-120.

Hughes, C., & Rusch, F. R. (1989). Teaching supported employees with severe mental retardation to solve problems. *Journal of Applied Behavior Analysis, 22*, 365-372.

Hughes, C., & Rusch, F. R. (1990). *Teaching self-instruction utilizing multiple exemplars to produce generalized problem-solving among individuals with severe mental retardation.* Manuscript submitted for publication.

Israel, A. C. (1978). Some thoughts on correspondence between saying and doing. *Journal of Applied Behavior Analysis, 11*, 271-276.

Johnston, M. B., Whitman, T. L., & Johnson, M. (1980). Teaching addition and subtraction to mentally retarded children: A self-instruction program. *Applied Research in Mental Retardation, 1*, 141-160.

Keogh, D. A., Faw, G. D., Whitman, T. L., & Reid, D. (1984). Enhancing leisure skills in severely retarded adolescents through a self-instructional treatment package. *Analysis and Intervention in Developmental Disabilities, 4*, 333-351.

Langer, J. (1969). *Theories of development.* New York: Holt, Rinehart & Winston.

Leon, J. A., & Pepe, H. J. (1983). Self-instructional training: Cognitive behavior modification for remediating arithmetic deficits. *Exceptional Children, 50*, 54-60.

Luria, A. R. (1961). Psychological studies of mental deficiency in the Soviet Union. In N. R. Ellis (Ed.), *Handbook of mental deficiency.* New York: McGraw-Hill.

Mahoney, M. J., & Mahoney, K. (1976). Self-control techniques with the mentally retarded. *Exceptional Children, 42*, 338-339.

Malott, R. W. (1984). Rule-governed behavior, self-management, and the developmentally disabled: A theoretical analysis. *Analysis and Intervention in Developmental Disabilities, 4*, 199-209.

Matthews, B. A., Shimoff, E., & Catania, A. C. (1987). Saying and doing: A contingency-space analysis. *Journal of Applied Behavior Analysis, 20*, 69-74.

Meichenbaum, D. (1977). *Cognitive behavior modification: An integrative approach.* New York: Pergamon.

Meichenbaum, D., & Goodman, J. (1971). Training impulsive children to talk to themselves: A means of developing self-control. *Journal of Abnormal Psychology, 77,* 115-126.

Moore, S. C., Agran, M., & Fodor-Davis, J. (1989). Using self-management strategies to increase the production rates of workers with severe handicaps. *Education and Training in Mental Retardation, 24,* 324-332.

Patterson, G. R. (1979). A performance theory for coercive family interaction. In R. B. Cairns (Ed.), *The analysis of social interactions: Methods, issues, and illustrations* (pp. 119-162). Hillsdale, NJ: Lawrence Erlbaum.

Peters, R. D., & Davies, K. (1981). Effects of self-instructional training on cognitive impulsivity of mentally retarded adolescents. *American Journal of Mental Deficiency, 85,* 377-382.

Rusch, F. R., Martin, J. E., Lagomarcino, T. R., & White, D. M. (1987). Teaching task sequencing via verbal mediation. *Education and Training in Mental Retardation, 22,* 229-235.

Rusch, F. R., McKee, M., Chadsey-Rusch, J., & Renzaglia, A. (1988). Teaching a student with severe handicaps to self-instruct: A brief report. *Education and Training in Mental Retardation, 23,* 51-58.

Rusch, F. R., Morgan, T. K., Martin, J. E., Riva, M., & Agran, M. (1985). Competitive employment: Teaching mentally retarded employees self-instructional strategies. *Applied Research in Mental Retardation, 6,* 389-407.

Salend, S. J., Ellis, L. L., & Reynolds, C. J. (1989). Using self-instruction to teach vocational skills to individuals who are severely retarded. *Education and Training in Mental Retardation, 24,* 248-254.

Shaver, J. P. (1983). The verification of independent variables in teaching methods research. *Educational Researcher, 12,* 2-9.

Stokes, T. F., Osnes, P. G., & Guevremont, D. C. (1987). Saying and doing: A commentary on a contingency-space analysis. *Journal of Applied Behavior Analysis, 20,* 161-164.

Thoresen, C. E., & Coates, T. J. (1977). Behavioral self-control: Some clinical concerns. In M. Hersen, R. M. Eisler, & P. M. Miller (Eds.), *Progress in behavior modification* (Vol. 2, pp. 308-352). New York: Academic Press.

Voeltz, L. M., & Evans, I. M. (1983). Educational validity: Procedures to evaluate outcomes in programs for severely handicapped students. *The Journal of the Association for Persons with Severe Handicaps, 8,* 3-15.

Wacker, D. P., Carroll, J. L., & Moe, G. L. (1980). Acquisition, generalization, and maintenance of an assembly task by mentally retarded children. *American Journal of Mental Deficiency, 85,* 286-290.

Wacker, D. P., & Greenebaum, F. T. (1984). Efficacy of a verbal training sequence on the sorting performance of moderately and severely mentally retarded adolescents. *American Journal of Mental Deficiency, 88,* 653-660.

Watson, D., & Tharp, R. G. (1989). *Self-directed behavior: Self-modification for personal adjustment.* Pacific Grove, CA: Brooks/Cole.

Wehman, P. (1975). Behavioral self-control with the mentally retarded. *Journal of Applied Rehabilitation Counseling, 6,* 27-34.

Whitman, T., & Johnson, M. B. (1983). Teaching addition and subtraction with regrouping to educable mentally retarded children: A group self-instructional training program. *Behavior Therapy, 14,* 127-143.

Whitman, T. L., Spence, B. H., & Maxwell, S. (1987). A comparison of external and self-instructional teaching formats with mentally retarded adults in a vocational training setting. *Research in Developmental Disabilities, 8,* 371-388.

BEHAVIORAL ASSESSMENT AND TREATMENT OF BRAIN-IMPAIRED INDIVIDUALS

MICHAEL D. FRANZEN
West Virginia University School of Medicine

I. INTRODUCTION

At first glance, it might seem that clinical neuropsychology and behavior therapy might not have too much in common. Neuropsychologists are believers in the black box, and their work often relies on cognitive constructs such as visual-spatial perception. On the other hand, behaviorists concentrate on observable behaviors without reference to central nervous system structures. Behaviorists tend to eschew inferential, abstract constructs, relying instead upon descriptive assessment terms. Many clinical neuropsychologists were traditionally trained in the use of the Rorschach, an instrument that enjoys great notoriety and little popularity among behaviorists.

Recently, there has been increased interest in neuropsychology by behaviorists as witnessed by groups such as the Behavioral Neuropsychology Special Interest Group of the Association for the Advancement of Behavior Therapy. There has been a parallel interest in behavioral treatment techniques developing among neuropsychologists. The topic of behavioral assessment and intervention with brain-impaired individuals has been the focus of two previous chapters in *Progress in Behavioral Modification* (Horton & Miller, 1985; Webster & Scott, 1988). The Horton and Miller (1985) chapter focused on general issues in recovery from brain injury and on conceptual models for treatment. The Webster and Scott (1988) chapter presented general models of assessment of the brain-impaired individual and reviewed cognitive retraining studies. This chapter will present a general conceptual model for behavioral treatment of brain impairment and review the studies that used a basic behavioral methodology in treating the individual. This chapter is not intended to be a comprehensive review. Instead, the chapter can be seen as an attempt to highlight important concepts and recent trends in the behavioral assessment and treatment of brain impairment.

II. BEHAVIORAL CLINICAL NEUROPSYCHOLOGY

A. Background

Clinical neuropsychological assessment is an evolving area that has changed under the influence of multiple sources. One of those sources is the types of clinical questions asked of neuropsychologists. When questions were related to the presence of organic factors, assessment techniques were qualitative in nature and provided binary information—organic versus functional, impaired versus normal. When the questions asked were related to localization for planning surgery, the assessment techniques provided information related to the most likely site of the lesion (Franzen & Lovell, 1987a). As Reitan (1989) points out, these general trends occurred contemporaneously with neuropsychologists' intellectual interest in general tests of cerebral functioning. Those questions are still asked, but, increasingly, clinical neuropsychologists are being asked to help plan treatment for individuals with central nervous system involvement because of better survival rates from traumatic injuries, because of the increasingly older population of this country, and because of increasing social and political pressure to provide some form of treatment (Franzen & Sullivan, 1987).

Although many people agree that treatment of the brain-impaired individual is important, there is little agreement as to what constitutes the best treatment or even what skill areas are amendable to treatment. Treatment of cognitive deficits might be implemented by retraining the skill through repetition, by teaching an alternate functional system, or by teaching use of a behavioral prosthetic (a technique to facilitate functional improvement, if not actual improvement, in the skill itself).

In addition, there may be treatment of the emotional or behavioral disturbances secondary to the brain injury. For the sake of simplicity, all of these forms of treatment will be referred to as *neuropsychological rehabilitation.*

There are two areas in which behavioral theory and techniques have been adapted to clinical neuropsychological problems: in behavioral assessment and in behavioral treatment. The interest in behavioral assessment techniques has come with growing acknowledgment that traditional neuropsychological assessment techniques do not always generalize well to real-life situations. Traditional testing may identify specific lesions or molecular skill deficits, but real life often requires molar collections of skills. Localizing a lesion will not help predict whether the individual can return to independent living. An example of newer assessment techniques can be found in the Direct Assessment of Functional Status (Loewenstein et al., 1989), which involves standardized observation of the patient using a telephone directory and telephone, performing personal hygiene tasks, using a memorized shopping list, and balancing a checkbook.

The development of instruments such as Loewenstein's is not the only way that traditional clinical neuropsychological assessment can interface with behavioral assessment. Although early behavioral assessors tended to eschew psychometric, norm-referenced assessment techniques, more recent conceptualizations have included a role for psychometric testing. Traditional assessment may not always identify the exact target behavior at a level that allows for intervention planning, but comparison to norms can help identify whether a given individual's level of performance is consistent with premorbid functioning or with the general level expected of an individual in a given setting. The next stage of assessment can then concentrate on identifying target behaviors associated with adequate functioning in the setting where the client is to be placed. Standardized testing also allows for a comparison of individual strengths and weaknesses, which can be useful in developing a treatment plan. The use of a standardized memory test may indicate that a client's new learning of verbal material is superior to his or her new learning for visual material, thereby suggesting a treatment to encourage encoding of verbal representations of visual information that needs to be remembered. Finally, norm-referenced tests can be used as pre-post measures to evaluate the effectiveness of a treatment program.

Aside from the use of norm-referenced test results, idiographic assessment techniques can be adapted to neuropsychological assessment. Little actual work has been done in this area, but the implications are interesting. Rosenberger, Mohr, Stoddard, and Sidman (1968) used matching-to-sample laboratory techniques to investigate organic communication deficits. This procedure allowed a greater specification of deficit type in that matching spoken single letters to either tactile or visual stimuli was intact whereas matching letters to their homonymous word counterparts was impaired even when both the stimulus and the response were visual, that is, intramodal. A subsequent paper classified aphasic deficits as some breakdown in stimulus control of the language-related behaviors (Sidman, Stoddard, Mohr, & Leicester, 1971), whereby language deficits could be classified as impairments in input, output, or relational categories. Although there were no treatments attempted in these cases, greater specification of deficits has obvious treatment implications.

III. BEHAVIORAL AND TRADITIONAL NEUROPSYCHOLOGY

A. Conceptual Differences

Behavioral assessment assumes that behavior is under the control of a wide range of variables. This assumption also holds for behavioral neuropsychological assessment, although the likelihood is greater that organismic, physiological variables determine major limits on the behavior. This may be one of the most important differences between traditional and behavioral neuropsychological assessment. Traditional neuropsychological assessment assumes that the level of test performance obtained is a true representation of the level of ability. Of course, such an assumption requires that the optimal performance has been obtained from the patient. On the other hand, behavioral neuropsychological assessment does not make any assumptions about the level of underlying skill. Instead, the testing situation is seen as a stimulus setting that elicits certain behaviors from the patient. The test scores are interpreted as a sample of behavior elicited by the test stimuli in the framework of the social motivational system constructed by the examiner. These two conceptual systems may seem similar, but they differ in the extent to which assumptions about generalizability are made. The traditional neuropsychological assessment assumes that ability level is invariant across situations. The behavioral neuropsychological assessment views the situation as an interesting source of variability in the determinants of the patient's behavior. (For a more complete discussion of generalizability theory and its relation to behavioral assessment, see Cone, 1988.)

A related contrast is the conceptualization of ability in traditional neuropsychological assessment versus the conceptualization of skill in behavioral neuropsychological assessment. *Ability* can be defined as a basic description of capacity to perform some behavior. For traditional neuropsychological assessment, abilities are cognitive constructs such as visual-spatial construction, and the absence of ability is a deficit such as visual-spatial apraxia. This conceptualization can be traced to the early origins of neuropsychology in behavioral neurology, where it was important to uncover a deficit by demonstrating the lack of ability to perform some behavior. *Skill* can be defined as the capacity of an individual to perform a behavior at some level of accuracy under certain conditions. This definition allows for a continuum of performance level as well as variability of performance of the same individual under differing conditions. Instead of viewing variability of performance as nuisance or error, behavioral neuropsychological assessment views it as an interesting source of control over the dependent measure, the explication of which can help us better understand and help our patients.

B. Treatment Goals of Behavioral Neuropsychology

Behavioral techniques have been applied to both the treatment of cognitive deficits and the treatment of problematic behaviors. The treatment of cognitive deficits may be further broken down into treatments that aim at actually improving the performance level in a skill and those that aim at teaching a compensatory strategy to remediate the skills deficit. The three basic approaches are to retrain a skill, train an alternate function system, or teach a behavioral prosthetic. Retraining a skill involves breaking the skill down into the smallest observable components and training the individual to improve in level of performance by some design such as the changing criterion design. Teaching an alternate system involves conditioning an individual to substitute an intact molecular skill for an impaired one so that the molar behavior will be exhibited. This approach was articulated by Aleksandr Luria and is deeply tied to his notion of functional system. An example would be teaching an individual with auditory discrimination deficits to use proprioceptive cues to evaluate the accuracy of his or her own verbal production. Finally, teaching behavioral prosthetics involves the use of topographically dissimilar behaviors to achieve the intended goal. An example would be teaching an individual with a memory deficit to use lists and written reminders. The decision to use one of these three methods rather than another involves a complicated set of considerations. For example, Rothi and Horner (1983) suggest that the more recent the injury, the more likely that retraining or teaching an alternate functional system would be effective.

C. Conceptual Considerations in Behavioral Neuropsychology

Probably the earliest attempt to provide a conceptual framework for behavioral interventions in the treatment of brain-impaired individuals is a book edited by Edelstein and Couture (1984). In that book, a chapter by Goldstein (1984) discusses some of the relations between neuropsychology and behaviorism. Goldstein (1984) accurately points out the discrepancies between the two areas in terms of theoretical frameworks and suggests that the commonality between the two would be the interest in treating brain-impaired individuals. This is a view shared by Horton and Wedding (1984).

Part of the problem is the discrepancy between the theories of measurement subscribed to by the two fields. Neuropsychology subscribes to the classical theory in which measurement numbers are thought to reflect an underlying reality in the form of an abstract construct, such as visual construction skills, or in the form of uncovered relations between variables. Behavioral assessment subscribes to an operational theory of measurement in which numbers are thought to be the product of some operation without reference to the construct. Relations between variables are described and, in part, constructed by the measurement process (Franzen, 1989).

The two fields also differ in the theory of truth used to draw conclusions. Neuropsychology tends to use a categorical theory of truth in which conclusions are drawn with reference to a set of theoretical standards. Behaviorism uses a pragmatic theory of truth in which conclusions are drawn on the basis of demonstrated differences. It may be that progress in behavioral neuropsychology is attendant upon the achievement of some common ground of measurement theory and theory of truth, but clinicians are providing the impetus for developing the area and the evidence for the fruitfulness of the endeavor.

Wilson (1987a) states that behavioral single-subject designs can be helpful in evaluating the effectiveness of neuropsychological treatments but does not state how to integrate neuropsychological test data with behavioral treatment. Franzen and Iverson (1990) present a model for integrating behavioral and neuropsychological assessment in the treatment of specific cognitive deficits. They suggest using a battery of neuropsychological assessment instruments to identify problematic areas and then assessing those areas in a more fine-grained manner with the use of idiographic assessment methods. Treatment is applied sequentially across behaviors in a modified multiple-baseline design. Short neuropsychological tests are used as probe measures for changes in treatment phases, and the neuropsychological battery is repeated at the termination of treatment. The choice of target behaviors is conducted by comparison with normative information regarding level of performance as well as by comparison with the demands of the environment on the particular individual.

D. Pragmatic Considerations in Behavioral Neuropsychology

The general methods thought to be useful in treating brain-impaired individuals are not very different from the general behavioral methods for treating other problems. Goldstein and Ruthven (1983) describe a program used at the Wichita Veterans Administration Hospital. It is a cognitive retraining program; that is, one focus is on repetition of skill-related behaviors to improve performance. The authors discuss the use of feedback, shaping, positive reinforcement, and other behavioral techniques applied to the problems of cognitive deficits as well as the use of behavioral techniques to reduce inappropriate social behavior and emotional problems in the brain impaired.

Gianutsos and Gianutsos (1987) describe the application of the single-subject design to neuropsychological rehabilitation. Most of their work has been in the area of memory treatment, although they also describe the use of biofeedback to facilitate recovery of motor function in hemiparesis. They advocate the use of single-subject designs because it allows a separation of individual increments of gain, a position with which Webster, McCaffrey, and Scott (1987) agree. Seron (1987) presents a scheme for manipulating both antecedents and consequences in treating cognitive impairments. Most of Seron's work has been in treating language deficits, where stimulus control and antecedent relations to behavior can be more readily used than in the treatment of other deficits, such as in visual-spatial skills.

The treatment of brain-impaired individuals involves a complex set of target problem areas as well as a mix of techniques and methods. Perhaps more than most physical illnesses and injuries, a brain injury can affect an extremely large number of variables related to adjustment and adaptive behavior. The result of brain injury may be related to circumscribed areas of cognitive functioning, such as the language impairments associated with stroke, or to global areas of dysfunction, such as the memory, attention, and information processing deficits associated with significant closed head injury. There may be problems with self-care behaviors or interpersonal behaviors. There also may be dysfunctional internal affective states. This chapter is organized using a conceptual system based on target behaviors. I will separately review attempts to treat cognitive deficits, attempts to improve adaptive behaviors, attempts to improve social and interpersonal behaviors, and attempts to treat internal, affective states. Unfortunately, with the exception of angry outbursts, there are no published accounts of attempts to behaviorally treat emotional dysfunction in brain-impaired patients.

The application of behavioral methods to treating brain-impaired individuals has been accomplished in a large-scale fashion without an accompanying understanding of the ethos of behaviorism. The definition of behavioral assessment and treatment is not contained in some recognized canon but is instead open to public debate. Although this flexibility may be optimal for the development and adaptation of a field, it poses problems for the author of review papers in deciding which studies to include. Turkat and Behner (1989) correctly remind us that the crux of behavior therapy is not the application of reinforcement or punishment systems to problematic targets but is instead the method of conceptualizing the problem and the relation between the problem and the eventual treatment. Therefore, this chapter will review studies that have used a behavioral conceptualization resulting in the application of some behavioral method rather than those studies that may have used some method labeled *behavioral*.

IV. TREATMENT STUDIES

A.   General Considerations in the Application of Behavioral Treatments

There is some evidence to suggest that the application of specific behavioral techniques may have special requirements in brain-impaired individuals. Because brain injury has an effect on abstraction skills, the generalization curve may be attenuated in comparison with non-brain-impaired individuals. Ribes-Inesta and Guzman (1974) compared various forms of behavioral interventions and found that punishment resulted in lesser generalization across settings. Additionally, the use of punishment raises ethical concerns.

Different schedules or learning paradigms may be differentially effective in treating brain impairment. Bleiberg, Freedman, Scheuneman, Merbitz, and Swartz (1985) presented evidence to suggest that head-injured subjects were less likely than stroke victims or nonimpaired subjects to learn a laboratory task using an avoidance paradigm, but that there were no differences using an escape paradigm. There is also evidence to suggest that language skill learning by aphasics varied with the paradigm used, namely, verbal reinforcers, token reinforcers, self-reinforcement, self-punishment, or delayed reinforcement (Goodkin, 1966, 1969). Kushner, Hubbard, and Knox (1973) found differences in effectiveness for time-out, response cost, and aversive consequences when teaching aphasics a nonverbal task with the greatest effect occurring when punishment was coupled with positive reinforcement. In contrast to the Bleiberg et al. (1985) study, there were no systematic attempts to identify the relevant variables controlling the effectiveness of treatment methods in these studies, but the general results indicate that there may be either individual differences or idiographic relations among variables that affect the effectiveness of a given procedure. The results also suggest that data from nonimpaired individuals should not be used to suggest treatment methods for impaired individuals.

Zencius, Wesolowski, and Burke (1989) compared behavioral contracting and point systems with response-cost procedures in the treatment for refusal to attend therapy sessions and for impulse control deficits. For the first subject, each of the treatments improved compliance. For the second subject, although each of the treatments improved compliance, the combined treatment of point system with response cost produced optimal results.

It may be that, with reduced self-evaluative and/or hedonic response systems, the brain-impaired individuals need combined treatments to effect significant change. Hegel (1988) reported that goal setting and extinction were insufficiently powerful to significantly increase compliance in a head-injured patient. When a token system was added, the level of compliance increased, and the effect was demonstrated in a reversal design. It is interesting that the rate of angry outbursts was found to covary with the implementation of the token system. This result underlies the importance of evaluating behaviors that are functionally but not necessarily topographically related to the behavior of interest.

There might be some concerns regarding the ability of an individual with deficits in learning to benefit from a treatment that relies heavily on learning and memory. Tate (1987a) suggests that the limited neural integrity of the brain-impaired individual may require more repetitions for learning to occur. Goldman (1983) agrees and lists impaired abstraction, overlearned rigidity, disinhibition, and deficits in sensory, perceptual, attention, and memory processes as limiting factors. However, rather than ruling out behavioral methods entirely, Goldman (1983) suggests that repeated use of overcorrection procedures may be the treatment of choice for extremely impaired individuals. Bayle and Greer (1983) report that comatose individuals were able to demonstrate moderate degrees of responsiveness when music was contingent upon their responding, and Haley (1983) reports success in behavioral treatment of a woman with multiple sensory and cognitive deficits. This is not to say that operant techniques are a panacea, only that the limits of their applicability in this population are unknown at this time.

Jacobs (1988) discusses some of the limits and applications of behavior analysis to treatment of brain-impaired individuals. He lists philosophical benefits accrued from the application of behavior modification, including the fact that behaviorism subscribes to the doctrine of least restrictive environment and that behavioral programs are better to the extent that they are facilitative (teach new skills) rather than restrictive (reduce the available repertoire). However, he warns that the application of behavior modification techniques should always be in the service of the individual and not in the service of the institution, with guarantees for the dignity and rights of the client. Behavioral treatments may be best implemented when a behavioral conceptualization of the skill exists, and different schedules may be differentially effective in changing the behavior of brain-impaired individuals. The question remains whether behavioral treatments are actually effective in treating the deficits attendant upon brain impairment. Let us now examine some of the treatment studies in individual skill areas.

V. ATTENTION

As with many neuropsychological concepts, attention is a multidimensional entity. Attention can be divided into tonic, phasic, and selective aspects. Attention span can be divided into vigilance (a temporal aspect) and density (a quantitative aspect). Furthermore, Posner (1980) divided selective attention for spatial information into disengage, move, and engage functions with separate neuroanatomical referents. Because attention is a metacognitive skill, that is, a skill that is considered to be modality nonspecific and basic to other neuropsychological skills, treatment has not been directed at teaching alternate functional systems or behavioral prosthetics. Instead, retraining methods have been used. Gummow, Miller, and Dustman (1983) indicate that retraining or stimulation may be the appropriate method of treating attentional problems caused by traumatic injury.

The relation of attention to other neuropsychological skills presents problems for documenting the effects of treatments designed to improve attention. As discussed earlier, the multiple-baseline across-behaviors design can be used to evaluate the effectiveness of treatments above the effects of spontaneous recovery. Gray and Robertson (1989) described what they term a *multiple-baseline across-behaviors design* to remediate deficits in attention. Unfortunately, the authors used only two behaviors and implemented treatment only in the area of attention. Therefore, the design is more accurately described as a *treatment baseline design with a control measure*. In all three cases presented, there seemed to be improvement in the target behavior but not in the control measure.

Sohlberg and Mateer (1987) evaluated the effectiveness of a package designed to improve attention. The study utilized a hybrid multiple-baseline across-behaviors design using three treatments—attention, visual-spatial processing, and memory—but only two dependent measures—attention (PASAT scores) and visual-spatial processing (the spatial relations subtest from Woodcock-Johnson).

For each of four patients, the gains appeared to be maintained following termination of the specific training phase.

Attention can be assessed either by observation of behavior or by examination of some behavioral by-product. Although attention is actually unobservable, attending behavior can be observed. Otherwise attention is inferred from the score on a task that has heavy attentional demands. Wood (1986) administered token reinforcement to two subjects contingent upon exhibition of attending behavior, significantly increasing the percentage of time attending. Four other patients were reinforced for attending behavior resulting in increases in percentage of attending behavior in response to an auditory task but somewhat more variable results for the standardized measures of auditory attention/memory.

Ponsford and Kinsella (1988) evaluated both attending behavior and the behavioral by-products of performance on tasks with attentional demands in 10 subjects using a multiple-baseline across-subjects design. Additionally, the patients' therapists completed a rating scale of attending behavior. There was a general trend of spontaneous recovery on two of the tasks with attention demands but no apparent effect of treatment on attending behavior. It is interesting that inspection of the trends indicated that 3 of the subjects improved significantly when feedback and reinforcement were added to the computer exercise, indicating limited support for operant procedures but not for the computerized exercises. These results are especially important given the proliferation of computerized cognitive retraining exercises available commercially.

Ben-Yishay, Piasetsky, and Rattok (1987) describe a treatment program involving a series of five tasks that overlap in skills related to attentional processes. The five skill areas are training the patient to attend and react to environmental signals, training the patient to time responses to changing environmental cues, training the patient to be actively vigilant, training in time estimation, and training to synchronize responding with complex rhythms. A group of subjects were run in a modified baseline design in which the treatment was feedback regarding performance with positive reinforcement for improvement. Generalization of effects was assessed by the use of psychometric instruments and behavioral observations during targeted activities. All of the data were presented in group form, precluding any attempt to evaluate process variables. This last point is especially important because of the problems in generalization of treatment effects. For example, Webster, Gouvier, and Doerfler (reported in Webster & Scott, 1988) trained a brain-impaired individual to decrease his reaction time but reported no generalization to other tasks.

As noted above, aspects of attention may be best ameliorated by direct retraining; however, certain aspects of selective attention may be addressed using a self-instructional intervention. Webster and Scott (1983) present the results of a single-subject (A-B) design that taught an individual to self-cue to attend. The use of self-cuing resulted in improvement in attentional skills, memory performance, and problem solving, which was maintained at an 18-month follow-up.

Visual neglect is one of the aspects of attention deficits that may be ameliorated by self-cuing strategies. Robertson, Gray, and McKenzie (1988) applied a computerized visual search treatment program in conjunction with self-cuing to scan left to treat three patients with unilateral visual neglect. The authors described their design as *multiple baseline across behaviors,* but, because only two behaviors were measured and only one behavior received treatment, the design may be more accurately described as a *simple A-B design with a control measure.* In the first case, the target behavior was score on a word reading task while the control measure was score in copying a single Bender-Gestalt design. In the second case, the target behaviors were a letter cancellation task, a word-finding search task, and a playing-card search task. The control measures were a motor impersistence task and the Bender-Gestalt copy task. The choice of control tasks was completed without any indication of impairment in those particular skills, and the internal validity of the experiment is compromised. The third case used the same control measure, but there was an indication that performance was impaired on this task. In the third case, the target measures were accuracy in reading prose passages and word lists, telephone dialing, address copying, and letter cancellation. The control measures were score on the Bender copying task, score on the PASAT, and performance on a go/no-go reaction time procedure. The results were more convincing in this case than in the first two.

Deficits in sustained attention (rather than attention density) might be more amenable to behavioral intervention because sustained attention requires more of an overt behavioral component in the form of facing the relevant stimuli and engaging in the behavioral task. Wood (1987, pp. 140-142) presents some interesting data regarding training brain-impaired individuals to sustain attention on a rehabilitation task. By presenting the individual with tokens for sustained attention in an A-B-A-B design, Wood was able to demonstrate improvement in the rate of attending behavior from 40% to over 60% of a session, contingent upon reinforcement. Attempts to replicate this finding with other patients resulted in clear success for a second patient and less remarkable gains for a third patient. To improve auditory attention, Wood used a combination of reinforcement and response cost. This hybrid method appeared to reduce the rate of false positive responses in the subject.

Although attention may seem to be a skill area in which behavioral interventions are limited in their effect, the studies discussed above demonstrate effectiveness in increasing the amount of attending behavior. The extent to which behavioral treatments can increase the density of attention is less sure and is in need of further study.

VI. TREATMENT OF SENSORY AND PERCEPTUAL DEFICITS

A. Basic Sensation and Perception

Sensation and perception are basic skills, and the remediation of their deficit has relied on the use of retraining and behavioral prosthetics. It is difficult to teach an alternate functional system to an individual with basic sensory loss. Although more complex perceptual skills, such as being aware of body position in space, can be performed using visual input instead of proprioceptive input, most of the work has focused on using the first two strategies.

Early work by Zihl and von Cramon (1979), replicated by subsequent reports (Zihl, 1981; Zihl & von Cramon, 1982), indicates that retraining may be effective in treating individuals with centrally mediated visual field defects. Balliet, Blood, and Bach-y-Rita (1985) criticize Zihl for the use of subjective impressions as a dependent measure, the use of large visual stimuli response variability, and allowing compensatory eccentric fixation. It should be pointed out that Zihl also used objective dependent measures and the application of infrared sensors to detect eye movement. The question is largely unresolved, although the responsibility rests with the researcher who challenges the conventional wisdom.

One of the designs used to acquire perceptual discrimination skills is the changing criterion design. Mosk and Bucher (1984) report the results of their attempts to train six retarded children to perform a pegboard-insertion task with increasingly difficult discriminations between patterns of placement of pegs in an array of holes. Prompting was compared with combined shaping and prompting and found to be less effective than the combination.

B. Perceptual Field Defects

Field neglect is usually considered an attentional problem rather than a perceptual problem but is considered here because of the conceptualization used in these studies, namely, that neglect can be remediated by treatment aimed at changing behavioral aspects of perception. Perceptual deficits can be very difficult to improve, as indicated in Taylor, Schaeffer, Blumenthal, and Grisell (1971), who compared the effectiveness of using only physical motor training and the combination of physical motor training with exercises that activated alternate scanning procedures, other gross sensory-related behaviors, or constructional skills in treating individuals with hemiplegia and hemi-inattention. There were no differences between the individuals who received simply the motor treatment and the individuals who received both forms of treatment.

In an application of behavioral prosthetics, Weinberg et al. (1977) trained right-hemisphere-injured patients in a visual scanning procedure to obviate the hemi-inattention problems. There was improvement in a variety of tasks that required visual attention to the entire field. Weinberg et al. (1979) subsequently trained subjects in spatial organization of sense of touch on their own backs and in accurate line bisection resulting in improvements in sense of spatial location. Gordon et al. (1985) describe a program that includes training of visual scanning, somatosensory awareness, and size estimation in right-hemisphere stroke patients. They found increases in performance on spatial-perceptual tasks and decreases in emotional dysfunction.

Webster and his colleagues have also used behavioral prosthetics to remediate perceptual deficits. Webster et al. (1984) treated three male subjects with left-sided hemi-inattention and left homonymous hemianopsia by training the subjects in visual scanning resulting in improvement in a visual scanning task as well as wheelchair navigation. Gouvier, Cottam, Webster, Beissel, and Wofford (1984) subsequently replicated these results and also investigated the addition of training subjects to scan while their wheelchair was moving. Training in mobile scanning resulted in further decreases in wheelchair navigation errors. Webster et al. (1988) subsequently conducted a group comparison of similar data from 12 subjects and concluded that wheelchair ambulation errors result from more than just neglect in right-hemisphere stroke patients. More fine-grained assessment of the impaired skill areas may lead to more effective treatments.

In one of the few studies examining retraining for perceptual skills, Carter, Howard, and O'Neil (1983) tried to improve visual scanning skills, visual spatial (design matching) skills, and time estimation skills in stroke patients through the use of immediate feedback and positive reinforcement in a changing criterion design. Comparison of pre- and post-treatment scores for the experimental and control groups indicated much more improvement for the treated group. There was no evaluation of the extent to which improvement on analog tests generalized to real-world tasks, but the results are suggestive and future efforts may help determine the effectiveness of other such treatments aimed at complex perceptual skills.

VII.   SPEECH AND LANGUAGE DEFICITS

Brain impairment may affect language use in several ways: in impaired production, either as the result of reduced fluency or inaccurate usage; in impaired pronunciation (dysarthria); or in reduced comprehension of verbal communication directed at the subject. The treatment of fluency has been attempted only in terms of amount of language output, not in terms of lexical versus semantic access to language.

A.   Fluency and Production Deficits

Rothschild, Guilford, and McConnell (1975) report the results of their attempt to increased verbalization in a 64-year-old aphasic patient. The patient exhibited groaning sounds, and these sounds were shaped into phonemes and words. The reinforcers used were social praise, followed by a point system whereby the patient could earn points toward purchasing breaks, ice cream, orange juice, or coffee. Finally, in the third phase of the treatment, reinforcement was provided by showing the patient pictures from *Playboy* and *Penthouse* magazines. Although there was great variability in all of the data, there appeared to be the most consistent improvement in the number of words emitted each session as compared with the number of sounds or phrases.

Goodkin (1969) investigated the utility of verbal reinforcement, token reinforcement, self-reinforcement, punishment (of the same three types), delayed feedback, and modeling in increasing desired language production and in decreasing undesired language production. Goodkin (1969) reports increases in frequency of words and sentences and decreases in unclear, perseverative, and irrelevant productions. The most effective paradigms appeared to be modeling, self-punishment, and delayed reinforcement. Ayers, Potter, and McDearmon (1975) treated four adult aphasic patients with deficits mainly in expressive speech problems. Positive reinforcement resulted in increases in frequency of correct responses as well as improvement in score on the Minnesota Test for Differential Diagnosis of Aphasia.

As mentioned above, the issue of generalization is an extremely important issue. Although it is possible to improve a patient's performance on standardized test measures or on laboratory tasks, the important question is whether these procedures make any difference in the patient's performance in the free environment. Campbell and Stremel-Campbell (1982) used a procedure called "loose training" to facilitate generalization. They implemented a within-subject across-behaviors multiple baseline to teach accurate use of the word *is* versus the word *are*. There was a functional reduction in stimulus control by using a variety of naturally occurring stimulus events to elicit the behavior. Generalization occurred across settings and over time.

Wood (1987, pp. 109-114) conceptualized dysarthria following head injury as being due to problems in attention, that is, deficits in the patient's ability to divide attention between breathing pattern and word rate, among other word production variables. He speculated that schedules such as interval schedules would be ineffective because the patient would be unable to benefit from information transmitted by such a schedule. He instead used a form of time-out in which the consequences would be more noticeable to the patient and more easily associated with aspects of attending to language production. Using a three-subject, multiple-baseline across-subjects design, Wood demonstrated improvement when the time-out procedure was coupled with speech therapy aimed at improving the patient's articulation. The time-out appears to have aided in generalization of gains.

Basso (1987) states that, although the operant approach might be effective in eliciting improvement, the reason for a skill deficit must be identified for treatment to be most effective. Although she does not use the lexicon of behaviorists, she is alluding to the problem of target behaviors. The ultimate goal of rehabilitation is to increase functional adaptibility. Just as in other areas of behavioral intervention, the functional behavior goal may not be the best target behavior. Although improving conversation may be the functional behavior goal, the target behavior may be increased fluency or minimization of perseverations, depending upon the actual molecular deficit of the patient.

In choosing a target behavior, it is important to determine the etiological and maintenance factors in disturbed neurobehavioral performance. McMordie (1976) presents a case of an individual who exhibited perseverative speech mainly in relation to the appearance of his injuries and his prognosis. Although the target was reduction in perseverative speech patterns, evaluation of the individual indicated that the problem was related to the presence of severe anterograde memory deficits and the concern that the individual experienced when repeatedly recognizing that he had right-eye blindness and disturbed function of his right leg and arm. Treatment aimed at the hypothesized etiological agent of emotional arousal resulted in reduction of the frequency of inappropriate verbalizations, and removal of the intervention resulted in an increase in perseverative verbalizations.

Giles, Fussey, and Burgess (1988) report the results of a treatment to increase the appropriate verbalizations of a head-injured patient with a high rate (52%) of circumlocutory and jargon-like speech. The subject was cued to keep his verbalizations short and to pause to think out his reply. Successful exhibition of the desired behaviors resulted in reinforcement, and failure to exhibit the desired behavior resulted in time-out. Treatment was successful across structured conversations, semistructured conversations, and unstructured conversations.

Impaired rate of verbalization may be manifested in low frequency of word production or use of inappropriate language. Green, Linsk, and Pinkston (1986) present two cases: in the first, the goal was to reduce an aspect of language production, and, in the second, the goal was to increase some aspect of language production in two elderly men who had suffered strokes. The spouses of both men were taught to implement the contingencies, and an A-B-A-B design was used with a six-month follow-up. The target behaviors were affected during the treatment phases and returned to baseline during the withdrawal phases. Gains were maintained at six months. Using overcorrection, Wood (1987) was able to reduce verbal perseverations and, using DRO, he was able to reduce use of obscene language in a frontal-lobe-injured patient.

VIII. MEMORY

A. Single Treatments

Memory is a multifaceted construct. Impairment of memory can occur globally, for registration or retrieval, for different stages of the memory consolidation process, or for different modalities. Although memory is generally considered to be under the control of internal variables, Dolan and Norton (1977) report success in using operant procedures to improve the memory performance of brain-impaired patients. Perhaps the greatest challenge is presented by the densely amnesic patient who has marked deficits in new learning. Because repetition does not seem to be an efficient method of increasing retention, Goldstein et al. (1985) utilized the Premack Principle, for example, pairing new information (the patient's ward number) with old information (the name of the patient's daughter). Distributed practice with multiple repetitions was used with eventual success. A multiple baseline across behaviors (five different places of information) indicated that gains generally followed implementation of treatment but that long-term retention of the information was variable for the different pieces of information.

Schacter and his colleagues have reported on a series of studies that investigated the applicability of implicit learning technique to remediating memory deficits in amnesic patients. The technique is based on the observation that amnesic patients can learn perceptual, cognitive, or motor skills even when they cannot verbalize any memory of having been taught the skills. Glisky, Schacter, and Tulving (1986) trained amnesic patients to perform computer operation skills using repetitions with decreasing levels of cues to the correct response. The amnesic patients required many more repetitions to learn to criterion level than did the normal control subjects, but retention was seen at one month following termination of treatment. Generalization was limited in that the amnesic subjects could not provide correct responses to questions that differed from the original wording used in the training sessions or transfer their skills to a novel task with the same skill requirements.

A similar study investigated the ability of amnesic patients to learn vocabulary words by gradually decreasing the number of lexical cues needed to retrieve a word when presented with its definition. There was decay of information between sessions, but a gradual learning curve emerged. Subjects retained the vocabulary over a six-week follow-up period (Glisky, Schacter, & Tulving, 1988). Other studies have indicated that, using these methods, programming skills themselves can be taught to densely amnesic patients sufficient to allow them to work (Glisky & Schacter, 1987). Follow-up studies indicate that the skills are retained for intervals up to nine months (Glisky & Schacter, 1988) and that as many as 250 discrete pieces of information can be learned (Glisky & Schacter, 1989). The applications of this type of intervention may be limited to actual behaviors and not to learning verbal information. For example, Wilson (1987b, pp. 120-123) used motor cues to teach a patient the names of his therapists, but, even though the patient was able to learn the motor cues, he was unable to associate them with the names.

Gianutsos and Gianutsos (1979) evaluated the effectiveness of a retraining exercise on the verbal memory of four impaired individuals. Using what was described as a multiple-baseline across-subjects design, the researchers were able to demonstrate improvement in the task due to introduction of a mnemonic device of constructing a story to encode unrelated words. Unfortunately, there was no attempt to evaluate the generalizability of the gains across other memory tasks or to real-life situations.

Gianutsos (1981) used the multiple-baseline across-behaviors design to investigate the effect of treating different types (short term and long term) of memory impairment in a postencephalitic patient. The two tasks consisted of memory span practice and a mnemonic elaboration task. The results indicate positive effects of the treatments on both types of memory, but, again, no information regarding generalization to extratest behaviors is provided.

Classical conditioning in amnesic patients may be possible even though the subjects are unable to state the contingencies used. Weiskrantz and Warrington (1979) demonstrated classical conditioning of the eye-blink reflexive response. Daum, Channon, and Canavan (1989) demonstrated that, although amnesic subjects showed normal patterns of eye-blink conditioning, they showed ambiguous patterns for extinction of the conditioned response and abnormal patterns of discrimination learning and classical reversal learning. Apparently, the operation by which basic classical learning takes place is intact in amnesic patients, but other aspects of classical learning are different from those in nonimpaired individuals. Zencius, Wesolowski, Burke, and McQuade (1989) applied antecedent control (prompting) procedures to three brain-impaired individuals who were unable to comply with other treatment programs because of memory deficits, suggesting that antecedent control procedures can supplement consequent control procedures, increasing their effectiveness.

Wilson (1982) reports the results of a multiple-baseline design attempt to improve the memory of an individual who had received a cerebral vascular accident. The four target areas were memory of his daily timetable at the treatment center, memory for names of people who treated him, memory for a shopping list, and memory for his way around the treatment center. Different treatments were effective for different targets.

Wilson (1981) treated deficits in memory for the names of 10 people involved in the treatment of the patient by visually encoding the information to be remembered. Although the treatment was successful, there did not appear to be generalization to other behaviors. A follow-up study investigated whether the visual imagery or the rehearsal was in fact the effective component (Wilson, 1987b, pp. 113-115). The results indicate that, although both treatments were effective, the visual imagery was slightly superior.

Because of the modest rate of success in treating memory problems with purely psychological methods, some researchers have investigated the effectiveness of chemical treatments. Most of these studies have been conducted with elderly patients with progressive dementias, and the results have been mixed (Franzen & Rasmussen, 1990). McLean, Stanton, Cardenas, and Bergerud (1987) used retraining in combination with administration of physostigmine. The memory treatment was a self-cuing instructional method that taught the subject to focus on the information to be learned. The drug and memory treatments were implemented as a package in an A-B-A design. Implementation of the package resulted in memory improvement in immediate and 30-minute delay recall of reading passages, which was reversed when the treatment was removed. The authors then replicated the effects with a second patient.

A commonly reported problem in the memory retraining literature is the fact that, even if you can teach a memory disordered individual some form of mnemonic or external memory aid, the individual will forget to use it. Gouvier (1982) has developed an intervention in which a wrist alarm clock will sound a "beep" to prompt the subject to check his or her schedule book; however, this procedure also only works when the subject remembers to use the prompt. There is some evidence to suggest that a behavioral intervention such as verbal praise can increase the probability that such prompts will result in the wanted response (Fowler, Hart, & Sheehan, 1972). In a modification of the prompting procedure, Daniel, Webster, and Scott (1986) successfully taught a patient to use self-cueing to facilitate use of a visual imagery technique to improve memory.

B.   Comparisons Across Different Types of Memory Treatment

Crosson and Buenning (1984) investigated the effectiveness of three different strategies to improve verbal memory in an individual who had suffered a closed head injury. The three strategies were to have the patient self-cue for sustained concentration, visualize the content of a paragraph as it was being read, and ask a pertinent question following each sentence in the paragraph. Visual imagery and questioning appeared to be most effective in improving memory, but the effects of the different treatments cannot be easily disentangled. The interventions were implemented sequentially on the same task, but they overlapped by a few days. The treatment also seemed to improve memory as assessed using the Wechsler Memory Scale. There was good generalization to the open environment (assessed by informal report), perhaps because the training exercise was chosen to resemble behaviors required at the subject's workplace. There was a small drop in gain at the nine-month follow-up, and the patient was encouraged to continue use of the mnemonics.

Imagery training has shown limited generalization effects. Lewinsohn, Danaher, and Kikel (1977) were able to train brain-impaired individuals to use visual imagery to strengthen the relations between paired associates and between faces and names. Imagery reduced the number of repetitions needed for acquisition and increased rates of recall after a 30-minute delay, but results were no different from those of the control procedure at a one-week follow-up. Goldstein et al. (1988) administered a mnemonic training procedure to improve list and face-name associations. The treatments were effective in decreasing the number of trials needed to learn the lists each time and appeared to generalize to nonadministered lists or face-name pairs. Although these results are encouraging, the generalization to different response structures, such as everyday memory tasks, remains unknown.

IX. SOCIAL AND ADAPTIVE BEHAVIOR

Although implementation of behavioral methods to treat cognitive deficits seems to elicit the most excitement and controversy from behavioral neuropsychologists, the treatment of social behavior is equally important in the overall rehabilitation of a brain-impaired individual. There are multiple changes in social behavior following brain injury. There may be changes in the ability to inhibit impulses. There may be difficulty in control of emotional expression. These individuals may be easily irritated or may show apathy. Although these changes in behavioral functioning may have their origin in physical trauma, they are amenable to behavioral intervention.

A. Aggression

Aggression following brain impairment is a problem that receives attention inordinate to its rate of occurrence but appropriate to its potential for deleterious effects. Franzen and Lovell (1987b) review some methods of behavioral intervention that might be appropriate for treating aggressive behavior. They recommend activities in two broad classes: (a) identifying and reducing possible antecedents for the aggressive event and (b) identifying and reducing possible positive consequents. The authors also discuss increasing the repertoire of the individual to include behaviors incompatible with the undesired behavior (differential reinforcement of incompatible behavior—DRI) and differential reinforcement of other behavior (DRO) in the category of reducing antecedents. Hollon (1973) used DRO to reduce the rate of aggressive behaviors in two brain-impaired adults. Tate (1987b) reports the use of DRO to reduce the rate of aggressive behavior directed at staff. Lira, Carne and Masri (1983) report a case in which stress inoculation was used to decrease the rate of angry outbursts in a brain-impaired person. Horton and Howe (1981) report a case in which a response-cost method was used to decrease the rate of aggressive behavior directed toward staff.

Aggressive behavior is a complex phenomenon that is likely to be under the control of multiple variables. Jacobs, Lynch, Cornick, and Slifer (1986) report a case of an aggressive adolescent with Reye's syndrome who engaged in behavior injurious both to himself and to others. Aggressive behavior seemed to be elicited when rehabilitation procedures were implemented or when the patient entered a new environment, such as a shower room. The implementation of DRO contingencies was effective in reducing the frequency of aggressive events, but contingent restraint resulted in a discontinuity and even greater decreases in the frequency of aggressive events. The authors next implemented what they termed *systematic desensitization* (although, from their description, it seems closer to simple graduated exposure). The procedures were taught to family members to facilitate generalization and maintenance.

The application of behavioral methods such as systematic desensitization may have limited efficacy in the treatment of brain-impaired subjects, but the limitations are likely to be determined by the extent to which the individual can comply with the instructions regarding covert deconditioning. Schloss, Smith, Santora, and Bryant (1989) report the results of an application of systematic desensitization in the treatment of an individual with anger responses to three stimuli—joke telling, criticism, and heterosexual talk (dating, childbearing, and so on). Through use of a multiple-baseline across-behaviors design, the researchers were able to demonstrate the effectiveness of the treatment. It should be pointed out that the IQ of this individual was 70 and that he was able to comply with the instructions for progressive muscle relaxation and imaginal deconditioning.

Aggression may be the result of frustration experienced by the brain-impaired individual who has limited success in acquiring his or her wants from the environment. For example, Wood (1987, pp. 115-118) describes a patient who had multiple deficits in communication and physical ambulation skills. Treatment of these deficits was hampered by his aggressive responses to frustration in training exercises. Time-out procedures greatly reduced the rate of aggressive behaviors and coincidentally reduced the rate of choking while being fed, a behavior that may have been functionally, if not topographically, related to aggressive behavior.

As another example of special considerations in the application of behavioral methods to this population, let us examine a case reported in Crewe (1980). A young head-injured man frequently used obscene language and grabbed parts of women's bodies. DRI coupled with punishment had variable results. The subject had marked memory deficits, and frequent reminders as to the contingencies in place had to be given to him. When the reminders were given, the rate of inappropriate behaviors decreased quickly.

Social skills packages have been described in the treatment of non-cognitively impaired individuals. Turner, Hersen, and Bellack (1978) report the results of an application of such a package to a 19-year-old male whose previous IQ evaluations ranged in value from 20 to 80. The program included modeling, rehearsal, instruction, feedback, and reinforcement. The target behaviors included latency of verbal responses, amount of words spoken in conversation, duration of eye contact, quality of intonation, and frequency of smiling during interactions. Treatment was successful, but the gains were differentially maintained across a six-month period. Booster sessions were able to reinstitute the gains.

Some treatments have been directed at individuals with minor cerebral dysfunction. For example, Brannigan and Young (1978) treated a 13-year-old boy who had been diagnosed with minimal brain dysfunction. The patient had been demonstrating problems in adjustment, interpersonal relations, emotional control, and repetitive behaviors. The therapist provided treatment in social skills, including imaginal success scenes, role-playing, coaching, and practice with feedback and social reinforcement. There were improvements in interpersonal behaviors, academic performance, and emotional behaviors, pointing out the possible multiple beneficial effects of treatment.

B. Inappropriate Behaviors

In some cases, behaviors exhibited by the subject will interfere with the rehabilitation process. Many of these behaviors are related to the emotional liability common in closed head injury patients. Sand, Trieschman, Fordyce, and Fowler (1970) treated a young brain-impaired boy who threw a tantrum when asked to work on rehabilitation tasks. The authors successfully implemented a combination of time-out procedures to reduce the frequency of tantrums and positive reinforcement (in the form of tokens) to increase compliance to treatment regimen.

Whaley, Stanford, Pollack, and Lehrer (1986) report the results of an attempt to compare the efficacy of behavioral management and lithium treatment in the control of inappropriate behaviors in a subject with a frontal-lobe injury. The design used was an A-B-BC-C design, where B was a token exchange for a minute absent of inappropriate behavior and C was the use of lithium. The use of the token economy resulted in significant decreases in inappropriate behavior as did the use of lithium, but there were no additional gains from the combined use of both interventions.

The reduction of unwanted behaviors can be accomplished by either directing contingencies specifically at the behavior or by substituting a functionally or topographically related behavior with higher social valence. For example, Lane, Wesolowski, and Burke (1989) treated a hoarding brain-impaired individual by teaching him to collect baseball cards and by using a time-out procedure when inappropriate hoarding occurred. One-year follow-up indicated that the gains were maintained, possibly because of the sustained use of the alternate behavior.

C. Activities of Daily Living

Many brain-impaired individuals require assistance in completing hygiene and feeding behaviors. These are more complex behaviors and at a more molar level than skills such as visual scanning or memory. Behavioral programs may be effective in teaching these behaviors. Suggestive evidence is provided by Giles and Clark-Wilson (1988), who report the results of a behaviorally based intervention to decrease the time taken for four patients to perform their morning toilet routine. When the program was discontinued, three of the four patients maintained their gains. The program was reinstituted in the fourth patient, resulting in improvement. The results are remarkable in that none of the patients had washed or dressed him- or herself in over three years. Wood (1987, pp. 94-97) describes a series of three patients who received a similar prompt and reward paradigm and showed improvement in the same dependent variables.

Jain (1982) describes a case in which a stroke patient received differential contingencies to improve activities of daily living (ADLs), self-feeding, and attendance at therapy sessions. The ADLs were affected by a token system. Eating behavior was reinforced with more physical therapy time (the only treatment she attended regularly and seemed to enjoy). Attendance at therapy was reinforced by visits home. The interventions resulted in improvement sufficient to allow discharge home, and the gains were maintained at a one-year follow-up. Cohen (1986) reports the results of an application of Foxx and Azrin's toilet training program to a severely neurologically impaired woman. The patient was discharged to home, where her mother reported that, with the treatment in place, the patient was still continent at the one-year follow-up.

Eames and Wood (1985) reports the results of a token economy program to treat 24 patients with severe brain damage. The intervention was effective in increasing success in ADLs, reducing aggressive behaviors, and decreasing the amount of supervision necessary at follow-up periods ranging from 6 to 39 months.

X. PLANNING AND ORGANIZATION DEFICITS

Patients with frontal-lobe injuries may exhibit deficits in metaskills such as planning and organization. Some researchers have suggested that self-instructional cueing, similar to that used in the treatment of impulsive children, may be helpful. Cicerone and Wood (1987) increased effective planning skills by teaching self-cueing during performance on an analog task. Generalization was affected by having the individual discuss problem solving for personal difficulties using the principles learned in the self-cueing treatment. There were no increases in performance on the WISC-R Mazes subtest, but target behaviors of self-stimulating and off-task verbalizations and unplanned moves on the analog task were reduced in frequency. Subjective ratings of generalization by staff indicated reasonable improvement.

XI. COMBINATIONS OF TREATMENTS

Early reports of behavioral interventions with brain-impaired individuals focused on the application of a single treatment. For example, Hall and Broden (1967) report on the successful application of social reinforcement in increasing the rate of desired social behaviors emitted by brain-injured children. However, for some behaviors, such as self-abusive behaviors or other behaviors that may interfere with therapy for other problems, a combination of multiple techniques may be needed to more quickly effect control over the relevant behaviors. For example, Cinciripini, Epstein, and Kotanchik (1980) used a combination of overcorrection and differential reinforcement of incompatible behaviors to control the self-stimulatory behaviors of a 7-year-old boy with cerebral palsy and a seizure disorder. Similarly, Waye (1980) successfully treated an adolescent with Huntington's chorea using time-out and positive reinforcement for desired behaviors.

Foxx and Azrin (1972) described quick success from the use of a treatment package (restitution training) for decreasing the rate of aggressive and disruptive behaviors. This package involves the removal of environmental reinforcers for undesired behaviors (time-out) and guided implementation of a behavior designed to reverse or atone for the effects of the target behavior extended over time and requiring effort on the part of the subject.

XII. OTHER BEHAVIORS

Frequently, the brain-impaired individual will show problematic behaviors in areas that are not easily conceptualized as involving either direct cognitive skills or social interaction skills. Behavioral interventions can be helpful in these areas as well. For example, Kumchy and Kores (1981) reported the results of using reinforcement to facilitate attendance and participation in various therapy sessions. The client had exhibited inappropriate behaviors such as pinching, hitting, and abusive language directed at the therapists. The frequency of desired behaviors increased and the frequency of undesired behaviors decreased during the course of six sessions, allowing greater gains to be made in the therapy sessions.

Rinke, Williams, Lloyd, and Smith-Scott (1978) investigated the effectiveness of prompting and reinforcement, separately and in combination, for increasing the rate of self-bathing in six elderly subjects with diagnoses of chronic brain syndrome. There did not seem to be any difference between the combination treatment and the individual treatments, but this lack may have been a result of the order of implementation, namely, that the combination treatment was always implemented first.

Reidy (1979) discusses the effects of a treatment to increase appropriate eating behaviors of a 7-year-old brain-impaired boy using verbal cues, social reinforcement, and manual guidance (interruption and correction). The treatment was implemented as a package. The baseline lasted for 2 consecutive meals, where appropriate eating behavior occurred 21% of the time. The treatment lasted for 10 consecutive meals, where, for the last 2 meals, the level of appropriate eating behavior was 100%. Treatment was then withdrawn for two and a half days while the child had a home visit. Following return to the hospital, the rate of appropriate eating behavior was 69%. Treatment was reinstated, and the parents were trained in the program. The rate of appropriate eating behavior was 90%. Finally, the staff were all trained in the implementation of the program, and the rate stayed at about 90%.

The last aspect of the Reidy (1979) study points out some of the special problems in using behavioral programs with the brain impaired. As mentioned earlier in this chapter, generalization may be limited unless efforts are made to enhance generalizability. Part of these efforts may involve training individuals in the patient's environment in the use of the treatment procedures as, for example, in the cases of Green et al. (1986) or Jacobs et al. (1986). Operant methodology may not always be positively valued or understood by the general public, and education of the parent, spouse, or other individual may be the first step. Salzinger, Feldman, and Portnoy (1970) instructed the parents of brain-impaired children in the use of behavior analytic techniques to record and change the children's behaviors. The parents were given written and oral instructions as well as quizzes on operant principles to assess their level of understanding. At the end of two years, the parents who had understood and implemented the programs reported success in changing their children's behavior. Failure in changing the children's behavior appeared to be related to incomplete or inaccurate understanding of operant principles. It is interesting that the level of education of the parents did not seem to influence whether or not the programs were initiated but did seem to positively influence whether or not the programs were maintained once initiated.

The treatment of emotional responses, especially fear and agitation, is a difficult issue in brain-impaired subjects. Several of the successful treatment programs used with cognitively intact subjects involved the use of covert techniques or other cognitive processes, which may be limited in application for impaired subjects. For these problems, the use of flooding combined with extinction may be helpful (Sellick & Peck, 1981).

XIII. CONCLUSIONS

The interaction between behavioral psychology and clinical neuropsychology has been largely in the area of treatment. Usually, traditional neuropsychological assessment instruments are used to identify problem areas, and behavioral, usually operant methods, are used to improve the patient's skill level. These treatments have been directed toward the actual skill (retraining), some variant of the molecular behaviors required to produce a similar behavior (alternate functional systems), or a substitute behavior (behavioral prosthetics). In some instances, the treatment has been directed toward behaviors that are nonadaptive but marginally related to the actual skill deficits (anger outbursts, noncompliance).

The development or adaptation of behavioral assessment techniques for neuropsychological assessment will probably help advance the field. The hallmark of behavior assessment and therapy in other problems areas has been the close and reiterative link between assessment and treatment. By attending to this link, treatments may become more effective.

Some of the interesting areas for future research include examination of the various schedules and their relative effectiveness and efficiency for treating different types of cerebral impairment. Although some of the variables controlling effects of schedules and paradigms will no doubt be related to learning history factors that are idiographic, group research may help us identify general trends in relations between frontal-lobe injuries and the most likely schedules or paradigms for effective treatment, narrowing the search for interventions that are effective.

Another area for future research is in forging links between theory and practice. Currently, many neuropsychological skill deficits are conceptualized as abstract constructs. An example of this conceptualization can be found in the area of aphasia. Aphasics are thought to be missing an abstract ability related to connecting symbols with objects, and no amount of training should be able to improve this abstract ability, although training in the use of alternate functional systems or behavioral prosthetics might be helpful. The success of operant methods in improving the functional status of aphasics points toward a conceptualization involving skill rather than abilities, but these studies have used head-injured patients rather than stroke patients. The etiology of language deficits following head injury may be very different. Head-injury language deficits may be related to confusion or secondary to deficits in divided attention, whereas language deficits following stroke may be related to compromise of one of the more basic, particular skills unique to language production.

Unless specifically mentioned in this chapter, cited studies did not address the issue of generalization. This issue is critical because of the hypothesized attenuation of the generalization curve in brain-impaired individuals. The one area in which generalization has been addressed to the largest extent is memory, and it was found that improvement on a laboratory task was not associated with improvement in everyday memory. This issue needs to be addressed in all neuropsychological treatment studies. The relevant dimensions include generalization across time, settings, eliciting stimuli, and tasks.

Selection of target behaviors is another area for future development. Most extant interventions select targets either on the basis of identification of skills that are deficient or on the basis of functional behaviors that are inappropriate. Because most neurobehavioral skills are multidimensional, evaluation of functionally related as well as topographically related behaviors may be important in the choice of targets.

The application of behavioral methodology has occurred informally without consideration of the implications of modifying the methodology. Although the designs are often described as multiple baselines, frequently there are fewer than the suggested minimum of three behaviors used. In addition, the treatments applied across phases are not similar, and the order of treatment is not randomized. Frequently, the dependent variables are not measured continuously. Although single-subject design is a robust methodology that has undergone evolutionary development, the changes mentioned above were conducted without any consideration of the consequences. There should be greater attention paid to the changes made and the effects of those changes. Franzen and Iverson (1990) provided a theoretical rationale for some of the necessary changes in applying behavioral treatment methods to cognitive rehabilitation, but more work needs to be done. Unless the application of behavioral methods and techniques is accompanied by the development of a theoretical rationale, the use of these methods and techniques may lead to inaccurate conclusions regarding the effectiveness of a specific intervention and inadequate tests of the general proposition that behavioral methods are useful with the brain-impaired population.

REFERENCES

Ayers, S. K. B., Potter, R. E., & McDearmon, J. R. (1975). Using reinforcement therapy and precision teaching techniques with adult aphasics. *Behavior Therapy & Experimental Psychiatry, 6,* 301-305.

Balliet, R., Blood, K. M. T., & Bach-y-Rita, P. (1985). Visual field rehabilitation in the cortically blind? *Journal of Neurology, Neurosurgery, and Psychiatry, 48,* 1113-1124.

Basso, A. (1987). Approaches to neuropsychological rehabilitation: Language disorders. In M. Meier, A. Benton, & L. Diller (Eds.), *Neuropsychological rehabilitation.* New York: Guilford.

Bayle, M. E., & Greer, R. D. (1983). Operant procedures and the comatose patient. *Journal of Applied Behavior Analysis, 16,* 3-12.

Ben-Yishay, Y., Piasetsky, E. B., & Rattok, J. (1987). A systematic method for ameliorating disorders in basic attention. In M. Meier, A. Benton, & L. Diller (Eds.), *Neuropsychological rehabilitation.* New York: Guilford.

Bleiberg, J., Freedman, P. E., Scheuneman, A. L., Merbitz, C., & Swartz, J. (1985). Anticipatory behavior deficits following brain injury. *International Journal of Clinical Neuropsychology, 7,* 153-156.

Brannigan, G. G., & Young, R. G. (1978). Social skills training with the MBD adolescent: A case study. *Academic Therapy, 13,* 401-404.

Campbell, C. R., & Stremel-Campbell, K. (1982). Programming "loose training" as a strategy to facilitate language generalization. *Journal of Applied Behavior Analysis, 15,* 295-301.

Carter, L. T., Howard, B. E., & O'Neil, W. A. (1983). Effectiveness of cognitive skill remediation in acute stroke patients. *American Journal of Occupational Therapy, 37,* 320-326.

Cicerone, K. D., & Wood, J. C. (1987). Planning disorder after closed head injury: A case study. *Archives of Physical Medicine and Rehabilitation, 68,* 111-115.

Cinciripini, P. M., Epstein, L. H., & Kotanchik, N. L. (1980). Behavioral intervention for self-stimulatory, attending, and seizure behavior in a cerebral palsied child. *Journal of Behavior Therapy and Experimental Psychiatry, 11,* 313-316.

Cohen, R. E. (1986). Behavioral treatment of incontinence in a profoundly neurologically impaired adult. *Archives of Physical Medicine and Rehabilitation, 67,* 883-884.

Cone, J. D. (1988). Psychometric considerations in the multiple models of behavioral assessment. In A. S. Bellack & M. Hersen (Eds.), *Behavioral assessment: A practical handbook* (3rd ed., pp. 42-66). New York: Pergamon.

Crewe, N. M. (1980). Sexually inappropriate behavior. In D. S. Bishop (Ed.), *Behavioral problems and the disabled: Assessment and management* (pp. 39-53). Baltimore: Williams & Wilkins.

Crosson, B., & Buenning, W. (1984). An individualized memory retraining program after closed-head injury: A single-case study. *Journal of Clinical Neuropsychology, 6,* 287-301.

Daniel, M., Webster, J. S., & Scott, R. R. (1986). Single-case analysis of the brain-injured patient. *The Behavior Therapist, 10,* 71-75.

Daum, I., Channon, S., & Canavan, A. G. M. (1989). Classical conditioning in patients with severe memory problems. *Journal of Neurology, Neurosurgery, and Psychiatry, 52,* 47-51.

Dolan, M., & Norton, J. (1977). A programmed training technique that uses reinforcement to facilitate acquisition and retention in brain-damaged patients. *Journal of Clinical Psychology, 33,* 496-501.

Eames, P., & Wood, R. (1985). Rehabilitation after severe brain injury: A follow-up study of a behavior modification approach. *Journal of Neurology, Neurosurgery, and Psychiatry, 48,* 613-619.

Edelstein, B. A., & Couture, E. T. (1984). *Behavioral assessment and rehabilitation of the traumatically brain-damaged.* New York: Plenum.

Fowler, R., Hart, J., & Sheehan, M. (1972). A prosthetic memory: An application of the prosthetic memory concept. *Rehabilitation Counseling Bulletin, 16,* 80-85.

Foxx, R. M., & Azrin, N. H. (1972). Restitution: A method of eliminating aggressive-disruptive behavior of retarded and brain damaged patients. *Behavior Therapy and Research, 10,* 15-27.

Franzen, M. D. (1989). *Reliability and validity in neuropsychological assessment.* New York: Plenum.

Franzen, M. D., & Iverson, G. L. (1990). Applications of single subject design to cognitive rehabilitation. In A. M. Horton (Ed.), *Behavioral clinical neuropsychology across the lifespan* (pp. 155-174). New York: Springer.

Franzen, M. D., & Lovell, M. R. (1987a). Neuropsychological assessment. In R. E. Hales & S. C. Yudofsky (Eds.), *Textbook of neuropsychiatry* (pp. 41-53). Washington, DC: American Psychiatric Press.

Franzen, M. D., & Lovell, M. R. (1987b). Behavioral treatment of aggressive sequelae of brain injury. *Psychiatric Annals, 17,* 389-396.

Franzen, M. D., & Rasmussen, P. R. (1990). Clinical neuropsychology and older populations. In A. M. Horton (Ed.), *Behavioral clinical neuropsychology across the lifespan* (pp. 81-102). New York: Springer.

Franzen, M. D., & Sullivan, C. R. (1987). Cognitive rehabilitation of patients with neuropsychiatric disabilities. In R. E. Hales & S. C. Yudofsky (Eds.), *Textbook of neuropsychiatry* (pp. 439-449). Washington, DC: American Psychiatric Press.

Gianutsos, R. (1981). Training the short- and long-term verbal recall of a post-encephalitic amnesic. *Journal of Clinical Neuropsychology, 3,* 143-153.

Gianutsos, R., & Gianutsos, J. (1979). Rehabilitating the verbal recall of brain-injured patients by mnemonic training: An experimental demonstration using single-case methodology. *Journal of Clinical Neuropsychology, 1,* 117-135.

Gianutsos, R., & Gianutsos, J. (1987). Single-case experimental approaches to the assessment of interventions in rehabilitation. In B. Caplan (Ed.), *Rehabilitation psychology desk reference* (pp. 453-470). Rockville MD: Aspen.

Giles, G. M., & Clark-Wilson, J. (1988). The use of behavioural techniques in functional skills training after severe head injury. *American Journal of Occupational Therapy, 42,* 658-665.

Giles, G. M., Fussey, I., & Burgess, P. (1988). The behavioral treatment of verbal interaction skills following severe head injury: A single case study. *Brain Injury, 2,* 75-79.

Glisky, E. L., & Schacter, D. L. (1987). Acquisition of domain-specific knowledge in organic amnesia: Training for computer-related work. *Neuropsychologia, 25,* 893-906.

Glisky, E. L., & Schacter, D. L. (1988). Long-term retention of computer learning by patients with memory disorders. *Neuropsychologia, 26,* 173-178.

Glisky, E. L., & Schacter, D. L. (1989). Extending the limits of complex learning in organic amnesia: Computer training in a vocational domain. *Neuropsychologia, 27,* 107-120.

Glisky, E. L., Schacter, D. L., & Tulving, E. (1986). Computer learning by memory-impaired patients: Acquisition and retention of complex knowledge. *Neuropsychologia, 24,* 313-328.

Glisky, E. L., Schacter, D. L., & Tulving, E. (1988). Learning and retention of computer-related vocabulary in memory-impaired patients: Method of vanishing cues. *Journal of Clinical and Experimental Neuropsychology, 8,* 292-312.

Goldman, J. J. (1983). A fundamental problem in behavior modification with institutional mental retardates. *Psychiatric Quarterly, 55,* 65-69.

Goldstein, G. (1984). Methodological and theoretical issues in neuropsychological assessment. In B. A. Edelstein & E. T. Couture (Eds.), *Behavioral assessment and rehabilitation of the traumatically brain-damaged* (pp. 1-21). New York: Plenum.

Goldstein, G., McCue, M., Turner, S. M., Spanier, C., Malec, E. A., & Shelly, C. (1988). An efficacy study of memory training for patients with closed-head injury. *The Clinical Neuropsychologist, 2,* 251-259.

Goldstein, G., & Ruthven, L. (1983). *Rehabilitation of the brain-damaged adult.* New York: Plenum.

Goldstein, G., Ryan, C., Turner, S. M., Kanagy, M., Barry, K., & Kelly, L. (1985). Three methods of memory training for severely amnesic patients. *Behavior Modification, 9,* 357-374.

Goodkin, R. (1966). Case studies in behavioral research in rehabilitation. *Perceptual and Motor Skills, 23,* 171-182.

Goodkin, R. (1969). Changes in word production, sentence production, and relevance in an aphasic through verbal conditioning. *Behavior Research and Therapy, 7,* 93-99.

Gordon, W. A., Hibbard, M. R., Egelko, S., Diller, L., Shaver, M. S., Lieberman, A., & Ragnarsson, K. (1985). Perceptual remediation in patients with right brain damage: A comprehensive program. *Archives of Physical Medicine and Rehabilitation, 66,* 353-359.

Gouvier, W. (1982). Using the digital alarm chronograph in memory training. *Behavioral Engineering, 7,* 134.

Gouvier, W. D., Cottam, G., Webster, J. S., Beissel, G. F., & Wofford, J. D. (1984). Behavioral interventions with stroke patients for improving wheelchair navigation. *International Journal of Clinical Neuropsychology, 6,* 186-190.

Gray, J. M., & Robertson, I. (1989). Remediation of attentional difficulties following brain injury: Three experimental single case designs. *Brain Injury, 3,* 163-170.

Green, G. R., Linsk, N., & Pinkston, E. M. (1986). Modification of verbal behavior of the mentally impaired elderly by their spouses. *Journal of Applied Behavior Analysis, 19,* 329-336.

Gummow, L., Miller, P., & Dustman, R. E. (1983). Attention and brain injury: A case for cognitive rehabilitation. *Clinical Psychology Review, 3,* 255-274.

Haley, W. E. (1983). Behavioral management of the brain-damaged patient: A case study. *Rehabilitation Nursing, 8,* 26-28.

Hall, R. V., & Broden, M. (1967). Behavior changes in brain-injured children through social reinforcement. *Journal of Experimental Child Psychology, 5,* 463-479.

Hegel, M. T. (1988). Application of a token economy with a noncompliant closed head-injured male. *Brain Injury, 2,* 333-338.

Hollon, T. H. (1973). Behavior modification in a community hospital rehabilitation unit. *Archives of Physical Medicine and Rehabilitation, 54,* 65-68.

Horton, A. M., & Howe, N. R. (1981). Behavioral treatment of the traumatically brain-injured: A case study. *Perceptual and Motor Skills, 53,* 349-350.

Horton, A. M., & Miller, W. G. (1985). Neuropsychology and behavior therapy. In M. Hersen, R. M. Eisler, & P. M. Miller (Eds.), *Progress in behavior modification* (Vol. 19, pp. 1-85). Orlando, FL: Academic Press.

Horton, A. M., & Wedding, D. (1984). *Clinical and behavioral neuropsychology.* New York: Praeger.

Jacobs, H. E. (1988). Yes, behaviour analysis can help, but do you know how to harness it? *Brain Injury, 2,* 339-346.

Jacobs, H. E., Lynch, M., Cornick, J., & Slifer, K. (1986). Behavior management of aggressive sequelae after Reye's syndrome. *Archives of Physical Medicine and Rehabilitation, 67,* 558-563.

Jain, S. (1982). Operant conditioning for management of a noncompliant rehabilitation case after stroke. *Archives of Physical Medicine and Rehabilitation, 63,* 374-376.

Kumchy, C. I. G., & Kores, P. J. (1981). Behavioral management of a neurologically impaired pediatric inpatient. *Archives of Physical Medicine and Rehabilitation, 62,* 289-291.

Kushner, H., Hubbard, D. J., & Knox, A. W. (1973). Effects of punishment on learning by aphasic subjects. *Perceptual and Motor Skills, 36,* 283-289.

Lane, I. M., Wesolowski, M. D., & Burke, W. H. (1989). Teaching socially appropriate behavior to eliminate hoarding in a brain injured adult. *Journal of Behavior Therapy and Experimental Psychiatry, 20,* 79-82.

Lewinsohn, P. M., Danaher, B. G., & Kikel, S. (1977). Visual imagery as a mnemonic aid for brain-injured persons. *Journal of Consulting and Clinical Psychology, 45,* 717-723.

Lira, F. T., Carne, W., & Masri, W. (1983). Treatment of anger and impulsivity in a brain damaged patient: A case study applying stress innoculation. *International Journal of Clinical Neuropsychology, 5,* 159-160.

Loewenstein, D. A., Amigo, E., Duara, R., Guterman, A., Hurwitz, D., Berkowitz, N., Wilkie, F., Weinberg, G., Black, B., Gittelman, B., & Eisdorfer, C. (1989). A new scale for the assessment of functional status in Alzheimer's disease and related disorders. *Journal of Gerontology: Psychological Sciences, 44,* 114-121.

McLean, A., Stanton, K. M., Cardenas, D. D., & Bergerud, D. B. (1987). Memory training combined with the use of oral physostigmine. *Brain Injury, 1,* 145-159.

McMordie, W. R. (1976). Reduction of perseverative inappropriate speech in a young man with persistent anterograde amnesia. *Journal of Behavior Therapy and Experimental Psychiatry, 7,* 67-69.

Mosk, M. D., & Bucher, B. (1984). Prompting and stimulus shaping procedures for teaching visual-motor skills to retarded children. *Journal of Applied Behavior Analysis, 17,* 23-34.

Ponsford, J. L., & Kinsella, G. (1988). Evaluation of a remedial program for attentional deficits following closed-head injury. *Journal of Clinical and Experimental Neuropsychology, 10,* 693-708.

Posner, M. I. (1980). Orienting of attention. *Quarterly Journal of Experimental Psychology, 32,* 3-5.

Reidy, T. J. (1979). Training appropriate eating behavior in a pediatric rehabilitation setting: Case study. *Archives of Physical Medicine and Rehabilitation, 60,* 226-230.

Reitan, R. M. (1989). A note regarding some aspects of the history of clinical neuropsychology. *Archives of Clinical Neuropsychology, 4,* 385-391.

Ribes-Inesta, E., & Guzman, E. (1974). Effectiveness of several suppression procedures in eliminating a high-probability response in a severely brain-damaged child. *Interamerican Journal of Psychology, 8,* 29-39.

Rinke, C. L., Williams, J. J., Lloyd, K. E., & Smith-Scott, W. (1978). The effects of prompting and reinforcement on self-bathing by elderly residents of a nursing home. *Behavior Therapy, 9,* 873-881.

Robertson, I., Gray, J., & McKenzie, S. (1988). Microcomputer-based cognitive rehabilitation of visual neglect: Three multiple-baseline single-case studies. *Brain Injury, 2,* 151-163.

Rosenberger, P. B., Mohr, J. P., Stoddard, L. T., & Sidman, M. (1968). Inter- and intramodality matching deficits in a dysphasic youth. *Archives of Neurology, 18,* 549-562.

Rothi, L. J., & Horner, J. (1983). Restitution and substitution: Two theories of recovery with applications to neurobehavioral treatment. *Journal of Clinical Neuropsychology, 5,* 73-81.

Rothschild, A., Guilford, A. M., & McConnell, J. V. (1975). An investigation of the use of operant conditioning techniques in the treatment of a 64 year-old aphasic. *Journal of Biological Psychology, 17,* 33-36.

Salzinger, K., Feldman, R. S., & Portnoy, S. (1970). Training parents of brain-injured children in the use of operant conditioning procedures. *Behavior Therapy, 1,* 4-32.

Sand, P. L., Trieschmann, R. B., Fordyce, W. E., & Fowler, R. S. (1970). Behavior modification in the medical rehabilitation setting: Rationale and some applications. *Rehabilitation Research and Practice Review, 1,* 11-24.

Schloss, P. J., Smith, M., Santora, C., & Bryant, R. (1989). A respondent conditioning approach to reducing anger responses of a dually diagnosed man with mild mental retardation. *Behavior Therapy, 20,* 459-464.

Sellick, K. J., & Peck, C. L. (1981). Behavioral treatment of fear in a child with cerebral palsy using a flooding procedure. *Archives of Physical Medicine and Rehabilitation, 62,* 398-400.

Seron, X. (1987). Operant procedures and neuropsychological rehabilitation. In M. Meier, A. Benton, & L. Diller (Eds.), *Neuropsychological rehabilitation* (pp. 132-161). New York: Guilford.

Sidman, M., Stoddard, L. T., Mohr, J. P., & Leicester, J. (1971). Behavioral studies of aphasia: Methods of investigation and analysis. *Neuropsychologia, 9,* 119-140.

Sohlberg, M. M., & Mateer, C. A. (1987). Effectiveness of an attention-training program. *Journal of Clinical and Experimental Neuropsychology, 9,* 117-130.

Tate, R. L. (1987a). Issues in the management of behavior disturbance as a consequence of severe head injury. *Scandinavian Journal of Rehabilitation Medicine, 19,* 13-18.

Tate, R. L. (1987b). Behavior management techniques for organic psychosocial deficit incurred by severe head injury. *Scandinavian Journal of Rehabilitation Medicine, 19,* 19-24.

Taylor, M. M., Schaeffer, J. N., Blumenthal, F. S., & Grisell, J. L. (1971). Perceptual training in patients with left hemiplegia. *Archives of Physical Medicine and Rehabilitation, 52,* 161-169.

Turkat, I. D., & Behner, G. W. (1989). Behavior therapy in the rehabilitation of brain-injured individuals. *Brain Injury, 3,* 101-102.

Turner, S. M., Hersen, M., & Bellack, A. S. (1978). Social skills training to teach prosocial behavior in an organically impaired and retarded patient. *Journal of Behavior Therapy and Experimental Psychiatry, 9,* 253-258.

Waye, M. F. (1980). Treatment of an adolescent behavior disorder with a diagnosis of Huntington's chorea. *Journal of Behavior Therapy and Experimental Psychiatry, 11,* 239-242.

Webster, J. S., Cottam, G., Gouvier, W. D., Blanton, P., Beissel, G. F., & Wofford, J. (1988). Wheelchair obstacle course performance in right cerebral vascular accident victims. *Journal of Clinical and Experimental Neuropsychology, 11,* 295-310.

Webster, J. S., Jones, S., Blanton, P., Gross, R., Beissel, G. F., & Wofford, J. D. (1984). Visual scanning training with stroke patients. *Behavior Therapy, 15,* 129-143.

Webster, J. S., McCaffrey, R., & Scott, R. R. (1987). Single case design for neuropsychology. In D. Wedding, A. M. Horton, & J. Webster (Eds.), *The neuropsychology handbook: Behavioral and clinical perspectives* (pp. 219-258). New York: Springer.

Webster, J. S., & Scott, R. R. (1983). The effects of self-instructional training on attentional deficits following head injury. *Clinical Neuropsychology, 5,* 69-74.

Webster, J. S., & Scott, R. R. (1988). Behavioral assessment and treatment of the brain-injured patient. In M. Hersen, R. M. Eisler, & P. M. Miller (Eds.), *Progress in behavior modification* (Vol. 22, pp. 48-87). Orlando, FL: Academic Press.

Weinberg, J., Diller, L., Gordon, W. A., Gerstman, L. J., Lieberman, A., Lakin, P., Hodges, G., & Ezrachi, I. (1977). Visual scanning training effect on reading-related tasks in acquired right brain damage. *Archives of Physical Medicine and Rehabilitation, 58,* 479-486.

Weinberg, J., Diller, L., Gordon, W. A., Gerstman, L. J., Lieberman, A., Lakin, P., Hodges, G., & Ezrachi, O. (1979). Training sensory awareness and spatial organization in people with right brain damage. *Archives of Physical Medicine and Rehabilitation, 60,* 491-496.

Weiskrantz, L., & Warrington, E. K. (1979). Conditioning in amnesic patients. *Neuropsychologia, 17,* 187-194.

Whaley, A. L., Stanford, C. B., Pollack, I. W., & Lehrer, P. M. (1986). The effects of behavior modification vs. lithium therapy on frontal lobe syndrome. *Journal of Behavior Therapy and Experimental Psychiatry, 17,* 111-115.

Wilson, B. (1982). Success and failure in memory training following a cerebral vascular accident. *Cortex, 18,* 581-594.

Wilson, B. A. (1981). Teaching a man to remember people's names after removal of a temporal lobe tumor. *Behavioral Psychotherapy, 9,* 338-344.

Wilson, B. A. (1987a). Single-case experimental designs in neuropsychological rehabilitation. *Journal of Clinical and Experimental Neuropsychology, 9,* 527-544.

Wilson, B. A. (1987b). *Rehabilitation of memory.* New York: Guilford.

Wood, R. L. (1986). Rehabilitation of patients with disorders of attention. *Journal of Head Trauma Rehabilitation, 1,* 43-53.

Wood, R. L. (1987). *Brain injury rehabilitation: A neurobehavioral approach.* Rockville, MD: Aspen.

Zencius, A., Wesolowski, M. D., & Burke, W. H. (1989). Comparing motivational systems with two non-compliant head-injured adolescents. *Brain Injury, 3,* 67-71.

Zencius, A. H., Wesolowski, M. D., Burke, W. H., & McQuade, P. (1989). Antecedent control in the treatment of brain-injured clients. *Brain Injury, 3,* 199-205.

Zihl, J. (1981). Recovery of visual function in patients with cerebral blindness. *Experimental Brain Research, 24,* 159-169.

Zihl, J., & von Cramon, D. (1979). Restitution of visual function in patients with cerebral blindness. *Journal of Neurology, Neurosurgery, and Psychiatry, 42,* 312-322.

Zihl, J., & von Cramon, D. (1982). Restitution of visual field in patients with damage to the geniculostriate visual pathway. *Human Neurobiology, 1,* 5-8.

HARNESSING COMPUTER TECHNOLOGY FOR BEHAVIORAL THERAPY TRAINING AND RESEARCH

MATTHEW E. LAMBERT
MARALYN BILLINGS
Texas Tech University

I. INTRODUCTION

The computer revolution of the past 25 years has brought significant technological advances. Computers, once the restricted purview of the federal government and select institutions of higher learning, are now widely available. Moreover, the computing power that formerly required a building wing or entire building to house can now sit on a desktop or be carried in one hand. Computers have also become easier to use, incorporating such features as *user friendly* interfaces and alternative input devices (e.g., mice, light pens, touch screens). Computers, furthermore, are

Authors' Note: We would like to express thanks to James L. Hedlund and Susan S. Hendrick for their helpful comments during the preparation of this chapter.

no longer relegated to numeric processing tasks but are now used to collect, process, manage, and present information for tasks that range from word processing to simulation of complex human physiological or cognitive processes to teaching first graders their multiplication tables.

With these advances, computer technology has also been applied to the complex tasks of psychological, psychiatric, and social work training and research. And, although many areas of psychological, psychiatric, and social work training and research have benefited from computer technology, behavior therapy training and research can be said to have especially profited. Thus, with the advent of a new decade, it is worthwhile to review the current state of computer applications for behavior therapy training and research as well as issues related to the use of those applications.

II. BEHAVIOR THERAPY TRAINING

Bootzin and Ruggill (1988) indicated that behavior therapy training involves the acquisition of assessment, intervention, relationship enhancement, and problem-solving or decision-making skills. Moreover, training strategies involving information acquisition, practice, and feedback activities are often most effective for building those skills. Numerous computer applications have been developed during the past two decades that can provide those particular learning activities for behavior therapy trainees.

A. Information Acquisition Applications

Although various authors (e.g., Berven, 1985; Sampson, 1986) have discussed using computer programs to disseminate psychological information, few such applications have been developed primarily for use in behavior therapy training. More commonly, programs have been developed to provide information about clinical skills generic to many theoretical orientations. For example, several programs have been reported for teaching differential diagnosis of psychiatric disorders based upon DSM-III criteria (e.g., Stout, 1988; Swartz & Pfohl, 1981).

Yet, one computer application that has been specifically developed for use in behavioral training is *Behavior Analysis: A Computer-Based Tutorial* (Graf, 1988). This program was designed to teach basic principles of operant and respondent conditioning. Using a modular teaching approach, *Behavior Analysis* provides instruction in the history of behavior analysis and relevant ethical issues, operant conditioning principles and schedules of reinforcement, and respondent conditioning principles. Each module presents basic definitions found in the behavioral literature and uses embedded questions and unit quizzes to facilitate content mastery.

Additionally, other computer applications that use a self-directed approach for behavioral information acquisition (Lambert, Intrieri, & Hollandsworth, 1986;

Shavalia & Delprato, 1980) make use of the computer's information storage and retrieval capacities to create data bases of references related to behavioral assessment and treatment of diverse psychological dysfunctions. These data bases can then be accessed by behavior therapy trainees to facilitate client assessment and treatment during practice or to provide starting points when exploring specific behavioral technologies. Although a great deal of behavioral information can be made available through these systems, the data bases must be continually updated and managed.

B. Practice Applications

In addition to applications designed for information acquisition, many more practice-oriented applications have been developed. These applications provide practice activities for a broad range of generic as well as behaviorally oriented clinical skills, the formulation and practice of which are important to behavior therapy training (Bootzin & Ruggill, 1988).

Among the diverse practice applications that have been described, computer simulations are by far the most common. Simulations are working analogues of real-life situations that are designed to behave as a person or system, thus allowing users to experiment with alternative behaviors and strategies and learn their likely effects (Berven, 1985). Furthermore, computer simulations enable vicarious experiences over a wide range of clinical problems that may not be available in vivo, while reducing the concern for patient welfare during the time trainees develop and practice new clinical skills (Lambert, Hedlund, & Vieweg, 1990). Standardized computer simulations can also be used to evaluate areas of clinical competence (Berven, 1987).

McMinn (1988), for example, described a simulation application designed to facilitate acquisition and practice of ethical principles by psychology students. Simulations can also be used to help trainees learn to apply various therapeutic approaches. One such application was developed to help trainees learn four diverse marital and family therapy approaches (Fine & McIntosh, 1986). Using an interactive video format, trainees worked with the same simulated couples by applying strategic, structural, behavioral, or experiential/communication therapy approaches to the couples' problems. By simulating the same couples, students could compare how interventions from each approach would affect the problems presented, thus learning what to expect from each approach and to differentiate the four approaches. Another simulation application, *The Great Therapists Program* (Halpain, Dixon, & Glover, 1987), used an interview format to contrast Rogerian, Gestalt, behavior therapy, and rational emotive therapy approaches. In this program, transcripts of interviews found in books written by major proponents of the approaches were used to guide separate interviews. For each interview, actual client statements made during that interview were presented to trainees in one section of the computer screen. In another area of the screen, trainees typed their own responses to the client statements. Following entry of the trainee's response, the actual response made during that interview by the approach's proponent would be presented adjacent to the trainee's response. Subsequent statements and responses would then be generated until the transcript was exhausted, and, at that point, the trainee could obtain a printout of his or her own responses and compare them with those made by the "great therapists."

Despite training contributions made by the applications just discussed, many simulations have been designed to facilitate practice of somewhat more circumscribed sets of clinical behaviors. Basic interviewing or relationship enhancement skills development, for example, have been the focus of several interviewing simulations. The ways in which these simulated interviews have been structured, however, differ considerably.

The *Client 1* simulation (Hummel, Lichtenberg, & Shaffer, 1975; Lichtenberg, Hummel, & Shaffer, 1984), for instance, employed a complex coding system through which users constructed interview responses to natural language client statements presented on a computer screen. In constructing their responses, users selected numeric codes from computer-presented menus of counselor leads; affect, content, and person references; and prepositional phrases, which were then converted to verbal equivalents and presented on the computer's video screen. A subsequent computer-generated client response was presented, and the user was then prompted to create another statement. Through this process, trainees were able to practice constructing appropriate interview statements.

Another interviewing simulation described by Alpert (1986) used a somewhat different menu-based approach to responding. Here, users did not construct responses but selected from a menu of three to five response options that appeared following a client statement. Then, depending upon the point in the program and the chosen response's appropriateness, the simulation offered feedback, redirected the user to make a more appropriate response, or moved to the next client statement. Despite the somewhat *canned* nature of the user responses, analysis of usage data collected from beginning therapists indicated that simulation use led to improvements in basic interviewing skills (Alpert, 1986).

Although the above interviewing simulations used menuing strategies to construct or select therapists statements, others have used natural language input schemes. The *Clinical Interviews: Mental Health Series* is one example (Lambert, 1989a). This application consists of five patients portraying diverse problems. For each patient, the user responds to client statements by typing a natural language response at the computer keyboard. The simulation program analyzes the user's statement and, depending upon presence or absence of certain key words, generates the next client statement. The interview can then continue until the user terminates it or the available informational areas are exhausted. A verbatim transcript of the interview can also be printed for later review. Quizzes are used to assess users' comprehension of the interviews.

Similarly, Santo and Finkel (1982) described a diagnostic interviewing simulation. What differentiates this program from others, however, is the inclusion of both teacher and monitor functions. The teacher function provides advice to the user when the interview goes astray, while the monitor function serves to ensure that the user enters understandable statements into the computer. Through these functions, the user's interviewing behavior can be more specifically shaped.

In addition to interviewing simulations, several clinical diagnosis/treatment decision (CDTD) simulations have been developed to provide trainees with opportunities to practice and refine developing diagnostic and treatment planning skills (Lambert et al., 1990) and are particularly relevant to the development of behavioral skills. Two CDTD simulations, for example, have been designed to help teacher trainees develop classroom behavior management decision-making and planning skills. The *Microgames* program (Semmel, Varnhagen, & McCann, 1981) simulates six different students with behavior problems and requires that trainees select interventions to reduce those problem behaviors. Trainees then receive feedback on their intervention selections through indications of whether the problem behavior(s) became better or worse or had no change. Other interventions can then be selected, and the game progresses. Additional instructional modules are also integrated into the application to facilitate skill development and the subsequent transfer of those skills to actual classroom behavior management problems. The second program, described by Gorrell and associates (Gorrell, Cuevas, & Downing, 1988), used a similar strategy by simulating eight classroom problems. Rather than allowing users to select interventions and see their results, however, the program prompted them to develop a treatment plan for dealing with the problem behavior. Once the treatment plan was developed, the computer analyzed it and predicted the plan's success for managing the behavioral problem and gave a justification for that determination.

Another type of CDTD simulation, however, involves a less structured approach to behavioral decision-making and treatment planning skills development and is exemplified by four behavior therapy case simulations described by Lambert (1987a, 1987b; Lambert & Lenthall, 1988). These simulations require users to act as behavior therapists when assessing, diagnosing, and treating each case. In acting as behavior therapists, users may select any combination of approximately 60 assessment and treatment options displayed via menu screens. After making selections, users are presented with results that would typically (or presumedly) occur if the procedure had actually been conducted for that type of case. Users can then continue selecting assessment or treatment strategies until successful problem resolution occurs or users give up. At that point, a narrative case summary of an ideal treatment process is presented, which can be compared with a listing of the user's actual treatment process.

Reports of these simulations being used in training programs suggest that they are well accepted by trainees for practicing behavioral decision-making and treatment planning skills (Lambert, 1989b; Lambert, Lewis, & Pryor, 1989). Additionally, comparisons of simulation performance patterns generated by doctoral psychology trainees, master's degree in social work trainees (Lambert, 1990a), and psychology trainees at three experience levels (Lambert & Meier, 1990) suggest that these simulations may also be useful for evaluating various aspects of clinical behavior.

C. Feedback Applications

Although information and skills can be broken down into relatively distinct units, the process of rendering feedback to trainees, especially during supervision, is less precise. Lack of precision, however, may be a function of the trainee performance data collected and strategies then used to generate trainee feedback. Often, the available performance data are superficially or vaguely defined, while strategies for providing feedback regarding that performance data are rarely ever discussed, much less enumerated or consistently applied. Nevertheless, several innovative computer programs have been developed that address these data collection and feedback strategy issues and offer some structured supervisory feedback options.

Three programs designed to aid in the collecting and quantifying of trainee performance data were presented by Froehle (1984). The three programs used monitoring equipment and behavioral coding systems to collect a variety of psychophysiological, observational, and self-report data (from the therapist and client) during therapy sessions and directly input that data into the computer for analysis. Data tabulations can then be retrieved for use during supervision or, for the psychophysiological data, matched to session videotapes and viewed concomitantly with activities that occurred during the session. Hence, with these programs, events often evaluated in retrospect can be anchored to quantifiable data, enabling the feedback process to be more focused toward facilitating trainees' skill development.

Advances in the design and development of computer-based expert systems may also offer a method for facilitating structured feedback about trainees' skills. Expert systems are computer programs designed to imitate human cognitive processes. They require that discrete sets of rules be developed from which decisions or judgments can be made about such issues as diagnoses, case conceptualizations, or intervention strategies (Hedlund, Vieweg, & Cho, 1985). And because they are computer models, expert systems apply those decision rules reliably, making these systems particularly appropriate for use as models against which to gauge a supervisee's own diagnostic, case conceptualization, or intervention formulations, thus having a supervisor always present.

Nevertheless, only one expert system has been described for such use in behavior therapy training. The *Behavioral Consultant System* (*BCS*) (Lambert, 1990b) is an expert system developed to act as an auxiliary supervisor to behavior therapy trainees. The *BCS* program operates by querying users about behavioral assessment information gathered from physiological, motoric, and cognitive domains; it then generates treatment suggestions based upon that information. Furthermore, progress through the decision model proceeds top down, as domains related to various behavioral excesses or deficits are excluded as contributing to the patient's problems. The *BCS* program also allows patient problems to be addressed, should they arise following initial problem remediation, or changes in intervention strategies, when the behavioral problems do not respond to specific treatments. Teaching and hypotheses testing functions have been included in the system as well. Hence, by using the *BCS* during practica and other training experiences, trainees may always

have a supervisor available against whom their actual or hypothetical case conceptualizations and problem-solving strategies and skills can be compared.

Although the *BCS* was specifically designed for use in training, other clinical
expert systems could also be used in this manner. For example, the *Computer
Assisted Treatment Consultation for Emotional Crises* (*CATCEC*) program
(Hedlund, Vieweg, & Cho, 1987; Levin, Hedlund, & Vieweg, 1983) and the *Mental
Retardation-Expert* program (M. G. Hile, personal communication, June 11, 1990)
could easily be used by trainees needing supervision and feedback on crisis
intervention skills or behavioral management skills when working with developmentally disabled persons.

D. Issues and Limitations

Although computer technology holds many potential contributions and benefits
for behavior therapy training, several issues need to be considered when evaluating
computer-based training applications (Lambert, 1988). First, most applications
described in this review have resulted from demonstration projects that received
little further work after their initial development. Thus it is unclear whether these
programs are actually effective in bringing about their stated goals. Even programs
that reported substantive learning effects have not undergone sufficient testing to
distinguish generalizable learning effects from potential novelty effects related to
computer use. Some researchers (e.g., Alpert, 1986; Lambert & Meier, 1990) are
now attempting to systematically evaluate computer-based training applications,
but sufficient evidence is not currently available to warrant general endorsement of
the computerized training applications now available.

Furthermore, little is known about the best way to use computerized training
programs. Do all trainees benefit from computer use? Do stand-alone programs
facilitate learning to a greater or lesser degree than programs used as supplements
to traditional training activities? Should computer-based training programs replace
some traditional training activities? What are the best programs for accomplishing
specific training tasks? How should data collected during computer-based training
be used to evaluate trainees? Should computer-avoidant students be required to use
computerized training applications? How should computer-based training activities
be integrated into a training program, and what infrastructure is needed to accom-
plish that? These are just some of the questions that need to be asked when
considering the use of computer applications for behavior therapy training. And, as
yet, few answers are available.

III. BEHAVIOR THERAPY RESEARCH

Compared with behavior therapy training, computers have played a much larger
role in behavior therapy *research* activities. Sophisticated statistical software packages (e.g., BMDP, SAS, SPSS) are widely available for both mainframe and

microcomputers. Specialized computer routines are also available for specific statistical functions, such as calculating interobserver reliability statistics (Burns & Cavallaro, 1982; MacLean, Tapp, & Johnson, 1985). Yet, computer technology may be harnessed for a much broader range of behavior therapy research activities. Computers may also be used to collect data and conduct assessments as well as deliver or control treatment protocols. Thus the remainder of this chapter will focus on computer applications used in behavior therapy research activities. Because of the vast number of such applications, however, any comprehensive coverage of those applications is beyond the scope of this review. Rather, examples of applications that harness computer technology to perform a wide range of behavior therapy research activities will be presented. Issues relevant to using computer technology in behavior therapy research will also be addressed.

A.   Computer-Based Data Collection and Assessment

The expanded computer revolution of the 1970s and 1980s heralded the advancement of computer-based testing. Psychological tests (e.g., MMPI, CPI, MCMI), structured interviews, and self-report inventories (e.g., Beck Depression Inventory) have all been converted to computer-based formats that allow for efficient administration and scoring without sacrificing reliability or validity (e.g., Lambert, Andrews, Rylee, & Skinner, 1987). Readers interested in the current state of these applications are directed to a review by Hedlund et al. (1985) or the 1985 "Perspectives on Computerized Psychological Assessment" special issue of the *Journal of Consulting and Clinical Psychology*. Nonetheless, numerous computer applications have also been developed recently for facilitating the collection and analysis of cognitive, motoric, and physiological data particularly relevant to behavior therapy researchers. It is to those applications that this discussion now turns.

1. COGNITIVE AND MOTORIC DATA COLLECTION

Kratochwill, Doll, and Dickson (1985) noted that computerization of behavioral assessment activities can lead to standardization of both psychometric and procedural aspects of behavioral assessment and provide portable vehicles for such assessment procedures. These potential benefits can be seen particularly in the computerized assessment procedures that have been used to assess cognitive and motoric behavioral domains. For example, in the cognitive domain, Markman and Poltrock (1982) used a computer-based self-monitoring system to help couples systematically record their perceptions about dyadic interactions during therapy sessions. Similarly, Holden (1985, 1988) used computer simulations to provide a structured assessment of how parents conceptualize and make decisions about child-rearing problems. One especially interesting example of an innovative computer application used to assess cognitive behavior is the *Body Build* program described by Dickson-Parnell, Jones, Braddy, and Parnell (1987). The *Body Build* program makes use of computer-generated images of different body dimensions that users manipulate to provide perceptions of their current and ideal body shapes.

The two perceptions are subsequently codified and stored, hence allowing for quantified comparisons of those perceptions. Lang (1980) has also described how computer graphics can be used to assess subjects' self-reported feelings through the use of his *Self-Assessment Mannequin.*

Computer technology has also benefited the collection and analysis of motoric (overt) behavior, with applications ranging from the content analysis of verbal transcripts to determine anxiety levels (Gottschalk & Bechtel, 1982), to measuring children's attending behavior (Murphy-Berman, Rosell, & Wright, 1986), to measuring response times for written problem-solving protocols (Sawyer & Castellan, 1985). The collection and analysis of self-monitored eating behavior has also been systematized through computerization. The *Self-Monitoring Assessment System* (Schlundt & Bell, 1987, p. 216) "enables users to design data bases that correspond to the information collected by subjects in self-monitoring diaries" and "enables the user to create, maintain, and modify self-monitoring data bases." Routines are also built into the system to facilitate the organization and analysis of data across subjects.

Although many applications have been developed for collecting and analyzing discrete cognitive or motoric behavioral data, computer applications that can be used to simultaneously or sequentially assess numerous discrete behaviors probably have greater utility for behavior therapy researchers. Behavioral coding systems in particular can be enhanced through computerization. By computerizing behavioral coding systems, codings may be directly input into the computer and simultaneously time stamped. The efficient monitoring of a larger number of coding categories is also possible. Furthermore, because of these features, a number of otherwise unavailable data (i.e., frequencies, durations, latencies, response order, and lag sequential analyses) can be easily provided (e.g., Repp, Harman, Felce, Van Acker & Karsh, 1989; Unwin & Martin, 1987). Other applications have also been developed to collect broader ranges of cognitive and motoric behavioral data to facilitate therapy outcome research (e.g., *Computerized Assessment System For Psychotherapy Evaluation and Research*, McCullough, Farrell, & Longabaugh, 1986) and assess psychomotor and cognitive impairments (e.g., *Walter Reed Assessment Battery*, Thorne, Genser, Sing, & Hegge, 1985).

2. PHYSIOLOGICAL ASSESSMENT

Physiological behavior assessment procedures have also demonstrated improvement through the use of computer technology. Specifically, computer technology facilitates the collection and organization of extensive amounts of data collected by specialized monitoring equipment and helps to ensure data quality (Kratochwill et al., 1985). Computer applications for collecting and organizing high-rate physiological data have been developed for measuring skin conductance (Spinks, Dow & Chiu, 1983; White & Charles, 1983; Wojtaszek & Zawaszki, 1987) and cortical-event-related potentials (Lorig, 1985, 1986). Additionally, computer technology has been innovatively used to encode, for computer use, physiological data collected without a direct measurement device to computer interface. Motley (1987) developed the *Strip Charter* program, which enables users to trace physiographic strip-chart pen deflections as a means of entering that data into an Apple Macintosh microcomputer. Moreover, in an attempt to increase the portability of psychophysiological assessment, Otto, Baumann, and Robinson (1985) designed the *Pearl II* system to facilitate collection of neurobehavioral data and to conduct neurotoxicity assessments of children in rural areas.

Finally, because not all physiological assessments occur during discrete time periods, and numerous physiological systems are often of interest, systems capable of monitoring diverse physiological data over extended periods are needed. Hence, Kaplan (1982) developed a computer-based continuous monitoring system capable of recording multiple physiological and behavioral measures during studies lasting several hours. Among the measures that can be collected by this system are skin conductance, dermal temperature, blood pressure, heart rate, postural stability, hand tremor, and pursuit tracking.

B. Treatment Protocol Delivery and Control

Computers have increasingly been used to deliver or enhance behavioral treatment protocols. The use of computers requires that treatment components be explicitly specified, thus ensuring that treatments are reliably and completely implemented as well as allowing for individual components to be systematically investigated (Ghosh & Greist, 1988). Nevertheless, the use of computers to investigate the individual components of specific treatments (e.g., dismantling or treatment-constructive research strategies, Kazdin, 1986) or to deliver aspects of treatment protocols that are unrelated to the primary research questions (e.g., Doyle and Samson's, 1985, use of a computer game to study human adjunctive drinking based on differential reinforcement schedules) is often the exception rather than the rule. More frequently, the computer application is used to deliver an entire treatment protocol that is central to the research endeavor, or provide facilitative enhancements to standard treatment protocols.

1. TREATMENT PROTOCOL DELIVERY SYSTEMS

The variety of treatment protocol delivery systems that have been used mirrors the diversity of behavior therapy research areas. Computerized treatment protocols have been developed for smoking cessation (Burling et al., 1989; Schneider, 1986), social skills and assertiveness training (Muehlenhard, Baldwin, Bourg, & Piper, 1988; Muehlenhard & McFall, 1983), contingency management (Tombari, Fitzpatrick, & Childress, 1985), and problem-solving skills training (Wagman, 1980, 1981, 1982a, 1982b; Wagman & Kerber, 1980). Considerable variability exists, however, in the flexibility and sophistication of these applications.

With respect to flexibility, variation exists in how easily these programs can be adapted or modified, especially when a protocol calls for adapting the treatment components to each subject's needs. Two applications designed to provide systematic desensitization demonstrate these flexibility differences. One program developed by Biglan, Villwock, and Wick (1979) used a standard desensitization hierarchy for all subjects, whereas an alternative program by Chandler and associates (Chandler, Burck, & Sampson, 1986; Chandler, Burck, Sampson, & Wray, 1988) allows hierarchy customization for each subject.

Variations in application sophistication relate to the type of human-computer interaction used and the fidelity of computer-delivered treatment components as compared with their person-delivered counterparts. Human-computer interactions typically vary from natural language text entry to forced-choice entry systems. Limitations in current computer technology, however, make complete reliance on natural language interfaces infeasible. Thus the relatively sophisticated treatment protocol delivery applications that have been developed use a combination of multiple-choice and limited natural language input.

Given the limits of current human-computer interfaces, some of the fidelity of person-delivered protocols is necessarily lost through computerization. Nevertheless, integral treatment components, such homework assignments and their evaluation, cannot be sacrificed without an even greater loss in fidelity. Several innovative treatment delivery applications, however, developed to provide cognitive-behavioral treatment for depression (Selmi, Klein, Griest, Johnson, & Harris, 1982; Selmi, Klein, Griest, Sorrell, & Erdman, 1990), in vivo exposure treatment (Carr, Ghosh, & Marks, 1988; Ghosh & Marks, 1987; Ghosh, Marks, & Carr, 1984), and sexual dysfunction treatments (Binik, Servan-Schreiber, Friewald, & Hall, 1988; Servan-Schreiber & Binik, 1989) have addressed this fidelity issue by effectively incorporating homework assignment and evaluation components into their systems. Of note also is the inclusion of functions in the treatment program for sexual dysfunction that monitor potential adverse side-effects related to discussing specific sexual problems. Thus the computer's apparent *awareness* of potential secondary problem areas can give the subject a sense of relatedness similar to that found with person-delivered protocols, thereby increasing the programs' fidelity (Binik et al., 1988; Servan-Schreiber & Binik, 1989).

2. TREATMENT PROTOCOL ENHANCEMENTS

Several computer applications have been reported as adjunctive enhancements to non-computer-based treatment protocols. These applications typically involve using the computer to enhance treatment protocol adherence. Less frequently, however, computer applications are used to monitor treatment progress or treatment success, such as was reported by Holborn, Hiebert, and Bell (1987). In their study, a computer-based operant measurement system was used to monitor various sleep-related behaviors in an A-B single-case experimental design.

Nonetheless, computer-based adherence enhancements have been used with treatment protocols for obsessive-compulsive disorder (Baer, Minichiello, Jenike, & Holland, 1988), obesity (Burnett, Taylor, & Agras, 1985), smoking cessation (Schneider, Benya, & Singer, 1984), and tricyclic antidepressant therapy (Sorrell, Griest, Klein, Johnson, & Harris, 1982). For the majority of these applications, the computer acts as a prompt for complying with the treatment protocol. The notable exception is the application reported by Sorrell and associates (1982), which used a computer-based psychoeducational approach to enhance patient compliance. Nevertheless, the advantages of using computer applications to enhance compliance stem from the computer's capability to be programmed to prompt subjects to perform certain activities at specific times and offer immediate protocol adherence feedback. Moreover, as computers become progressively more concealable and portable, they may increasingly be used to ensure treatment protocol adherence across numerous settings and under a variety of conditions.

C. Biofeedback

Although the previous discussion has attempted to distinguish between computer applications used for data collection or assessment versus treatment protocol administration or enhancement, numerous computer systems have been developed that integrate data collection and protocol generation functions. And one area in which these integrated functions are essential is biofeedback research. Computer-based biofeedback systems introduce precision, accuracy, and reliability into the data acquisition process. Furthermore, these systems are generally able to quickly process large amounts of data and can be programmed to be self-modifying, hence meeting the changing needs of the biofeedback trainee.

Currently, microcomputer biofeedback systems can be classified as either partially or fully automated systems. Partially automated systems are designed to collect data, perform simple statistical operations, and create structured protocols, but they are not designed to be interactive. Interactive, fully automated systems can be programmed to be self-modifying according to the needs of the trainee. Such capability allows the shaping of responses by making the stimulus presentations during a trial dependent on antecedent trials. General-purpose microcomputers can also be used in biofeedback research, but, because they are not integrated systems, they may be harder to program, interface, and implement than systems designed specifically for biofeedback work.

Partially automated systems have been used in a variety of biofeedback research areas, such as training patients to control voice level (Zicker, Tompkins, Rubow, & Abbs, 1980), using EMG biofeedback to shape cerebral palsied children's behavior (Finley, Etherton, Dickman, Karimian, & Simpson, 1981), and evaluating relaxation control variables through the monitoring of GSR, EMG, body temperature, and heart rate (Costello, 1988). These microcomputer-based systems, however, are reprogrammable and easily interfaced with other components. In contrast, fully automated biofeedback systems are used when the systematic shaping of a subject's responses is necessary. Fully automated biofeedback systems are designed so that the experimenter can manipulate the biofeedback reinforcement contingencies during training (e.g., Kolotkin, Billingham, & Feldman, 1981).

Computers also offer biofeedback researchers a way of quickly acquiring and analyzing vast amounts of data. Various physiological variables can be simultaneously monitored, and performance can be immediately rewarded. Experimenter effects can also be reduced by using devices such as MBERT, the Multiparameter

Biofeedback Experimental Research Tool (Uliano & Carey, 1984). MBERT enables minimal experimenter contact with subjects, thereby controlling experimenter effects across subjects and groups.

D. Issues and Limitations

Clearly, computers have an integral role in behavior therapy research activities. Yet, as was the case for training applications, several caveats are needed when considering computer technology use. First, computerized assessment and treatment systems are subject to the same psychometric concerns as are any assessment and treatment technologies. Reliability and validity are not inherent properties of computer systems and must be empirically demonstrated. In addition, because computer-generated data are collected and stored differently than other types of data, special attention must also be given to storage and retrieval procedures. The ability to collect and store large amounts of data, and the potential for accessing data through computer networks, also raises confidentiality issues (Sampson & Pyle, 1983). Moreover, computer storage does not ensure data integrity over time, therefore, appropriate data integrity mechanisms must be utilized (Hartman, 1986).

A third concern relates to the need for ongoing human interaction with subjects to monitor potential problems. These problems can range from subjects' failure to understand the process of computer interaction and related anxiety to a need for subject intervention should some difficulty arise apart from the computer-based interaction (Sampson & Pyle, 1983). Finally, some concerns have been raised about the potentially dehumanizing effects of human-computer interaction (e.g., Engels, Caulum, & Sampson, 1984). Although there is a basic need to be concerned for the rights of all research participants regardless of any computer applications use, as Colby, Gould, and Aronson (1989, p. 106) have indicated, "the shop-worn cry of dehumanization is an expectable part of resistance to accepting a new technology."

IV. THE FUTURE

In the light of continuing advancements in computer technologies and the current state of computer use in behavior therapy training and research, musing about future computer uses is necessarily speculative. Technologies, such as voice recognition systems (e.g., Boles, 1988; Martin, 1989) and touch sensitive screens (e.g., Pickering, 1986), once thought to be possible only in the minds of science fiction writers are now practical realities. Similarly, new ways of using existing technologies are being developed. *Distance learning* may become an important way to instantaneously disseminate training activities over wide geographical areas using telecommunication and computing technologies (e.g., LaMendola, 1988). Similarly, interactive video technology is facilitating new training and research methodologies (Schwartz, 1984). Computer-assisted telephone interviewing (CATI, Shangraw, 1986), another currently available technology, can be used to collect behavioral data directly from subjects in vivo. Thus it appears that the only limitations to be imposed on future uses of computer technology for behavior therapy training and research are those stemming from our own limited creative skills.

As we expand computerization in behavior therapy training and research, however, we must not lose sight of the many unanswered questions related to computerization's impact on training and research activities. Nonetheless, at this time, the sky is the limit.

REFERENCES

Alpert, D. (1986). A preliminary investigation of counselor-enhanced counselor training. *Computers in Human Behavior, 2,* 63-70.

Baer, L., Minichiello, W. E., Jenike, M. A., & Holland, A. (1988). Use of portable computer program to assist behavioral treatment in a case of obsessive compulsive disorder. *Journal of Behavior Therapy and Experimental Psychiatry, 19*(13), 237-240.

Berven, N. L. (1985). Computer technology in professional education. *Rehabilitation Counseling Bulletin, 29*(1), 26-41.

Berven, N. L. (1987). Improving evaluation in counselor training and credentialing through standardized simulations. In B. Edelstein & E. Berler (Eds.), *Evaluation and accountability in clinical training* (pp. 203-229). New York: Plenum.

Biglan, A., Villwock, C., & Wick, S. 1979. The feasibility of a computer controlled program for the treatment of test anxiety. *Journal of Behavior Therapy and Experimental Psychiatry, 10,* 47-49.

Binik, Y. M., Servan-Schreiber, D., Freiwald, S., & Hall, K. S. K. (1988). Intelligent computer-based assessment and psychotherapy: An expert system for sexual dysfunction. *Journal of Nervous and Mental Disease, 176*(7), 387-400.

Boles, D. B. (1988). Voice recognition with the Apple-Psych system. *Behavior Research Methods, Instruments, and Computers, 20*(2), 158-163.

Bootzin, R. R., & Ruggill, J. S. (1988). Training issues in behavior therapy. *Journal of Consulting and Clinical Psychology, 56*(5), 703-709.

Burling, T. A., Marotta, J., Gonzalez, R., Moltzen, J. O., Eng, A. M., Schmidt, G. A., Welch, R. L., Ziff, D. C., & Reilly, P. M. (1989). Computerized smoking cessation program for the worksite: Treatment outcome and feasibility. *Journal of Consulting and Clinical Psychology, 57*(5), 619-622.

Burnett, K. F., Taylor, C. B., & Agras, S. (1985). Ambulatory computer-assisted therapy for obesity: A new frontier for behavior therapy. *Journal of Consulting and Clinical Psychology, 53*(5), 698-703.

Burns, E., & Cavallaro, C. (1982). A computer program to determine interobserver reliability statistics. *Behavior Research Methods and Instrumentation, 14*(1), 42.

Carr, A. C., Ghosh, A., & Marks, I. M. (1988). Computer-supervised exposure treatment for phobias. *Canadian Journal of Psychiatry, 33*(2), 112-117.

Chandler, G. M., Burck, H. D., & Sampson, J. P. (1986). A generic computer program for systematic desensitization: Description, construction and case study. *Journal of Behavior Therapy and Experimental Psychiatry, 17*(3), 171-174.

Chandler, G. M., Burck, H., Sampson, J. P., & Wray, R. (1988). The effectiveness of generic computer program for systematic desensitization. *Computers in Human Behavior, 4*(4), 339-346.

Colby, K. M., Gould, R. L., & Aronson, G. (1989). Some pros and cons of computer-assisted psychotherapy. *Journal of Nervous and Mental Disease, 177*(2), 105-108.

Costello, B. R. (1988). Assessing the relaxation qualities of persons undergoing psychological care with biofeedback. *College Student Journal, 22*(1), 15-21.

Dickson-Parnell, B., Jones, M., Braddy, D., & Parnell, C. P. (1987). Assessment of body image perceptions using a computer program. *Behavior Research Methods, Instruments, and Computers, 19*(3), 353-354.

Doyle, T. F., & Samson, H. H. (1985). Schedule-induced drinking in humans: A potential factor in excessive alcohol use. *Drug and Alcohol Dependence, 16*(2), 117-132.

Engels, D. W., Caulum, D., & Sampson, D. E. (1984). Computers in counselor education: An ethical perspective. *Counselor Education and Supervision, 24,* 193-203.

Fine, M., & McIntosh, D. K. (1986). The use of interactive video to demonstrate differential approaches to marital and family therapy. *Journal of Marital and Family Therapy, 12*(1), 85-89.

Finley, W. W., Etherton, M. D., Dickman, D., Karimian, D., & Simpson, R. W. (1981). A simple EMG-reward system for biofeedback training in children. *Biofeedback & Self Regulation, 6*(2), 169-180.

Froehle, T. C. (1984). Computer-assisted feedback in counseling supervision. *Counselor Education and Supervision, 24*(12), 168-175.

Ghosh, A., & Greist, J. H. (1988). Computer treatment in psychiatry. *Psychiatric Annals, 18*(4), 246-250.

Ghosh, A., & Marks, I. M. (1987). Self-treatment of agoraphobia by exposure. *Behavior Therapy, 18,* 3-16.

Ghosh, A., Marks, I. M., & Carr, A. C. (1984). Controlled study of self-exposure treatment for phobics: Preliminary communication. *Journal of the Royal Society of Medicine, 77,* 483-487.

Gorrell, J., Cuevas, A., & Downing, H. (1988). Computer simulation of classroom behavior problems. *Computers & Education, 12*(2), 283-287.

Gottschalk, L. A., & Bechtel, R. J. (1982). The measurement of anxiety through the computer analysis of verbal samples. *Comprehensive Psychiatry, 23*(4), 364-369.

Graf, S. A. (1988). The Sorcerer's Apprentice: A review of Hardy's Behavioral Analysis: A computer-based tutorial. *Behavior Analyst, 11*(1), 77-81.

Halpain, D. R., Dixon, D. N., & Glover, J. A. (1987). The Great Therapists program: Computerized learning of counseling theories. *Counselor Education and Supervision, 26*(4), 255-259.

Hartman, D. E. (1986). Artificial intelligence or artificial psychologist? Conceptual issues in clinical microcomputer use. *Professional Psychology: Research & Practice, 17*(6), 528-534

Hedlund, J. L., Vieweg, B. W., & Cho, D. W. (1985). Mental health computing in the 1980s: II. Clinical applications. *Computers in Human Services, 1*(2), 1-31.

Hedlund, J. L., Vieweg, B. W., & Cho, D. W. (1987). Computer consultation for emotional crises: An expert system for "non-experts." *Computers in Human Behavior, 3*(2), 109-127.

Holborn, S. W., Hiebert, D. E., & Bell, C. L. (1987). Computer-interfaced operant measurement in treating insomnia. *Journal of Behavior Therapy and Experimental Psychiatry, 18*(4), 365-372.

Holden, G. W. (1985). Analyzing parental reasoning with microcomputer-presented problems. *Simulation and Games, 16*(2), 203-210.

Holden, G. W. (1988). Adults' thinking about a child-rearing problem: Effects of experience, parental status, and gender. *Child Development, 59*(6), 1623-1632.

Hummel, T. J., Lichtenberg, J. W., & Shaffer, W. F. (1975). Client 1: A computer program which simulates client behavior in an initial interview. *Journal of Counseling Psychology, 22*(2), 164-169.

Kaplan, H. L. (1982). An operating subsystem for continuous monitoring studies. *Behavior Research Methods and Instrumentation, 14*(2), 146-159.

Kazdin, A. E. (1986). The evaluation of psychotherapy: Research design and methodology. In S. L. Garfield & A. E. Bergin (Eds.), *Handbook of psychotherapy and behavior change* (3rd ed., pp. 23-68). New York: John Wiley.

Kolotkin, R. L., Billingham, K. A., & Feldman, H. S. (1981). Computers in biofeedback research and therapy. *Behavior Research Methods and Instrumentation, 13*(4), 532-542.

Kratochwill, T. R., Doll, E. J., & Dickson, W. P. (1985). Microcomputers in behavioral assessment: Recent advances and remaining issues. *Computers in Human Behavior, 1*(3), 277-291.

Lambert, M. E. (1987a). A computer simulation for behavior therapy training. *Journal of Behavior Therapy and Experimental Psychiatry, 18*(3), 245-248.

Lambert, M. E. (1987b, November). *Computer simulation as an aid to behavior therapy training*. Paper presented at the annual convention of the Association for Advancement of Behavior Therapy, Boston.

Lambert, M. E. (1988). Computers in counselor education: Four years after a special issue *Counselor Education and Supervision, 28*(2), 100-109

Lambert, M. E. (1989a). Review of Clinical Interviews: Mental health series. *Measurement and Evaluation in Counseling and Development, 21*(4), 188-190.

Lambert, M. E. (1989b). Using computer simulations in behavior therapy training. *Computers in Human Services, 5*(3/4), 1-11.

Lambert, M. E. (1990a). *Computer simulation based assessment of behavioral mental health professionals*. Unpublished manuscript.

Lambert, M. E. (1990b, April). *Application of microcomputer technology to graduate training of professional psychologists*. Paper presented at the Advanced Computing for the Social Sciences Conference, Williamsburg, VA.

Lambert, M. E., Andrews, R. H., Rylee, K., & Skinner, J. R. (1987). Equivalence of computerized and traditional MMPI administration with substance abusers. *Computers in Human Behavior, 3*, 139-143.

Lambert, M. E., Hedlund, J. L., & Vieweg, B. W. (1990). Computer simulation in mental health education: Current status. *Computers in Human Services, 7* (314), 211-229.

Lambert, M. E., Intrieri, R. C., & Hollandsworth, J. G., Jr. (1986). Development of a computerized reference retrieval system: A behavior therapy training tool. *Journal of Behavior Therapy and Experimental Psychiatry, 17*(3), 167-169.

Lambert, M. E., & Lenthall, G. (1988). Using computerized case simulations in undergraduate psychology courses. *Teaching of Psychology, 15*(3), 132-135.

Lambert, M. E., Lewis, D. H., & Pryor, C. (1989, April). *Computer simulation utilization in graduate behavior therapy training*. Paper presented at the 35th Annual Convention of the Southwestern Psychological Association, Houston. (ERIC Document Reproduction Service No. ED 308 454).

Lambert, M. E., & Meier, S. T. (1990). *Utilization of computerized case simulations in therapist training and evaluation*. Manuscript submitted for publication.

LaMendola, W. (1988). Distance learning. In B. Glastonbury, W. LaMendola, & S. Toole (Eds.), *Information technology and the human services* (pp. 175-181). New York: John Wiley.

Lang, P. J. (1980). Behavioral treatment and biobehavioral assessment: Computer applications. In J. B. Sidowski, J. H. Johnson, & T. A. Williams (Eds.), *Technology in mental health care delivery systems* (pp. 119-137). Norwood, NJ: Ablex.

Levin, J. S., Hedlund, J. L., & Vieweg, B. W. (1983). Computer supported assessment and consultation for emotional crises in a submarine environment. In R. Dayhoff (Ed.), *Proceedings of the Seventh Annual Symposium on Computer Applications in Medical Care* (pp. 940-943). New York: Institute of Electrical & Electronics Engineers.

Lichtenberg, J. W., Hummel, T. J., & Shaffer, W. F. (1984). Client 1: A computer simulation for use in counselor education and research. *Counselor Education and Supervision, 24*, 155-167.

Lorig, T. S. (1985). Event-related potential data acquisition on the Apple II+/IIe. *Behavior Research Methods, Instruments, and Computers, 17*(4), 479-483.

Lorig, T. S. (1986). Microcomputer-based scalp topography mapping of event-related potentials. *Behavior Research Methods, Instruments, and Computers, 18*(3), 293-298.

MacLean, W. E., Tapp, J. T., & Johnson, W. L. (1985). Alternate methods and software for calculating interobserver agreement for continuous observation data. *Journal of Psychopathology and Behavioral Assessment, 7*(1), 65-73.

Markman, H. J., & Poltrock, S. E. (1982). A computerized system for recording and analysis of self-observations of couples' interaction. *Behavior Research Methods and Instrumentation, 14*(2), 186-190.

Martin, G. L. (1989). The utility of speech input in user-computer interfaces. *International Journal of Man Machine Studies, 30*(4), 355-375.

McCullough, L., Farrell, A. D., & Longabaugh, R. (1986). The development of a microcomputer-based mental health information system. *American Psychologist, 41*(2), 207-214.

McMinn, M. R. (1988). Ethics case-study simulation: A generic tool for psychology teachers. *Teaching of Psychology, 15*(2), 100-101.

Motley, M. T. (1987). "Strip charter": A microcomputer program to quantify psychophysiological and other strip-chart data. *Western Journal of Speech Communication, 51*(1), 78-99.

Muehlenhard, C. L., Baldwin, L. E., Bourg, W. J., & Piper, A. M. (1988). Helping women "break the ice": A computer program to help shy women start and maintain conversations with men. *Journal of Computer-Based Instruction, 15*(1), 7-13.

Muehlenhard, C. L., & McFall, R. M. (1983). Automated assertion training: A feasibility study. *Journal of Social and Clinical Psychology, 1*(3), 246-258.

Murphy-Berman, V., Rosell, J., & Wright, G. (1986). Measuring children's attention span: A microcomputer assessment technique. *Journal of Educational Research, 80*(1), 23-28.

Otto, D. A., Baumann, S., & Robinson, G. (1985). Application of a portable microprocessor-based system for electrophysiological field testing of neurotoxicity. *Neurobehavioral Toxicology and Teratology, 7*(4), 409-414.

Pickering, J. A. (1986). Touch sensitive screens: The technologies and their application. *International Journal of Man Machine Studies, 25*(3), 249-269.

Repp, A. C., Harman, M. L., Felce, D., Van Acker, R., & Karsh, K. G. (1989). Conducting behavioral assessments on computer-collected data. *Behavioral Assessment, 11*, 249-268.

Sampson, J. P., Jr. (1986). The use of computer-assisted instruction in support of psychotherapeutic processes. *Computers in Human Behavior, 2*(1), 1-19.

Sampson, J. P., Jr., & Pyle, K. R. (1983). Ethical issues involved with the use of computer-assisted counseling, testing and guidance systems. *Personnel and Guidance Journal, 61*, 283-287.

Santo, Y., & Finkel, A. (182). *Chris*: A computer simulation of schizophrenia. In B. I. Blum (Ed.), *Proceedings of the Sixth Annual Symposium on Computer Applications in Medical Care* (pp. 737-741). New York: Institute of Electrical & Electronics Engineers.

Sawyer, T. A., & Castellan, N. J. (1985). A microcomputer-based technique for measuring response times in written protocols. *Behavior Research Methods, Instruments, and Computers, 17*(4), 503-504.

Schlundt, D. G., & Bell, C. (1987). Behavioral assessment of eating patterns and blood glucose in diabetes using the Self-Monitoring Analysis System. *Behavior Research Methods, Instruments, and Computers, 19*(2), 215-223.

Schneider, S. J. (1986). Trial of an on-line behavioral smoking cessation program. *Computers in Human Behavior, 2*(4), 277-286.

Schneider, S. J., Benya, A., & Singer, H. (1984). Computerized direct mail to treat smokers who avoid treatment. *Computers and Biomedical Research, 17*, 409-418.

Schwartz, M. D. (1984). Interactive video. *Computers in Psychiatry/Psychology, 6*(1), 7-13.

Selmi, P. M., Klein, M. H., Greist, J. H., Johnson, J. H., & Harris, W. G. (1982). An investigation of computer-assisted cognitive-behavior therapy in the treatment of depression. *Behavior Research Methods & Instrumentation, 14*(2), 181-185.

Selmi, P. M., Klein, M. H., Greist, J. H., Sorrell, S. P., & Erdman, H. P. (1990). Computer assisted congnitive-behavior therapy for depression. *American Journal of Psychiatry, 147*(1), 51-56.

Semmel, M. I., Varnhagen, S., & McCann, S. (1981). *Microgames*: An application of microcomputers for training personnel who work with handicapped children. *Teacher Education and Special Education, 4*, 27-33.

Servan-Schreiber, D., & Binik, Y. M. (1989). Extending the intelligent tutoring system paradigm: Sex therapy as intelligent tutoring. *Computers in Human Behavior, 5*(4), 241-259.

Shangraw, R. F. (1986). Telephone surveying with computers: Administrative, methodological and research issues. *Evaluation and Program Planning, 9*(2), 107-111.

Shavalia, T. L., & Delprato, D. J. (1980). A computerized reference retrieval system for behavior therapy outcome studies. *Journal of Behavior Therapy and Experimental Psychiatry, 11*, 111-115.

Sorrell, S. P., Greist, J. H., Klein, M. H., Johnson, J. H., & Harris, W. G. (1982). Enhancement of adherence to tricyclic antidepressants by computerized supervision. *Behavior Research Methods and Instrumentation, 14*(2), 176-180.

Spinks, J. A., Dow, R., & Chiu, L. W. (1983). A microcomputer package for real-time skin conductance response analysis. *Behavior Research Methods and Instrumentation, 15*(6), 591-593.

Stout, C. E. (1988). Personal computer software for teaching differential psychodiagnostics. *Behavior Research Methods, Instruments, & Computers, 20*(2), 106-107.

Swartz, C. M., & Pfohl, B. (1981). A learning aid for DSM-III: Computerized prompting of diagnostic criteria. *Journal of Clinical Psychiatry, 42*(9), 359-361.

Thorne, D. R., Genser, S. G., Sing, H. C., & Hegge, F. W. (1985). The Walter Reed performance assessment battery. *Neurobehavioral Toxicology and Teratology, 7*(4), 415-418.

Tombari, M. L., Fitzpatrick, S. J., & Childress, W. (1985). Using computers as contingency managers in self-monitoring interventions: A case study. *Computers in Human Services, 1*(1), 75-82.

Uliano, K. C., & Carey, J. R. (1984). MBERT: A BASIC program to alleviate experimenter effect in biofeedback research. *Perceptual and Motor Skills, 58*(1), 206.

Unwin, D. M., & Martin, P. (1987). Recording behaviour using a portable microcomputer. *Behaviour, 101*(1-3), 87-100.

Wagman, M. (1980). PLATO DCS: An interactive computer system for personal counseling. *Journal of Counseling Psychology, 27,* 16-30.

Wagman, M. (1981). Autonomous mode of systematic dilemma counseling. *Psychological Reports, 48,* 231-246.

Wagman, M. (1982a). Solving dilemmas by computer or counselor. *Psychological Reports, 50,* 127-135.

Wagman, M. (1982b). A computer method for solving dilemmas. *Psychological Reports, 50,* 291-298.

Wagman, M., & Kerber, K. W. (1980). PLATO DCS, an interactive computer system for personal counseling: Further development and evaluation. *Journal of Counseling Psychology, 27,* 31-39.

White, C. D., & Charles, P. (1983). Telemetric skin conductance with computer interface. *Psychophysiology, 20,*(5), 597-599.

Wojtaszek, Z., & Zawaszki, R. (1987). On-line computer analysis of electrodermal activity (EDA). *Journal of Psychophysiology, 1*(3), 271-273.

Zicker, J. E., Tompkins, W. J., Rubow, R. T., & Abbs, J. H. (1980). A portable microprocessor-based biofeedback training device. *IEEE Transactions on Biomedical Engineering, 27*(9), 509-515.

INJURY CONTROL IN CHILDREN

EDWARD R. CHRISTOPHERSEN
PATRICIA C. PURVIS
Children's Mercy Hospital, Kansas City, Missouri

I. INTRODUCTION

For many years, the greatest threats to the health and welfare of children were attributed to infectious diseases and inadequate nutrition and sanitation. As medical science has discovered how to prevent and treat common childhood illnesses, the death rate from infectious diseases has declined. As more is known about nutrition and sanitation, the death rate from nutritional problems and inadequate sanitation has similarly declined. Injuries are now the cause of more deaths in children than the next six most frequent causes combined (cancer, congenital anomalies, pneumonia, heart disease, homicide, and stroke). Over the past 59 years, there has been a substantial increase in the percentage of deaths due to intentional and unintentional injuries (Butler, Starfield, & Stenmark, 1984).

Authors' Note: Preparation of this manuscript was partially supported by a grant (CR49-70360301) from the Centers for Disease Control to Edward Christophersen. Address reprint requests to Edward Christophersen, Children's Mercy Hospital, 2401 Gillham Road, Kansas City, MO 64108.

Injuries are now the leading cause of morbidity and mortality in the United States in persons up to 38 years of age (National Safety Council, 1986). Over half of the permanent spinal cord damage, noncongenital mental retardation, and epilepsy in the United States is caused by vehicular trauma (Christophersen, 1986). There is more human suffering, to more people of all ages, at greater expense to society, from unintentional and intentional injuries than from any disease or affliction. In the United States, one injury that is serious enough to require medical care occurs every four seconds and one death from injuries occurs every six minutes. This factors to 240 people who died from injuries every day and 21,350 who are injured every 24 hours (National Safety Council, 1986). Morbidity and mortality tolls from injury are grim, resulting in serious disability, mental retardation, high medical costs, and/or loss of life (Alpert & Guyer, 1985). Each year, 19 million children under the age of 15 seek medical care for an injury (Cataldo et al., 1986). In fact, injuries cause 46% of all deaths for children aged 1 to 4, 55% for children aged 5 to 14, and 79% for persons 15 to 24 (National Academy of Sciences, 1985). The National Safety Council (1986) reports that motor-vehicle-related injuries were the highest cause of death among the 15 to 24 age range, and this age group accounts for one third of all motor-vehicle-related deaths; home-related injuries were cited as the most prevalent cause of death among the 1 to 4 age range. Home-related mortalities are caused, in order of frequency, from fire (burns/scalds), suffocation, drowning, falls, poisoning, and firearm discharge.

Injuries are not a product of fate. They come from tragic intersections of changeable environments and alterable behavior (Peterson, Moreno, & Harbeck, 1988). Only recently have "accidents" been viewed as something other than fateful events. Preferring the term *injury* to accident, because it is no more likely to occur by chance than disease (Guyer & Gallagher, 1985), researchers are approaching this phenomenon as controllable and preventable rather than as a collection of random events (Rivara, 1984).

This chapter will review the current conceptualization of injury prevention, discuss recent societal approaches to injury prevention, and include future concerns and directions for research to diminish the high human cost of injuries.

II. CURRENT CONCEPTUALIZATION OF INJURY CONTROL

The past view of injuries as accidental provided limited insight into their causation or treatment (Jones & McDonald, 1986). By objectively analyzing the factors revolving around injuries, points of reference can be analyzed, predictions made, and treatments developed.

A. Haddon's Epidemiological Model

Haddon's (1980) epidemiological model defined three organizing categories: (a) the recipient of the injury, (b) the agent/vehicle/vector (i.e., the physical energy at the source of the injury—mechanical, thermal, radiant, chemical, or electrical—and its method of transmission to the recipient), and (c) the environment (physical and psychosocial). *Injury* was defined as damage to the body manifest within 48 hours of the energy exchange that produced it (Haddon, 1980).

B.   Characteristics of the Injured Child

The injured child has been variously described as "accident prone," poorly disciplined, extroverted, and impulsive, with impaired ability to cope with hazards (Manheimer & Mellinger, 1967). Using the Rutter Child Behavior Questionnaire, these children are also described as aggressive and overactive (Bijur, Steward-Brown, & Butler, 1986). More recently, Nyman (1987) found that youngsters admitted to hospitals as a result of an injury who suffered from contusions, poisoning, and burns demonstrated temperaments that were more persistent, had higher activity levels, and showed more negative reactions to new situations than other hospitalized children as indicated by results from the Infant Temperament Scale. The studies that have used parent ratings of their infants' temperament suggest that children with certain characteristics will have more accidents than children who do not have these characteristics.

Other factors correlated with injuries include developmental age/stage (e.g., infants are at greater risk for automobile accidents, falls, and suffocation) (Zucker-man & Duby, 1985), child perception of danger (Osborne & Garrettson, 1985), being male (Rivara & LoGerfo, 1982), and alcohol and/or drug abuse by automobile drivers (Rivara, 1982). Davidson, Hughes, and O'Connor (1989) recently reported conflicting evidence from a three-year study of 951 children that indicated that excessively fearful children were at greatest risk of injury. They found that the overactive child who showed poor concentration was no more prone to injury than any other child. Rivara and LoGerfo (1982) concluded that some injuries (foreign body ingestion, poisoning, and burns) do not show a differential rate by sex and that by correcting for sex-related exposure to certain products (e.g., bicycles in relation to number of falls), little difference is noted. Another study concluded that children are no more likely to be injured at a day-care center than in their homes, and they may be at greater risk in their homes (Rivara, DiGuiseppi, Thompson, & Calonge, 1989).

C.   Injury Causation

The most frequent cause of injuries varies among age groups, except for motor vehicle injuries, which are the most common cause of injury across all ages. More children receive damaging blows as occupants, pedestrians, and operators of motor vehicles than from any other source, according to Guyer and Gallagher's (1985) study. The most frequent source of injury for preschoolers is from burns; for school-age children, from bicycles; for teenagers, from sports (Guyer & Gallagher, 1985). Other origins of injury include cleaning agents, glass, toys (Cataldo et al.,

1986), recreational equipment, and home structures, furniture, and fixtures (Jones & McDonald, 1986).

In some studies, injury has been correlated with environmental factors. Social-environmental factors include race, level of income (Wise, Mills, Wilson, Kotelchuck, & Murphy, 1983), younger mothers, single-parent families, and large families (Wadsworth, Burnell, Taylor, & Butler, 1983). Padilla, Rosenow, and Bergman (1976) found that high scores on a Social Readjustment Rating Questionnaire were better predictors of injury than risk-taking behavior among 130 seventh grade boys. Those scoring high in life change had significantly (> .05 level) more accidents than low scorers.

The motivation to practice safe behavior may be affected by several factors, which suggests that observation of the interaction between the parent and child is crucial. Valsiner and Lightfoot (1987) indicate that parents' constant evaluation of their children's behaviors reflect both cultural norms and personal knowledge regarding their children in certain environmental contexts, and these integrated judgments influence decisions about intervening in a dangerous situation. By their behavior, children also may discourage intervening parents from rearranging the environment more safely, if the rearrangement is more restrictive to the child (Baer, 1986). Both sources state that infrequency of actual injury contributes to low motivation for parental intervention. For this reason, Peterson, Farmer, and Mori (1987) suggest the investigation into injury should include studying "near injury," thus allowing for more frequent observation of the antecedents, stages of response, and consequences for injury.

Naming the injury recipient as the cause of that injury focuses on blame instead of discovering methods for eliminating hazardous situations. The multiplicity of correlates suggests that a number of poorly understood factors and associations contribute to injury. However, causation remains difficult to demonstrate. More likely, age, sex, sex-role-appropriate play behavior, and child temperament coexist with parent/child interactions, perceptions, and other attributes of the environment.

III.   STRATEGIES OF INJURY CONTROL

Methods for intervention depend primarily on two factors: (a) whether the intervention actually will be used (considering the action required, effort, and deterrents or incentives) and (b) whether it will be used correctly (Baker, 1981). Additionally, the probability that a child will be protected by an intervention varies inversely with the frequency that an action is required by an adult each time that child needs protection. Interventions requiring no individual action (i.e., passive interventions, such as automobile airbags that inflate upon impact or slats on baby cribs that are close enough together to prohibit a baby's head from getting stuck) are most successful; those requiring a one-time action (e.g., installation of smoke detectors) are less successful; and those requiring repeated individual action (i.e.,

TABLE 1
Effort Required for Interventions

Passive	Effort		Active
None	Only Once	Occasional	Frequent
Automatic Seat belts	Lower hot water heater setting	Check smoke detector	Seat belts
Windowguards	Playground covering		
Safety caps			

active interventions, such as fastening an automobile seat belt each time one rides) are the least successful (see Table 1 for examples of passive versus active strategies).

Until recently, intervention has focused primarily on two approaches: (a) passing laws that mandate the implementation of injury control strategies such as the installation and use of child restraint seats and seat belts (Sanders, 1982), smoke detectors (Feldman, 1982), and guards on the windows of multistory buildings that house children (Speigel & Lindaman, 1977), and (b) modifying the behavior of the potential injury victim or the parent who is responsible for the child.

A. Active Versus Passive Programs

If all injury control strategies could be placed along a continuum, according to the amount of effort that is required by the individual who is responsible for implementing the strategy, passive strategies would be those strategies that require no effort from an individual. An example of passive strategy would be automobile seat belts that automatically wrap around the driver or passenger every time the car door is closed and that require no action on the part of the driver—thus the label *passive*. An example of an active strategy would be the traditional automobile seat belt that an individual must place around him- or herself every time he or she enters an automobile—thus the label *active*. Active approaches are more difficult to implement and less effective than passive approaches (Williams, 1982).

Although passive approaches to injury control are preferred, numerous researchers already have shown that there are many instances when a passive approach is simply impossible. For example, parents can turn down their water heaters' temperature to protect their children from scald burns, but it is not possible to remove all potential sources of drowning in a home (toilets, buckets, and bathtubs). In those instances where a totally passive approach is not feasible, then a combination of active and passive approaches is desirable. In actuality, injury control cannot be realized without the contributions of both passive and active approaches. Legislation that mandated the use of child-resistant caps on medicines and that restricted the number of pills contained in a bottle of children's aspirin has resulted in a decrease in the number of children treated for ingestion of aspirin. However, the very nature of young children dictates that parents must be constantly vigilant about their child's location and activity. Medicines and other hazardous substances must be stored in a place where children cannot access them. No amount of legislation will take away parents' responsibility for monitoring their children. Obviously, a combination of passive and active approaches are most likely to result in the highest level of protection for our nation's children and youth.

Dershewitz (1979) observed that parents are much more likely to follow recommendations if doing so does not involve a lot of effort. For example, he compared parents' compliance with two different recommendations. One recommendation was for the installation of small plastic covers for electrical outlets that could be installed in seconds without tools and with little effort. The other recommendation was for plastic safety latches that had to be individually installed on each kitchen cabinet door and drawer, using provided screws. The parents in his study were much more compliant with the outlet covers than they were with the safety latches.

B. Legislative Efforts

Impressive benefits have been reported as a result of efforts within the legislative domain. The passage of the Poison Prevention Packaging Act in 1970, which mandated placing potentially hazardous drugs and household products in child-resistant containers, was correlated with a 97% drop in poisonings for children under 5 years (Cataldo et al., 1986). Sanders (1982) was instrumental in getting the original legislation passed in 1978 that mandated the use of child-restraint devices in Tennessee. Restraint seat usage in Tennessee increased from 9% to 27% during the first three years the law was in effect. Since 1978, all 50 states have passed child restraint seat laws.

A more recent review of increased safe seating for children following state implementation of child passenger safety legislation was presented by Seekins et al. (1988). Although their data indicated an increase from an average use rate of 13% to an average of 26% in seven states where observational data were collected, only Virginia and Illinois showed a definite increase, while the other states showed modest increases or even declines in compliance.

In an effort to reduce the high incidence of falls from apartment windows, the "Children Can't Fly" program was developed by the New York City Department of Health. This effort resulted in a health code law that required landlords to install window guards in apartments housing children age 10 or under, resulting in a 50% decrease in the number of children seriously injured or killed by falls (Speigel & Lindaman, 1977).

Future research needs to address the impact that legislation has on the education of citizens and lawmakers about the serious effects of injuries. When lawmakers have enough information to pass legislation that requires injury-reducing procedures that have proven effectiveness, then the legislative approach has achieved the ultimate goal—injury control. Fawcett, Seekins, and Jason (1987) showed the effectiveness of using established marketing research methods to influence public policy development in the legislatures of Kansas and Illinois. By identifying those state representatives interested in child passengers, providing appropriate data on the number of children affected, outlining the importance of the problem and the general acceptability of legislation in this area, a policy research process was developed that could be applied to other safety legislation issues. The field of injury control must identify research priorities and exercise whatever influence is necessary to effect the changes that protect the majority of our nation's citizens.

C. Educational Efforts

Educational programs are the most widely used approach to preventing health problems; however, most naively assume that, once information is provided, action will follow (Roberts & Elkins, 1981). Early evidence on the benefit of educational approaches in effecting behavioral change or reducing hazards suggested that educational approaches alone are not sufficient to reduce injury potential (Gallagher, Hunter, & Guyer, 1985). A home-safety study by Dershewitz and Williamson (1977) compared two groups of mothers; the experimental group received a 20-minute tutorial, a booklet on how to make their homes safer, safety latches for their kitchen cabinets and plastic plugs for their electric wall outlets, and a follow-up phone call as review. The control group received only the safety latches and the plastic plugs. Results obtained by interviewers during unannounced visits to both groups' homes showed little difference between the two groups in the reduction of household hazards. Other educational strategies that showed no significant changes in the home environment or behavior included the use of "Mr. Yuk" labels as a poison-prevention aid (Fergusson, Horwood, Beautrais, & Shannon, 1982), use of a national television campaign to increase home safety (Colver, Hutchinson, & Judson, 1982), and a school-initiated educational campaign for burn prevention (MacKay & Rothman, 1982). Others have experienced success by providing brief, selected information that is repetitive and age appropriate at well-child visits (Dershewitz, Posner, & Paichel, 1983; Kelly, Sein, & McCarthy, 1987). Miller, Reisinger, Blatter, and Wucher (1982) increased installation of smoke detectors in an experimental group who were given a one-minute educational message in the clinic and discount coupons for the purchase of a smoke detector.

Educational programs that attempt to scare parents into implementing injury control strategies to protect their infants or young children have been notoriously ineffective. Data support the fact that such programs do not motivate parents to change. Janis (1983) researched the issue of getting parents to comply with health care providers' recommendations and arrived at a series of recommendations. First, parents need to be *informed* about the seriousness of the problem. With child passenger safety, this is relatively easy to do; many films and written materials are available that convey the seriousness of the issue. But, in other accident prevention areas, like water heater settings, few materials are available. The Public Information Officer of the American Academy of Pediatrics offers myriad educational materials, at no cost for samples and at low cost for quantity orders from physicians. Second, parents must be convinced that there is *hope*, that they can do something, within a reasonable time frame and without significant costs, that will offer protection to their infant or child. Third, the parents need *time* to think about the issue and to make up their minds about it. Christophersen (1985) added to Janis's recommendations, suggesting that parents be informed about the advantages and disadvantages of both complying and not complying with the provider's recommendations. For example, when discussing the need to lower water heater settings, he suggests that parents be told about the risk of burning children with tap water that is too hot, that turning down the water heater will save in utility bills, and that the detergents manufactured for dishes and clothes are engineered to work at 120 to 125 degrees Fahrenheit (all advantages in lowering water heater temperatures). Parents should also be told that the family will not be able to take as many baths in succession after the water heater temperature is lowered (a disadvantage). In a similar study that was done with automobile child-restraint devices, Treiber (1986) showed that a combination of both positive and negative information about auto safety was superior to either a negative approach or a positive approach alone in terms of parental compliance.

Williams, Barone, Hassanein, and Christophersen (1990) showed that health education messages were more likely to result in a behavioral change if the messages were given to expectant parents, as a part of prenatal education, than if they were given to parents of 2-year-old children. This study contrasted the results obtained using prenatal education groups and educational groups for parents of toddlers. The major educational message was that lowering water heater temperature settings can drastically reduce injuries from hot water scalds (the second leading cause of death in children). Families in the prenatal group who got the message had significantly lower water heater temperature settings than parents in the prenatal group who did not receive the message. There was no difference in the two groups from the toddler classes. When interviewed later, the expectant parents stated that they wanted to do anything they could to protect their children. The parents of toddlers made frequent comments to the effect that they hadn't turned down their water heater temperature settings before and their children had not received any scald burns. Apparently, parents have a false sense of security when they practice unsafe procedures in their home and do not experience any unpleasant effects from doing so. The authors suggest that expectant parents are more receptive to health education messages because they have a different history than the parents of toddlers. The time at which a health education message is delivered is obviously deserving of more study.

Future research needs to concentrate on developing more effective educational methods, either by changing the way the education is conducted or by changing the components that are included in the educational package. Because educational programs appear to be more effective when used in combination with other approaches, future research needs to concentrate on educational programs that are part of a more comprehensive strategy.

D. Media Campaigns

Kelley (1979) reported negative results with a carefully controlled study to measure the effectiveness of media campaigns for health education. Using a cable television system that allowed two different television inputs into different subscriber's homes, Kelley found no differences between homes that received messages on the need to use automobile safety belts and homes that did not receive the messages. However, conclusions that the media is ineffective for health education should not be based on this one study. Because media messages are typically used in combination with a variety of other procedures in an attempt to improve the effectiveness of a program, it has been very difficult for researchers to accurately assess the effects of a simple media campaign.

The national PTA several years ago began a "Get Home Safely" seat belt campaign that featured "E.T." in local school systems. Local health professionals who supported the program made appearances in the schools on behalf of the campaign. The combination of school exposure, media coverage, and personal appearances by interested community professionals produced a product that was highly visible to the city's youth. That the campaign, by itself, was enough to produce a change is unlikely, but it helped get exposure for a topic that needed visibility.

Given the apparent success of the media in the are of advertising, future research might profitably be spent exploring the use of sophisticated advertising campaigns in combination with other procedures. Research efforts (by the Harborview Injury Control Center in Seattle, Washington) aimed at increasing the protection of bicycle riders through the use of bicycle helmets is one example of such a program.

E. Hospital-Based Programs

In 1973, Vermont had no child-restraint seat programs. During the next five years, loaner programs were developed at over 90% of the hospitals in the state (Colletti, 1983). The majority of hospitals that offer obstetrical care also offer prenatal or childbirth preparation classes. Fifteen years ago, one of this chapter's authors (ERC) began offering a class on parenting as part of the prenatal classes at the University of Kansas Medical Center. Topics such as child passenger safety and home injury control (water heater settings and smoke detector installations) were presented (see Christophersen, 1988a). Safety issues usually are not discussed during a prenatal visit to a pediatric health care provider, but prenatal classes offer a logical forum to discuss safety because many expectant couples attend them. These classes are offered during the seventh and eighth months of pregnancy, a time when many infant care decisions are being made by the expectant couples.

F. Physician Counseling Programs

If educational efforts were the responsibility of several groups of professionals within the same community or state, the efforts would be more effective than would the efforts of one physician alone. The provider, acting as coordinator, could certainly be instrumental in including presentation of information on accident prevention during prenatal classes as well as including such materials within his or her own office visits. Local PTAs, already sensitized by the national PTA's accident prevention initiatives, would more than likely cooperate with the physician to effect a communitywide educational effort.

Much of the written material distributed by the American Academy of Pediatrics (1977) is intended for distribution to families from pediatricians' offices. Reisinger et al. (1981) described the most effective physician counseling program for auto safety in the literature. They prepared materials that were distributed to parents in addition to periodic verbal discussions in the office. They collected observational data at each office visit during the first 15 months of the child's life. Slightly more than 50% of the mothers were correctly restraining their children by 15 months of age, which was significantly more than in the control group.

Both Reisinger and his colleagues (Reisinger et al., 1981) and Dershewitz (1979) tried brief (less than two minutes) educational pep talks for restraint seat use and smoke detector installation, respectively. Both studies reported some improvement in parents' use of injury control procedures. Dershewitz (1985) organized accident prevention information chronologically, so that he could plan which material to present at different well-child visits.

Later studies have shown that promising results emerged when more time and effort were taken by the health care provider for the health education message. Christophersen, Sosland-Edelman, and LeClaire (1985) reported very high rates of compliance with infant automobile restraint seat use when a multidimensional program was used. Their program included the passage of state legislation, a hospital loaner program for provision of the restraint seats, nurses and physicians who encouraged and educated new parents about the need for restraint seat usage, and a communitywide educational program on the advantages of restraint seat usage. The parents in the study correctly used restraint seats more than 85% of the time at hospital discharge and at 3-month, 6-month, and 12-month follow-up observations. In an extension of this study, Treiber (1986) reported that similar health education approaches were effective in increasing parents' use of automobile restraint devices for young children. Treiber (1986) showed that parents had the highest compliance rates when they were informed about both the dangers of automobile travel and the advantages inherent in the use of child restraint devices. Discussions only about the dangers of automobile travel or only about the advantages of restraint-seat use produced lower rates.

One of the strongest deterrents to physician counseling programs is the physician's busy schedule (Bass, Mehta, Ostrovsky, & Halperin, 1985). Reisinger and Bires (1980) reported that the pediatricians in their study spent an average of 97 seconds on health education to mothers with infants less than 5 months of age and only 7 seconds with the parents of children 13 to 17 years of age. Within these time constraints, very little can be accomplished. However, Osborn (1985) reported on a relatively new concept in well-child care: group well-child care. The main advantage of delivering well-child care in groups is that the provider has significantly more time to spend in discussion and information exchange with each mother. Much more information can be covered in a 45-minute visit instead of the more traditional 15-minute visit. Also, because the provider can schedule five or six mothers at the same time, he or she has to repeat the same message only one fifth or one sixth as many times in one day. Osborn (1985) reported other benefits of groups: The parents learn a great deal from each other and from the group discussion and, in turn, the provider learns a lot from the families. The group format also gives providers an opportunity they normally would not have to see how the mother-infant dyads interact.

Thomas, Hassanein, and Christophersen (1984), using a similar group well-child format, showed that parents could be persuaded to lower the thermostat on their water heaters. Although 65% of the experimental group (who received the accident prevention materials) set their water heaters at a "safe level" (130 degrees Fahrenheit or below), none of the control group (who had not received the special accident prevention materials) did. These results, from two independent programs, suggest that the physician may be a more effective counselor if he or she will adopt and utilize a group well-child format.

A similar group format has been successfully used by Christophersen, Barrish, Barrish, and Christophersen (1984) for group parenting classes. These authors cataloged the material that the American Academy of Pediatrics, in its *Standards of Health Care,* suggests should be covered during well-child care and then deleted the material that is typically covered by pediatricians during well-child visits (see Reisinger and Bires, 1980). The material left uncovered was then presented during four two-hour classes. The classes included information and discussion on accident prevention at home and in vehicles, normal growth and development, day care and baby-sitters, parent stressors, and child management.

Future health education research should concentrate on basic health education in an attempt to identify those components that may be critical to the effectiveness of any health education campaign. A carefully designed program of research that builds upon and extends the work of earlier researchers is likely to contribute to the eventual design of effective injury control programs.

G. Behavioral Interventions

Behavioral interventions, although tested on a relatively small scale, attempt to decrease excessive unsafe behavior while (often simultaneously) trying to increase insufficient safe behavior (Roberts, Fanurick, & Layfield, 1987). Motivational procedures for getting parents to adopt injury control strategies have been identified. Christophersen and Gyulay (1981) found an increase in mothers' compliance in using car seats when they were taught how to interact appropriately with their safely restrained children. Not only were the children safer, the mothers were rewarded by the advantage of improved in-car behavior from their children.

Interventions targeted to increase safe behaviors in children have shown success. Krenzelok and Garber (1981) were successful in teaching preschoolers to identify poisons and their dangers. Yeaton and Bailey (1978) used verbal prompts and modeling to teach elementary school children some pedestrian safety skills that were maintained at high levels one year later. Mori and Peterson (1986) indicated that 3-year-olds can benefit from safety skills intervention. These researchers, using a safety skills manual with a game format, demonstrated that preschoolers as young as 3 could learn to respond safely to a variety of dangerous home situations (specifically, selecting and preparing snacks, reacting to strangers on the phone or at the door, responding to a fire, and reacting to a physical injury). Some research suggests that overrehearsing or continual role-playing of safety behaviors are the most critical aspect of safety skills education once the initial correct response has been acquired (Peterson et al., 1988). Most researchers, however, agree that parents' participation is an integral part of educating children in safe behaviors (Guyer, Talbot, & Pless, 1985).

Programs combining education with behavioral techniques have shown promise. Speigel and Lindaman (1977) used community education regarding death by falls, disseminated by door-to-door visits and a media campaign combined with distribution of free window guards and some assistance in installing the guards. A significant drop in the number of falls from windows was noted, and legislation followed. Tertinger, Greene, and Lutzker (1984) presented families with a treatment package that included identification of hazards in the home, education on accident prevention, modeling of safety techniques, installation of safety devices, and frequent home visits. Long-term decreases in accessible hazards were found. Barone, Greene, and Lutzker (1986) successfully streamlined this package by developing an audiovisual show to train families, thus making the intervention practical for use by other health professionals, such as home-health nurses. Gallagher, Hunter, and Guyer (1985) reported success with the Home Injury Prevention Project (HIPP), part of Massachusetts statewide approach to injury prevention. This package consisted of identifying housing code violations, educating parents about potential safety hazards, and distributing/installing inexpensive safety devices and products in the homes.

Behavioral researchers frequently have viewed problematic behavior as falling into one of two categories: (a) behaviors that need to be learned initially or increased in frequency and (b) behaviors that need to be eliminated or reduced in frequency. These two categories are easy to identify in the area of injury control. Behaviors that must be learned or increased in frequency include using seat belts and conscientiously monitoring children; behaviors that must be eliminated or decreased in frequency include playing in the street, playing with matches, exceeding highway speed limits, and driving while intoxicated. Many standard behavioral procedures, including the use of tangible rewards and incentives, have been widely used in past research. Several researchers have applied these or similar procedures to injury control research. For example, Roberts and Turner (1986) used behavioral procedures for encouraging parents and children to use automobile safety belts or child restraint devices by rewarding parents for correctly using child restraint devices. Parents were rewarded with lottery tokens redeemable for prizes if their children were appropriately secured with an automobile seat belt when they arrived at their child's day-care center. When the families began receiving rewards based upon their seat belt use, there was a dramatic increase in their use of seat belts. After the rewards were removed, there was a gradual decline in seat belt use. Sowers-Hoag, Thyer, and Bailey (1987) used behavioral practice, assertiveness training, and social and contrived reinforcers to establish and maintain automobile safety belt use in young children.

Geller and his colleagues (Geller, Bruff, & Nimmer, 1985) also published clear demonstrations of the effectiveness of rewards on increasing the use of child safety devices. These studies demonstrate that procedures initially developed in totally different settings can have applicability when used in injury control research. For example, Mathews, Friman, Barone, Ross, and Christophersen (1987) reported on a program for teaching mothers to use standard child management procedures (see Christophersen, 1988b) to reduce the amount of dangerous behaviors in which their young children engaged. Mathews et al. (1987) showed that the use of procedures originally developed to reduce other inappropriate behaviors in young children were effective in reducing dangerous behaviors in young children. In this study, teenage mothers were taught, through modeling and demonstration, how to reward their young children (who were less than 1 year old) with brief physical contact (which is often used as a reward for children) for age-appropriate behaviors. They were also taught to punish dangerous behaviors by placing their child in their playpen for a brief disciplinary procedure (time-out). The children in the study engaged in potentially dangerous behaviors approximately 55% of the time prior to training. After training, the children's potentially dangerous behaviors occurred less than 10% of the time. These results were maintained at six-month follow-up observations.

Jones and McDonald (1986) suggested a child training model targeting competencies to prevent initial injuries and to initiate appropriate actions once an accident has occurred. Baer (1986) additionally suggested parent training to target behaviors of providing a safe environment and taking appropriate action once an accident occurs while also teaching children to do the same. The intervention process is made complex by the multiplicity of human as well as environmental factors that are necessary to consider. Technology to present information through development of successful educational methods will be necessary to heighten parental awareness of developmentally hazardous activities and the necessity to monitor their children while, concurrently, identifying interventions that require the least amount of effort to implement. It will be necessary to have a better understanding of the behavioral antecedents and consequences of injury to do so. Ultimately, comprehensive programs that incorporate several different approaches are likely to be necessary for injury morbidity and morality rates to decrease.

Future research on behavioral approaches needs to explore the various reward/punishment parameters as well as a wide variety of other procedures for increasing or decreasing behaviors. Researchers can study the procedures that are used to teach parents how to monitor or change their child's behaviors. In the Mathews et al. (1987) study, mothers were trained using in-home demonstrations from behavior therapists. Future research can examine whether the same procedures might work when used in an office setting. Actually, the application of strategies and procedures from the behavioral sciences to the area of injury control has vast frontiers that are yet to be explored.

These types of studies contribute to our knowledge of how to encourage individuals to comply with injury control strategies, and the studies that should be forthcoming on long-term maintenance should contribute even more. The field of injury control must also be poised to identify more comprehensive programs that incorporate several different approaches. In the aggregate, these approaches are complementary and can produce an effect that could not be realized by using one of the approaches in isolation. Gallagher et al. (1985) reported very encouraging results from an evaluation of the HIPP. A three-part injury prevention strategy was evaluated. The three strategies were regulatory (identification and abatement of violations of existing housing codes), educational (counseling on potential safety hazards in the home), and technological (installation and/or distribution of inexpensive safety devices at no cost to the family). Gallagher et al. (1985) showed that the homes in the intervention group had decreases in household hazards, including both decreases in hazardous items in the house and decreases in water heater temperatures.

IV. INJURY CONTROL: FUTURE DIRECTIONS

The magnitude of injuries and their cost to society demand that any profession with a potential for making a contribution should make it. The loss that society experiences from injuries can be reduced using already available procedures as well as procedures that have yet to be developed. In *Injury in America* (National Academy of Sciences, 1985, p. 37), several major approaches were identified to prevent injuries. These include

(1) *persuading* persons at risk of injury to alter their behavior to increase their self-protection (for example, to use seat belts or to install smoke detectors);

(2) *requiring* individual behavior change by law or administrative rule (for example, by passing laws requiring seat belt use or requiring the installation of smoke detectors in all new buildings); and

(3) *providing automatic protection* with product and environmental design (for example, by the installation of seat belts that automatically encompass occupants of motor vehicles or built-in sprinkler systems that automatically extinguish fires).

All three of these major approaches could benefit from substantial input from behavioral scientists. Historically, behavioral scientists have conducted countless studies on persuasion and attitude change, and the results can be applied to injury control. Of all of the major mandates in health care today, injury control is perhaps the one to which behavioral scientists have the most to contribute, because the loss of human life to injuries is enormous.

V. CONCLUSION

As the result of promising research in the legislative, educational, and behavioral areas, morbidity and mortality as a result of injuries can be reduced in the next decade. The three areas of intervention research we addressed in this chapter have strengths and weaknesses. Legislative regulation, although providing environmental safety barriers, has several drawbacks. First, it cannot occur in a vacuum. For legislation to occur, recognition of need, credible research to support passage of a bill, and a socially acceptable way to regulate the source of injury must be presented (Fawcett et al., 1987). Additionally, although potentially broad in scope, laws can be applied only to certain identifiable hazards that lend themselves to legislative control (e.g., unit packaging limiting the number of pills per bottle or regulation of speed limits). Educational interventions have shown mixed results. Although educational approaches have been used for a long time, a systematic program of research is needed to identify critical variables that affect the effectiveness of education. For example, Williams et al. (1990) identified a critical time in parenthood when parents are more apt to alter their environment as a result of educational techniques. Behavioral approaches currently intervene on a small scale and are expensive in terms of labor intensity. Research in this area is beginning to describe necessary components for intervention, but operationalizing them on a larger scale is necessary.

Ten years ago, injury control had barely been identified as an area for research investigation. Few injury control laws had been passed, there were virtually no research monies available (see National Academy of Sciences, 1985), and the general public had little knowledge of the enormous number of citizens who were killed or injured by "accidents." Over the past decade, research monies have begun to become available, both through the National Institutes of Health and the Centers for Disease Control; educational and behavioral approaches have been explored and the results published in journals and books; and numerous laws have been passed mandating the implementation of injury control strategies. The academic community appears now to be acutely aware of the need for systematic research on all of the various topics that come under the general heading of injury control research. Although virtually every one of us has felt the impact of unintentional and intentional injuries, we are just now, as a society, beginning to recognize the enormous importance of injury control as a topic for research, legislation, and public discussion.

REFERENCES

Alpert, J. J., & Guyer, B. (1985). Foreword. *The Pediatric Clinics of North America, 32,* 1-4.
American Academy of Pediatrics. (1977). *Standards of health care* (3rd ed.). Evanston, IL: American Academy of Pediatrics.

Baer, D. M. (1986, September). *A behavioral analysis of children's injuries.* Paper presented at the conference of the National Institute of Child Health and Human Development, Bethesda, MD.

Baker, S. P. (1981). Childhood injuries: The community approach to prevention. *Journal of Public Health Policy, 2,* 235-246.

Barone, V. J., Greene, B. F., & Lutzker, J. R. (1986). Home safety with families being treated for child abuse and neglect. *Behavior Modification, 10,* 93-114.

Bass, J. L., Mehta, K. A., Ostrovsky, M., & Halperin, S. F. (1985). Educating parents about injury prevention. *Pediatric Clinics of North American, 32,* 233-242.

Bijur, P. E., Stewart-Brown, S., & Butler, N. (1986). Child behavior and accidental injury in 11,066 preschool children. *Child Behavior and Injury, 140,* 487-492.

Butler, J. A., Starfield, B., & Stenmark, S. (1984). Child health policy. In H. W. Stevenson & A. E. Siegel (Eds.), *Child development research and public policy* (pp. 110-188). Chicago: University of Chicago.

Cataldo, M. F., Dershewitz, R. A., Christophersen, E. R., Finney, J. W., Fawcett, S. B., & Seekins, T. (1986). Childhood injury control. In N. A. Krasnegor, J. Arasteh, & M. F. Cataldo (Eds.), *Child health behavior: A behavioral pediatrics perspective* (pp. 217-253). New York: John Wiley.

Christophersen, E. R. (1985). Enhancing the effectiveness of health education strategies. *Clinics in Perinatology, 12,* 381-389.

Christophersen, E. R. (1986). Anticipatory guidance on discipline. *Pediatric Clinics of North America, 33,* 789-798.

Christophersen, E. R. (1988a). *Baby owner's manual: What to expect and how to survive the first year* (3rd ed.). Kansas City, MO: Westport.

Christophersen, E. R. (1988b). *Little people: Guidelines for common sense child rearing* (3rd ed.). Kansas City, MO: Westport.

Christophersen, E. R. (1989). Injury control. *American Psychologist, 44,* 237-241.

Christophersen, E. R., Barrish, H. H., Barrish, I. J., & Christophersen, M. R. (1984). Continuing education for parents of infants and toddlers. In R. F. Dangel & R. A. Polster (Eds.), *Parent training: Foundations of research and practice* (pp. 127-143). New York: Guilford.

Christophersen, E. R., & Gyulay, J. (1981). Parental compliance with car seat usage: A positive approach with long-term follow-up. *Journal of Pediatric Psychology, 6,* 301-312.

Christophersen, E. R., Sosland-Edelman, D., & LeClaire, S. (1985). Evaluation of two comprehensive infant car seat loaner programs with 1-year follow-up. *Pediatrics, 76,* 36-42.

Colletti, R. B. (1983). Hospital-based rental programs in increased car seat usage. *Pediatrics, 71,* 771-773.

Colver, A. F., Hutchinson, P. J., & Judson, E. C. (1982). Promoting children's home safety. *British Medical Journal, 285* 1177-1180.

Davidson, L. L., Hughes, S. J., & O'Connor, P. A. (1989). Accident-prone child doesn't fit stereotype [Abstract]. *Growing Child Research Review, 9,* 6.

Dershewitz, R. A. (1979). Will mothers use free household safety devices? *American Journal of Diseases of Children, 133,* 61-64.

Dershewitz, R. A. (1985). Prenatal anticipatory guidance. *Clinics in Perinatology, 12,* 343-353.

Dershewitz, R. A., Posner, M. K., & Paichel, W. (1983). The effectiveness of health education on home use of Ipecac. *Clinical Pediatrics, 22,* 268-270.

Dershewitz, R. A., & Williamson, J. W. (1977). Prevention of childhood household injuries: A controlled clinical trial. *American Journal of Public Health, 67,* 1148-1153.

Fawcett, S. B., Seekins, T., & Jason, L. A. (1987). Policy research and child passenger safety legislation: A case study and experimental evaluation. *Journal of Social Issues, 43,* 133-148.

Feldman, K. W. (1982). Controlling scald burns. In A. B. Bergman (Ed.), *Preventing childhood injuries* (Report of the 12th Ross Roundtable on Critical Approaches to Common Pediatric Problems). Columbus, OH: Ross Laboratories.

Fergusson, D. M., Horwood, L. J., Beautrais, A. L., & Shannon, F. T. (1982). A controlled field trial of a poisoning prevention method. *Pediatrics, 69,* 515-520.

Gallagher, S. S., Hunter, P., & Guyer, B. (1985). A home injury prevention program for children. *Pediatric Clinics of North American, 32,* 95-112.

Geller, E. S., Bruff, C. D., & Nimmer, J. G. (1985). "Flash for life": Community-based prompting for safety belt promotion. *Journal of Applied Behavior Analysis, 18,* 309-314.

Guyer, B., & Gallagher, S. S. (1985). An approach to the epidemiology of childhood injuries. *Pediatric Clinics of North American, 32,* 5-15.

Guyer, B., Talbot, A. M., & Pless, I. B. (1985). Pedestrian injuries to children and youth. *Pediatric Clinics of North America, 32,* 163-174.

Haddon, W. (1980). Advances in the epidemiology of injuries as a basis for public policy. *Public Health Reports, 95,* 411-421.

Janis, J. L. (1983). The role of social support in adherence to stressful decisions. *American Psychologist, 38,* 143-160.

Jones, R. T., & McDonald, D. (1986). Childhood injury: A prevention model for intervention. *Education and Treatment of Children, 9,* 307-319.

Kelley, A. B. (1979). A media role for public health compliance? In R. B. Haynes, D. W. Taylor, & D. L. Sackett (Eds.), *Compliance in health care* (pp. 193-201). Baltimore: Johns Hopkins University Press.

Kelly, B. Sein, C., & McCarthy, P. L. (1987). Safety education in a pediatric primary care setting. *Pediatrics, 79,* 818-824.

Krenzelok, E. P., & Garber, R. J. (1981). Teaching poison prevention to preschool children, their parents, and professional educators through child care centers. *American Journal of Public Health, 71,* 750-752.

MacKay, A. M., & Rothman, K. J. (1982). The incidence and severity of burn injuries following burn prevention. *American Journal of Public Health, 72,* 248-252.

Manheimer, D. I., & Mellinger, G. D. (1967). Personality characteristics of the child accident repeater. *Child Development, 38,* 491-513.

Mathews, J. R., Friman, P. C., Barone, V. J., Ross, L. V., & Christophersen, E. R. (1987). Parental management of infants: Increasing positive maternal interactions and decreasing dangerous infant behaviors. *Journal of Applied Behavior Analysis, 20,* 165-169.

Miller, R. E., Reisinger, K. S., Blatter, M. M., & Wucher, F. (1982). Pediatric counseling and subsequent use of smoke detectors. *American Journal of Public Health, 72,* 392-393.

Mori, L., & Peterson, L. (1986). Training preschoolers in home safety skills to prevent inadvertent injury. *Journal of Clinical Child Psychology, 15,* 106-114.

National Academy of Sciences. (1985). *Injury in America: A continuing public health problem.* Washington, DC: National Academy Press.

National Safety Council (1986). *Accident Facts: 1986.* Chicago: National Safety Council.

Nyman, G. (1987). Infant temperament, childhood accidents, and hospitalization. *Clinical Pediatrics, 26,* 398-404.

Osborn, L. M. (1985). Group well-child care. *Clinics in Perinatology, 12,* 355-365.

Osborne, S. C., & Garrettson, L. K. (1985). Perception of toxicity and dose by 3- and 4-year-old children. *American Journal of Diseases of Children, 139,* 790-792.

Padilla, E. R., Rosenow, D. S., & Bergman, A. B. (1976). Predicting accident frequency in children. *Pediatrics, 58,* 223-226.

Peterson, L., Farmer, J., & Mori, L. (1987). Process analysis of injury situations: A complement to epidemiological methods. *Journal of Social Issues, 43,* 33-44.

Peterson, L., Moreno, A., & Harbeck, C. (1988). Obstacles to safety skills education. *Newsletter of the Society of Pediatric Psychology, 12,* 19-22.

Reisinger, K. S., & Bires, J. A. (1980). Anticipatory guidance in pediatric practice. *Pediatrics, 66,* 889-892.

Reisinger, K. S., Williams, A. F., Wells, J. K., John, C. E., Roberts, T. R., & Podgainy, H. J. (1981). Effect of pediatricians' counseling on infant restraint use. *Pediatrics, 67,* 201-206.

Rivara, F. P. (1982). Epidemiology of childhood injuries: Review of current research and presentation of conceptual framework. *American Journal of Diseases of Children, 136,* 399-405.

Rivara, F. P. (1984). Epidemiology of childhood injuries. In J. D. Matarazzo, S. M. Weiss, & J. A. Herds (Eds.), *Behavioral health* (pp. 1003-1020). New York: John Wiley.

Rivara, F. P., DiGuiseppi, C., Thompson, R. S., & Calonge, N. (1989). Risk of injury to children less than 5 years of age in day care versus home care settings. *Pediatrics, 84,* 1011-1016.

Rivara, F. P., & LoGerfo, J. P. (1982). Epidemiology of childhood injuries: Sex differences in injury rates. *American Journal of Diseases of Children, 136,* 502-506.

Roberts, M. C., & Elkins, P. D. (1981, August). *Prevention of health and accident problems in childhood.* Paper presented at "Applying General Principles of Behavior to Health and Accident Problems in Children," symposium conducted at the convention of the American Psychological Association, Los Angeles, L. Wright (Chair).

Roberts, M. C., Fanurik, D., & Layfield, D. A. (1987). Behavioral approaches to prevention of childhood injuries. *Journal of Social Issues, 43,* 105-118.

Roberts, M. C., & Turner, D. S. (1986). Rewarding parents for their children's use of safety seats. *Journal of Pediatric Psychology, 11,* 25-36.

Sanders, R. S. (1982). Legislative approach to auto safety: The Tennessee experience. In A. B. Bergman (Ed.), *Preventing childhood injuries* (Report of the 12th Ross Roundtable on Critical Approaches to Common Pediatric Problems, pp. 39-43). Columbus, OH: Ross Laboratories.

Seekins, T., Fawcett, S. B., Cohen, S. H., Elder, J. P., Jason, L. A., Schnelle, J. F., & Winett, R. A. (1988). Experimental evaluation of public policy: The case for state legislation for child passenger safety. *Journal of Applied Behavior Analysis, 21,* 233-243.

Sowers-Hoag, K. M., Thyer, B. A., & Bailey, J. S. (1987). Promoting automobile safety belt use by young children. *Journal of Applied Behavior Analysis, 20,* 133-138.

Speigel, C. N., & Lindaman, F. C. (1977). Children can't fly: A program to prevent childhood morbidity and mortality from window falls. *American Journal of Public Health, 67,* 1143-1147.

Tertinger, D. A., Greene, B. F., & Lutzker, J. R. (1984). Home safety: Development and validation of one component of an ecobehavioral treatment program for abused and neglected children. *Journal of Applied Behavior Analysis, 17,* 159-174.

Thomas, K. A., Hassanein, R. S., & Christophersen, E. R. (1984). Evaluation of group well-child care for improving burn prevention practices in the home. *Pediatrics, 74* 879-882.

Treiber, F. A. (1986). A comparison of the positive and negative consequences approaches upon car restraint usage. *Journal of Pediatric Psychology, 11,* 15-24.

Valsiner, J., & Lightfoot, C. (1987). Process structure of parent-child-environment relations and the prevention of children's injuries. *Journal of Social Issues, 43,* 61-72.

Wadsworth, J., Burnell, I., Taylor, B., & Butler, M. (1983). Family type and accidents in preschool children. *Journal of Epidemiology and Community Health, 37,* 100-104

Williams, A. F. (1982). Passive and active measures for controlling disease and injury. *Health Psychology, 1,* 399-409.

Williams, G., Barone, V., Hassanein, R., & Christophersen, E. R. (1990). *Group parent education classes: A comparison of educational approaches to expectant parents versus parents of toddlers.* Unpublished manuscript.

Wise, P. H., Mills, M., Wilson, M., Kotelchuck, M., & Murphy, M. (1983). The influence of race and socioeconomic status on childhood mortality in Boston [Abstract]. *American Journal of Diseases of Children, 137,* 538.

Yeaton, W. H., & Bailey, J. S. (1978). Teaching pedestrian skills to young children: An analysis and one-year follow-up. *Journal of Applied Behavior Analysis, 11,* 315-329.

Zuckerman, B. S., & Duby, J. C. (1985). Developmental approach to injury prevention. *Pediatric Clinics of North American, 32,* 17-29.

THE BEHAVIORAL MODEL AND ADOLESCENTS WITH BEHAVIOR DISORDERS: A REVIEW OF SELECTED TREATMENT STUDIES

ELLEN OLINGER
Northeastern Illinois University

MICHAEL H. EPSTEIN
Northern Illinois University

Authors' Note: Preparation of this chapter was supported in part by a research grant (G0087C3034) from the U.S. Department of Education. However, the opinions expressed in this chapter remain those of the authors.

I. INTRODUCTION

Approximately 1% of adolescents attending school have been identified as behaviorally disordered to the extent that they are receiving special education services for this disorder (U. S. Department of Education, 1986). Prior to the mid-1970s, adolescents whose behavior deviated markedly from their peers were encouraged to drop out of school, expelled, or ignored by the educational system. Legislation passed in 1975, Public Law 94-142, the Education for All Handicapped Children Act, ensured that all handicapped children and adolescents, including those with behavior disorders or emotional disturbances, had a right to a free, appropriate public education. The law stated that students with handicaps shall receive appropriate educational services, nondiscriminatory testing and evaluations, placement in the least restrictive environments, individualized educational planning, and due process safeguards of their educational rights. PL 94-142 has led to sweeping changes in how handicapped students are educated in our nation's schools. PL 94-142 defines *behavior disorders*[1] as

Condition[s] exhibiting one or more of the following characteristics over a long period of time and to a marked degree, which adversely affects educational performance: a) an inability to learn which cannot be explained by intellectual, sensory, or health factors; b) an inability to build or maintain satisfactory interpersonal relationships with peers and teachers; c) inappropriate types of behavior or feelings under normal circumstances; d) a general pervasive mood of unhappiness or depression; or e) a tendency to develop physical symptoms or fears associated with personal or school problems.

Unfortunately, the law does not state how the definition is to be operationalized for identification purposes. Thus the ambiguousness and vagueness in the terms have resulted in much controversy on who should or should not receive services (Cullinan & Epstein, 1989). For example, while the law required educational services for students with behavioral and emotional disorders, it specifically stated that students whose behavior reflected social maladjustments are not to be provided services. Yet, no assessment procedures or guidelines were given to reliably differentiate between these types of behavior problems. The problems of definition, identification, and, for research purposes, subject description are discussed later in this chapter.

Much of the research and program development in special education have been directed toward improving the social and academic performance of students with behavior disorders. Intervention strategies have included almost every possible approach to changing human behavior including psychotherapy, milieu therapy, psychopharmacology, ecological management, individual and group counseling, and affective education (Cullinan, Epstein, & Lloyd, 1983). Some of the most researched and successful interventions for teaching children and adolescents with behavior disorders have been based on a behavioral approach. While previous writers have reviewed behavioral interventions used primarily with preschool- and elementary-aged students (e.g., Schloss, Schloss, Wood, & Kiehl, 1986; Skiba & Casey, 1985), this review will focus on adolescents with behavior disorders.

This chapter provides a critical review of behavioral interventions with adolescents with behavior disorders. It begins with an overview of adolescent development and how special education has served adolescents. This is followed by a description of the parameters used to identify the studies included in this chapter. This review is, of necessity, selective in nature and is in no way intended to cover every study conducted on every behavior problem of adolescents. Intervention approaches are grouped and reviewed according to the major type of procedure used. Finally, future research issues and suggestions for building on the available data base are offered.

II. ADOLESCENTS AND SPECIAL EDUCATION

Adolescence is traditionally viewed as a difficult and ambivalent time of life; however, empirical study over the last 20 years has challenged the notion that adolescence is automatically tumultuous, and the outlook regarding the changes inherent in the second decade of life is now more optimistic (Braaten, 1985; Pomeroy & Gadow, 1986). In fact, about 80% of adolescents adapt quite well emotionally with this period of life, which is about the same percentage of adults who manage to cope (Lipsitz, 1985). However, not all adolescents make a smooth transition from childhood to adulthood. Some adolescents whose behavior and/or learning problems had been recognized earlier in life may continue to require special services, and some adolescents may experience failure for the first time as they face the increased demands of secondary school settings and the prospect of assuming the responsibilities of adulthood (Cullinan et al., 1983; Epstein, 1982; Mercer, 1987).

Theories of adolescent development vary (see Epstein & Cullinan, 1979), but some general statements about the nature of this period can be made. Adolescence begins around the time of puberty, and with the onset of puberty, every aspect of development changes (Cullinan et al., 1983; Pomeroy & Gadow, 1986). Biologically, there is a growth spurt and sexual maturation to which the adolescent must adjust emotionally. Socially, peer interactions become more important as do male-female relationships. Psychologically, thinking becomes more complex and abstract, which makes the questioning of adults more likely (Clarizio, 1979; Lipsitz, 1985). In accordance with this cognitive development, many of the task demands of the secondary school curriculum, such as applying a principle to mathematical data, require the student to deal with symbolic representations (Alley & Deshler, 1979). It should also be noted that human development is not perfectly uniform, and adults need to remember that adolescent development in these areas is not apt to be synchronized (Lipsitz, 1985).

Historically, appropriate special education for handicapped adolescents has not been adequately developed, and it has been particularly underdeveloped for adolescents with behavior disorders (Cullinan & Epstein, 1989). Prior to the Education for All Handicapped Children Act (PL 94-142), secondary students with behavior problems were often viewed as disciplinary cases and were the ones most likely to be excluded from school (Braaten, 1985). Fortunately, current thinking recognizes that the nature of behavior problems is considerably more complex. Some problems may be a reflection of natural maturational processes, others may be an extension of childhood behavioral difficulties into adolescence, and still others may resemble adult psychiatric syndromes (Pomeroy & Gadow, 1986). Another reason for underdeveloped programming for adolescents with behavior disorders is that, in the past, most administration and teacher preparation programs in special education were developed with younger students in mind (Epstein, 1982). Finally, the major part of the research pertaining directly to behaviorally disordered students has focused on the classroom conduct of elementary school pupils (Epstein, Cullinan, & Rose, 1980).

Interventions for behaviorally disordered adolescents have received comparatively less attention. Fortunately, these trends have changed, and, in the decade since the enactment of PL 94-142, special education programs and related education services have been developed to serve this population. One of the major approaches to treatment for these pupils has been the behavioral model, and thus one primary purpose of this chapter is to review and analyze the research on treatments with adolescents identified as behaviorally disordered.

As is generally now known, the behavioral model for understanding and improving human behavior has had a great impact upon the education and treatment of handicapped and nonhandicapped individuals alike (see Epstein et al., 1980; Repp, 1983, for a historical overview). Since the late 1960s, the effectiveness of many behavioral methods with behaviorally disordered children and adolescents has been studied under carefully controlled conditions (Cullinan et al., 1983). Consequently, significant empirical evidence supports the widespread application of behavioral interventions to the treatment of individuals who are handicapped by their behavior (Cullinan, Epstein, & Kauffman, 1982). This progress notwithstanding, additional work in this area is clearly needed.

Important questions must be addressed to further advance our knowledge and usefulness. A major concern has already been stated: More research and evaluation must continue to focus exclusively upon adolescent pupils specifically identified as behaviorally disordered. Given that adolescence is characterized by many developmental changes, it, of course, cannot be presumed that treatments found to be effective with younger children will produce similar results with adolescents. Another concern is that research populations do not appear to be sufficiently described. A recent review of 168 studies that described the use of various behavioral interventions with behaviorally disordered students found that the subjects could be more adequately described in terms of demographic information, selection criteria, academic skills, and social-emotional adjustment (Olinger, Epstein, Karsh,

Ormsby, & Pray, 1988). In view of the unresolved issues surrounding the definition and diagnosis of behavior disorders (Cullinan et al., 1983; Kavale, Forness, Alper, 1986), the provision of this information seems especially valuable. Finally, there is the familiar issue of quality versus quantity. Results of various studies done over the past few decades are obviously not of equal weight; therefore, attention to and analysis of the methodological quality of the literature would be helpful. For example, if diagnosis is to lead into prognosis, we need to determine how many studies included a follow-up phase to determine if any favorable gains were maintained.

III. SELECTION OF STUDIES

This review provides an analysis of 53 published studies that investigated the effectiveness of behavioral interventions with adolescents. The final selection of studies is from 17 behavioral (e.g., *Journal of Applied Behavior Analysis*), educational (e.g., *Behavioral Disorders*), or psychological (e.g., *Journal of Behavior Therapy and Experimental Psychiatry*) journals (1968-1989). Studies with behavioral interventions were selected if the subjects manifested behavior problems and were of adolescent age and/or placed in a junior or senior high school program. As Wood (1987) has noted, the group of students labeled *behaviorally disordered* or *seriously emotionally disturbed* is remarkably heterogeneous. Therefore, this chapter includes subjects who were identified with the term *behaviorally disordered* or some comparable term (e.g., *emotionally disturbed, emotionally handicapped, conduct disordered*), and/or were receiving treatment for a specific behavior problem (e.g., truancy, disruptive school behavior), and/or were receiving their education in a special setting (e.g., self-contained classroom, Achievement Place group home). Studies with predelinquent or delinquent subjects were also selected if they overlapped with the aforementioned criteria (e.g., junior high school setting, social skills deficits). However, subjects with profound disorders such as autism or schizophrenia were not the focus of the review. Due to the heterogeneous nature of this literature, subject descriptions were provided for each study (see the table included in each section), the adequacy of subject descriptions was critiqued, and suggestions for improvement in this area were offered.

The review was further restricted to studies with social, as opposed to academic, dependent variables (e.g., disruptive behavior, social skills). Historically, the majority of treatment studies have focused on these behaviors (Epstein et al., 1980), and, therefore, a separate review of progress in this area seems warranted. Finally, the quality of the research was analyzed, and several important issues emerged: service/research settings and the least restrictive environment (LRE) mandate, adequacy of subject descriptions, social validation, the provision of follow-up data, the prevention of mental health problems, and other critical concerns. Over 20 years of research on this topic was thus reviewed and critiqued.

IV. BEHAVIORAL INTERVENTIONS

Various types of behavioral interventions have been developed and investigated with respect to the treatment of social behaviors (e.g., truancy, classroom conduct, social skills). The tables corresponding to each section summarize the use of selected interventions with behaviorally disordered adolescents. Although some studies may be classified under more than one category, they are grouped in the tables according to the major type of procedure that was used in the investigation. Therefore, studies that used primarily token and/or social reinforcement, behavioral contracting, punishment and reinforcement, self-management, social skills treatments, and other approaches are discussed in turn.

A. Social and/or Token Reinforcement

Social and token reinforcers are classified as secondary reinforcers, and their value has been learned or conditioned (Alberto & Troutman, 1986). Tokens are reinforcers that are exchangeable for a wide variety of objects or events that are reinforcing for a person (Sulzer-Azaroff & Mayer, 1977). Although contingent adult attention can sometimes be effective in decreasing behaviors such as talk-outs (e.g., Hall et al., 1971) and is often a component of intervention programs (e.g., Schloss, Schloss, & Harris, 1984), token reinforcement has been used to a much greater extent with behaviorally disordered adolescents and predelinquent and delinquent youths (Epstein et al., 1980).

Paniagua (1985) investigated the effectiveness of a point (token) system with adolescents in a group home. Specifically, points were awarded for true reports regarding the self-care skills and helping behaviors that were to be performed at an earlier time. The procedure was thus termed a *do-report correspondence training procedure.* Points for true reports were exchanged both daily (e.g., for using the stereo) and weekly (e.g., for going out during the weekend). The results showed increased levels of the target behaviors when true reports were reinforced. Token or point systems have also been used to decrease absences and tardiness (Hargreaves & McLaughlin, 1981), improve conversational skills (Minkin et al., 1976), and increase self-government (Fixsen, Phillips, & Wolf, 1973). Parenthetically, it should be noted that response cost (fines for misbehavior) is often a component of token economies. Studies that address the use of this particular punishment procedure are included in this review under the category of punishment and reinforcement.

The generally accepted and proven effectiveness of token reinforcement notwithstanding, excessive reliance on token programs is not recommended, either. Repp (1983) cautioned against automatic adoption of methods that have become popular and recommended more analysis and treatment of the variables that may be influencing maladaptive behavior. For example, Schloss, Schloss, and Harris (1984) developed and administered questionnaires to parents, teachers, and truant

TABLE 1
Studies with Social Dependent Variables: Social and/or Token Reinforcement

Author	Label	N	Setting	Treatment	Implementor	Dependent Variable(s)	Results
Drabman (1973)	Schizophrenia or unsocialized aggressive reaction	22	Psychiatric hospital school	Student versus teacher-administered token programs	Students and teachers	Disruptive behaviors, teacher interactions	Peers as effective as teachers in administering tokens; feedback not solely responsible for token success; peer feedback may be more important then teacher; withdrawal from tokens to feedback may be a way to fade tokens successfully
Emshoff, Redd, & Davidson (1976)	Delinquent	4	Residential treatment	Generalization training (praise and redeemable points, varied trainers and activities) versus constant training (stimulus conditions did not vary)	Undergraduate trainers	Positive comments	Greater improvement and generalization for training group
Fixsen, Phillips, & Wolf (1973; Exp. 1)	Predelinquent	7	Community group home (Achievement Place)	Self-government versus preset consequences (token economy in operation)	Teaching parents and subjects	Participation in discussion and voting in "trials"	More participation by subjects under self-government
Fixsen et al. (1973; Exp. 2)	Predelinquent	6	Community group home (Achievement Place)	Trials called by subjects versus trials called by teaching parents (token economy in operation)	Teaching parents and subjects	Number of trials	More trials called when teaching parents responsible except when points awarded for calling trials

Study	Population	N	Setting	Intervention	Change agent	Target behavior	Results
Hall et al. (1971; Exp. 3)	Emotionally disturbed	1	Self-contained classroom	Contingent attention	Teacher	Talk-outs	Talk-outs decreased
Hargreaves & McLaughlin (1981)	Behavior and attendance problems	4	Self-contained classroom	Token reinforcement combined with delay-of-consequences (fading)	Teachers	Absences, tardiness, teacher ratings	Behavior improved
Jones & Van Houten (1985)	Disruptive	13	Regular and special classrooms	Performance feedback package to reinforce academic performance	Teachers	Disruptive behaviors, English and science quiz scores	Disruptive behavior markedly reduced; quiz scores increased
Lebsock & Salzberg (1981)	Emotionally disturbed behavior	2	Therapy room and special class	Role-play and reinforcement procedures	Experimenter	Maladaptive interpersonal behaviors (e.g., "talking back")	Behaviors decreased
Mastropieri, Jenne, & Scruggs (1988)	Behaviorally disordered	11	High school resource English class	Level system	Classroom teacher	Talk-outs, out of seat, self-reports	Talk-outs and out-of-seat behaviors decreased, student self-reports attributed change to level system
McNeil & Hart (1986)	Delinquents	31	Institutional	Self-government system with student rules, trials, and consequences	Staff	Aggression	Aggressive behavior reduced
Minkin et al. (1976; Exps. 2, 3)	Delinquent and predelinquent	4	Group home (Achievement Place)	Training in conversational skills, monetary reinforcement	Experimenters	Conversational skills	Behaviors increased

(continued)

TABLE 1 (Continued)

Author	Label	N	Setting	Treatment	Implementor	Dependent Variable(s)	Results
Paniagua, 1985	Borderline delinquency or placement due to family problems	6	Group home	Do-report correspondence training (point system to reward true reports)	Staff	Self-care skills and helping behaviors; reports to staff about same	Behaviors increased during reinforcement of true reports
Schloss, Kane, & Miller (1981)	Behavior disordered	3	Regular and self-contained class	Attendance motivation program	Teachers, parents, home interventionist	Attendance	Attendance rose to 100%

behaviorally disordered adolescents for the purpose of identifying factors that may be related to poor attendance. The successful truancy intervention they then implemented included a component that decreased the reinforcers associated with staying home from school and increased the reinforcers associated with attendance (e.g., more social reinforcement for completing work).

B. Behavioral Contracting

Behavioral or contingency contracting is often used to modify the deviant behavior of behaviorally disordered or delinquent children and adolescents (Rutherford & Polsgrove, 1981). A behavioral contract is a written specification of the contingency of reinforcement, and it should clearly state the target behaviors to be performed by the student, how student performance of these behaviors is to be evaluated, and the reinforcers available to the student contingent upon performance (Cullinan et al., 1983). The use of contracting with behaviorally disordered adolescents requires no procedural changes, although a high level of student and parental participation is desirable (Guetzloe, 1980).

Truancy is a serious problem that demands the attention of those who work with behaviorally disordered youth (Schultz, 1987), and behavioral contracting has been shown to be effective in improving school attendance. For example, Bizzis and Bradley-Johnson (1981) investigated the effectiveness of contracting with a 17-year-old truant female who was classified as delinquent and had been permanently placed in a foster home. Baseline data showed that the subject was attending school an average of 2.5 days per week. Because of this low rate, contracts for school attendance were negotiated with the student by a youth guidance volunteer and a youth guidance worker with whom the student had a positive relationship. The contracts were written for two-week intervals, as this level of commitment was appropriate for this student. A variety of social reinforcers (e.g., phone calls, letters, recreational activities) were used to avoid reinforcer satiation and to increase the social interactions of the student. The intervention was successful, as attendance increased to 5 days per week during treatment phases. Additionally, the student's grades rose to Cs, as the school's policy was that, if a student missed 15 days of school, an F would be given for each class missed. It is important to note that, in this case, a series of two-week contracts with effective reinforcers succeeded where the traditional school policy had failed. Other studies have also shown how contracting can be used to improve attendance (MacDonald, Gallimore, & MacDonald, 1970; Vaal, 1973) and other behaviors such as tantrums and compliance (Welch, 1985).

For behavioral contracting to be effective, the consequences (e.g., special privileges) selected as reinforcers must in fact be reinforcing for the adolescent. For one student, increased social contact with an esteemed role model may be reinforcing, while, for another student, a privilege such as increased time with a microcomputer may be reinforcing. The initial stages of negotiation should, therefore, include attention to selection of reinforcers, and a variety of reinforcers should be used to avoid satiation, as illustrated in the study by Bizzis and Bradley-Johnson (1981).

TABLE 2

Studies with Social Dependent Variables: Behavioral Contracting

Author	Label	N	Setting	Treatment	Implementor	Dependent Variable(s)	Results
Bizzis & Bradley-Johnson (1981)	Delinquent	1	Public high school	Contracting (using naturally occurring reinforcers and significant others)	Guidance counselors	Attendance	Perfect attendance last 4 weeks of school
MacDonald, Gallimore, & MacDonald (1970; Exp. 1)	"Chronic nonattenders"	6	Special motivation class in regular school	Contracting	Local parent hired as attendance counselor and people from community	Attendance	Improvement in attendance
MacDonald et al. (1970; Exp. 2)	"Chronic nonattenders"	35	Public high school	Contingency counseling	School counselors and people from community	Attendance	Contingency counseling improved attendance; counseling alone did not
Vaal (1973)	School phobia	1	Public junior high school	Contingency contracting	Author	Coming to school on time without tantrum, attending all classes on schedule, remaining in school until dismissed	Perfect attendance and zero tantrums
Welch (1985)	Delinquent	1	Home	Contingency contracting with subject and family	Author and family of subject	Control of temper, curfew compliance, performance of household responsibilities	Improvement in all areas

The schedule of reinforcement is also an important consideration, for some students require more frequent delivery of reinforcers than do others. Finally, although contracting has been shown to be effective in decreasing truancy, improved academic performance does not always follow naturally as a result of increased attendance (Schultz, 1987). Academic and social interventions need to be planned and implemented concurrently, as behaviorally disordered adolescents frequently have deficits in both areas (Epstein, Kinder, & Bursuck, 1989; Mastropieri, Jenkins, & Scruggs, 1985).

C. Punishment and Reinforcement

As stated earlier, token systems have been used frequently to modify the behavior of behaviorally disordered adolescents, and these systems may incorporate a response cost component (e.g., Hogan & Johnson, 1985; Phillips, 1968; Swanson, 1985). Response cost is a punishment procedure that attempts to decrease behavior through the withdrawal of specific amounts of a reinforcer contingent upon the occurrence of undesired behavior (Alberto & Troutman, 1986). As a general rule in planning interventions, reinforcement procedures are preferred over punishment procedures when both are likely to be effective, and reinforcement of adaptive behaviors should be provided whenever punishment is used to decrease maladaptive behaviors (Matson & Olinger, 1985; Sulzer-Azaroff & Mayer, 1977).

In accordance with the guidelines just mentioned, Hogan and Johnson (1985) investigated the elimination of response cost in a token economy program that had been developed for adolescents diagnosed as emotionally disturbed and/or socially maladjusted. This study, conducted with a total of 132 clients, took place in a community-based treatment and special education program. The authors first investigated the implementation of a token economy with response cost. Then they investigated the removal of response cost coupled with restatement of behavior goals in positive terms and an expansion of the token economy to cover the entire day's schedule. This shift to a more positive approach resulted in a decline in the use of the time-out room, episodes involving violence, and the frequency of misbehavior reports. However, Hogan and Johnson (1985) cautioned that the positive findings do not mean that a program with no punishment component would be effective under all circumstances. They hypothesized that the response cost component may have been necessary initially to gain control over the youths' behavior. There is thus the possibility of order effects in this study. As Kazdin (1982) summarized, the sequence in which treatments are provided partially restricts the conclusions that can be drawn about the relative effectiveness of alternative treatments.

In summary, a combination of punishment and reinforcement procedures have been used to treat a variety of behaviors, including physical assault and theft (Hogan & Johnson, 1985), classroom behavior (McNamara, 1971; Meichenbaum, Bowers, & Ross, 1968), peer interactions (Swanson, 1985), and punctuality and aggressive statements in a group home setting (Phillips, 1968). When two or more techniques have been used in the same problem area, a natural question arises

TABLE 3
Studies with Social Dependent Variables: Behavioral Contracting

Author	Label	N	Setting	Treatment	Implementor	Dependent Variable(s)	Results
Hogan & Johnson (1985)	Socially maladjusted or emotionally disturbed	107- 132	Community-based treatment and special education program	Study of elimination of response cost in a token economy and shift to more positive approach	Staff	Unacceptable behaviors (e.g., physical assault, theft)	Decrease in misbehavior reports, use of time-out room and episodes involving violence
Hunsaker (1984)	Dropouts, and/or public assistance, and/or had criminal arrest records	5	Federal project: work site and vocational class	Positive reinforcement versus positive reinforcement and response cost	Instructor	Achievement of goals	Most improvement with positive reinforcement in combination with response cost
McNamara (1971)	Behavior problem students	18	Special school	Removal of teacher attention versus response cost	Author	Hand raise, teacher attention to hand raise; call out, teacher attention to call out	Response cost more effective than contingent teacher control alone
Meichenbaum, Bowers, & Ross (1968)	Adolescent offenders	10	Institution	Different schedules of feedback and/or response cost	Teacher, psychology interns	Inappropriate classroom behavior	Appropriate behavior increased
Phillips (1968, Exp. 1)	"Dependent-neglected"	3	Group home	Response cost	House parents	Punctuality	Punctuality increased

| Swanson (1985) | Emotionally disturbed, socialized aggressive | Self-contained class | Individual contingency and response cost versus group contingency and response cost (token system) | Teacher, student teacher, author | Social interactions (same sex and heterosocial) | Group contingency more effective in both cases |
| Wasserman (1977) | Disruptive | Group home and day treatment center | Negative reinforcement/ return to residential facility | Teacher and group home parent | Completing school work, not destroying school property, not making animal noises, washing before coming to school | Behavior improved to criteria |

concerning which treatment is most effective (Van Houten, 1987). This question is actually a complex one to answer, as many factors such as cost, user preference, and treatment generality enter into the decision (Van Houten, 1987). Although researchers in this review (e.g., Hogan & Johnson, 1985; McNamara, 1971; Swanson, 1985) explored the relative effectiveness of treatments, their findings are not conclusive because replications are needed to establish the reliability and generality of the findings (Barlow & Hersen, 1984).

D.   Self-Management

In self-management procedures, individuals learn to modify their own behavior. Such procedures, when effective, are highly desirable for use with behaviorally disordered adolescents, for adolescents often seek more autonomy from adults and need the skills to manage themselves as they contend with "peer pressure" and learn responsible independence. Table 4 provides a summary of selected studies that incorporate self-management techniques, and it can readily be seen that a variety of techniques are currently included under the category of self-management (e.g., self-monitoring, self-instruction). Mace, Brown, and West (1987) have provided a discussion of the theoretical models of behavioral self-management. They noted that the term *self-management* subsumes most of the procedures identified in this literature, while leaving theoretical questions regarding the mechanisms underlying self-management strategies open and subject to further study. This review chapter does not attempt a theoretical analysis of self-management but instead presents several studies that were conducted with adolescents. As Kazdin (1982) observed in a commentary and analysis of cognitive-behavioral interventions, the evidence must ultimately be in support of specific techniques as applied in specific situations.

A self-management study that was conducted over a three-year period by Brigham, Hopper, deArmas, Hill, and Newsom (1985) was instructional in nature and incorporated the textbook *Managing Everyday Problems: A Manual of Applied Psychology for Young People* (Brigham, 1982). The subjects were 103 middle school (sixth, seventh, eight grade) disruptive students. They were taught the principles of behavior analysis and how to observe and measure behavior. The primary focus was on teaching the students how their behavior affected others, and role-playing, modeling, study guides, and quizzes were used in the program. Additionally, the students conducted a self-management project that incorporated a behavioral contract with the self-management class instructor. For example, a student could choose to increase a behavior such as appropriate class participation. Multiple-baseline and clinical replication analyses indicated that the vast majority of the participating students reduced their level of disruptive behavior and increased their ratings with teachers. Follow-up data for intervals as long as two years showed ongoing lower levels of detentions. However, the program was *not* sufficient for a predelinquent subgroup within the study. Brigham et al. (1985) noted that no contingencies were manipulated outside the self-management class, and their results suggest that the instructional program is not sufficient by itself for predelinquent students.

Self-management techniques have also been used to modify other behaviors. For example, Osborne, Kiburz, and Miller (1986) decreased the self-injurious behavior (i.e., hitting face) of a behaviorally disordered adolescent by videotaping the subject and then using self-monitoring. Another recent self-management study, conducted with 21 institutionalized male adolescents, was based on cognitive-behavioral techniques for self-control of anger and aggression (Feindler, Ecton, Kingsley, & Dubey, 1986). The training program included relaxation training, self-evaluation, self-instruction, problem-solving training, and other techniques. The treatment subjects improved on several dependent variables such as self-control ratings by staff and more appropriate behavior during role-play conflict situations. However, Feindler et al. (1986) noted that no assessment was made of the subjects' use of anger control techniques in natural settings. Such assessment is, of course, critical to the future development of self-management methods.

The self-management literature is likely to continue to expand, as the long-range goal of self-management is unquestioned. Additionally, self-management of behavior and other treatment options such as contracting are not mutually exclusive options. As Alberto and Troutman (1986, p. 338) summarized, "Although total independence is not possible for all handicapped students, most can be taught to be more self-reliant." A balance between self-management and additional external contingencies can thus be used according to the needs of the individual.

E. Social Skills

In an earlier review, Epstein et al. (1980) noted that the vast majority of adolescent studies were concerned with disruptive or acting-out forms of behavior disorders and that increased attention must be paid to interventions that address other types of behavior disorders that impede personal development, such as social skills deficits. Several more researchers in clinical psychology and special education are now actively investigating social skills training and its influence upon social competence, for it is more widely recognized that social skills deficits cut across multiple clinical and special education populations of all ages (Hops, Finch, & McConnell, 1985; Mastropieri & Scruggs, 1987).

Definitions of social skills or social competence vary among researchers, and a wide array of discrete responses are grouped under the rubric of *social skills*. Generally speaking, most writers conceptualize *social skills* as the "behaviors necessary for successful interactions at home, school, and in the community" (Mastropieri & Scruggs, 1987, p. 318). Examples include problem-solving and conversational skills (Christoff et al., 1985), helping others (Greenleaf, 1982), and greeting and thanking behaviors (Kiburz, Miller, & Morrow, 1984). Many different types of interventions have likewise been used to improve social skills. Elliott, Gresham, and Heffer (1987) have classified these procedures under four major headings: manipulation of antecedents, manipulation of consequences, modeling/ coaching, and combined procedures.

Many researchers in this review used combined procedures, that is, social skills training treatment packages (e.g., Christoff et al., 1985; Elder, Edelstein, & Narick,

TABLE 4
Studies with Social Dependent Variable: Self-Management

Author	Label	N	Setting	Treatment	Implementor	Dependent Variable(s)	Results
Brigham, Hopper, Hill, deArmas, & Newsom (1985)	Disruptive	103	Middle school (6th, 7th, 8th grades)	Self-management program based on behavior analysis procedures	Teacher, aide, students	Violations of school rules	Lowered levels of detentions, higher teacher ratings, improvement on student measures
Feindler, Ecton, Kingsley, & Dubey (1986)	Psychiatric BD/ED youths	21	Residential	Cognitive-behavioral group, anger control training	Authors and research team	Anger and aggression (11 classes of behavior, e.g., hostile comments)	Improvement noted on several measures (e.g., child care staff ratings)
Feindler, Marriott, & Iwata (1984)	Multisuspended delinquents	36	Junior high school	Group anger control training	Therapist and program aide	Disruptive/aggressive behavior	Improvement noted
Osborne, Kiburz, & Miller (1986)	Behaviorally disordered	1	Regular classrooms and BD resource room	Self-control techniques (self-monitoring of video-tape of own behavior)	Special teacher, aide, and student	Self-injurious behavior (hitting face)	Behavior decreased in all settings
Reynolds & Coats (1986)	Depressed adolescents (nonclinical group)	30	High school	Cognitive-behavioral therapy versus relaxation training	Author	Depression, self-esteem, anxiety (e.g., as measured by self-reports)	No significant difference between treatment groups; both superior to waiting list control group

Study		N	Setting	Treatment		Target behavior	Results
Smith, Young, West, Morgan, & Rhode (1988)	Behaviorally disordered	4	Junior high school resource class	Self-evaluation paired with a teaching matching procedure	Teacher	Off-task and disruptive behaviors	Behaviors decreased; fading of the matching procedure still maintained the lower levels; generalization to regular classrooms did not occur until it was programmed
Santogrossi, O'Leary, Romanczyk, & Kaufman (1973)	Emotionally disturbed	9	Psychiatric hospital	Self-evaluation and token program	Teacher	9 categories of disruptive behavior	Self-evaluation alone ineffective; token program controlled by teacher reduced disruptive behavior
Synder & White (1979)	Behaviorally disturbed	15	Residential	Cognitive self-instruction, contingency awareness, and assessment control (no treatment)	Authors	Absence from class, failures to complete social/ self-care responsibilities, impulsive behavior	Best results with cognitive self-instruction group

TABLE 5
Studies with Social Dependent Variables: Social Skills Training

Author	Label	N	Setting	Treatment	Implementor	Dependent Variable(s)	Results
Christoff et al. (1985)	"Shy adolescents" (referred by staff for study)	6	Junior high school	Social skills and social problem-solving training	Clinical psychology interns	Problem-solving and conversational skills	Improvement on most measures
Elder, Edelstein, & Narick (1979)	Psychiatric	4	Psychiatric ward	Social skills training	Staff therapists	Aggressive interpersonal behavior (e.g., responses to teasing)	Increase in social appropriateness of responses
Greenleaf (1982)	Disruptive	43	Junior high school	Structured learning therapy and/or transfer programming	Author and special education teacher	Helping others	Groups with structured learning therapy performed better
Jamison, Lambert, & McCloud (1986)	Conduct or adjustment disorder	12	Psychiatric hospital	Social skills training	Clinical psychologist and other staff members	Eye contact, facial expression, voice loudness, verbal responses	Verbal responses and eye contact improved
Kelly et al. (1983)	Behaviorally disordered	4	Residential setting	Role-playing and self-monitoring	Teacher	Vocational social skills (i.e., appropriate responses to supervisor's instructions)	Self-monitoring resulted in rapid generalization from classroom to vocational room
Kiburz, Miller, & Morrow (1984)	Behaviorally disordered, mild mental retardation	1	4 settings within residential facility	Structured learning therapy and self-monitoring with reinforcement	Teacher	Greetings, thanking behavior	Skills trained, maintained, and generalized to three natural settings
Leger et al. (1979)	Emotionally handicapped	17	Residential school	Instructional package	Teacher and school psychologist	Communication behaviors (e.g., simple sentence responses)	Behaviors improved and generalization occurred in lecture-type format

Study	Population	N	Setting	Intervention	Staff	Measures	Results
Ollendick & Hersen (1979)	Incarcerated juvenile	27	Residential	Social skills training versus discussion and control groups	Staff psychologists	Variety of self-report, role-play, and behavioral measures	Social skills group improved significantly more
Sanson-Fisher, Seymour, & Baer (1976)	Delinquent girls and institutional staff	6 girls 11 staff	Residential	Staff training	Author/staff	Girls' conversation about prosocial and antisocial behavior	Staff behavior changes were not enough in themselves to alter girls' behavior significantly
Sanson-Fisher, Seymour, Montgomery, & Stokes (1978)	Delinquent	5	Residential	Token reinforcement of self-recorded behavior	Author and staff	Prosocial comments, antisocial comments, and positive attention to other's comments	Prosocial comments and positive attention to same increased when self-recording implemented
Schloss, Schloss, & Harris (1984)	Depressed youth (schizo-affective disorder)	3	Training room and self-contained class; lived in residential setting	Social skills training package "Facilitator" (trained teacher)		Social responses (e.g., greeting adults)	Behaviors improved; maintenance data mixed
Spence & Marzillier (1979)	Adolescent offenders	5	Community home	Social skills training	"Adult trainer"	Social skills (e.g., eye contact)	Mixed results: some behaviors harder to train and maintain than others
Spence & Marzillier (1981)	Adolescent offenders	6	Residential	Social skills training versus attention placebo versus no treatment control	Therapists	Social skills (e.g., attention feedback during listening)	Mixed findings: Behaviors that improved were maintained at follow-up
Warrenfeltz et al. (1981)	Emotionally disturbed, behaviorally disturbed	4	Residential setting	Didactic instruction, role-play, and self-monitoring	Special education teacher	Appropriate response to instruction and appropriate responses to critical feedback and conversation	Behaviors improved; self-monitoring seemed to promote generalization and maintenance

141

1979; Jamison, Lambert, & McCloud, 1986; Ollendick & Hersen, 1979; Schloss, Schloss, & Harris, 1984). For instance, Jamison et al. (1986) investigated the effectiveness of social skills training with 12 hospitalized adolescents who ranged in age from 15 to 17 years and had a diagnosis of conduct disorder or adjustment disorder according to DSM-III criteria. The subjects had also been identified by treatment staff prior to the study as having social skills deficits. The training included modeling and role-playing exercises, group discussion, and observing videotapes. The behaviors treated were eye contact, facial expression, voice loudness, and verbal response (i.e., nonassertive and assertive responses). Anger scenarios were incorporated into the five one-hour training sessions to provide the subjects with opportunities to role-play appropriate responses. During pre- and post-testing sessions, the experimental and control group subjects were presented individually with 10 scenarios that staff had judged likely to elicit an anger response. The videotaped responses of the subjects were scored by raters who were unaware of the purpose of the study. The results showed significant differences between groups in verbal responses and eye contact. However, the authors acknowledged that no in vivo generalization data were collected and that the transfer of these improvements from role-playing conditions to natural conditions is unknown. Additionally, Bornstein, Bellack, and Hersen (cited in Jamison et al., 1986) recommended that validation data be obtained from normally functioning persons to find out which social skills contribute most to effective social performance. In this way, behaviors could be targeted for treatment more precisely.

Although the social skills research with behaviorally disordered adolescents is promising, there are several unresolved issues, and some researchers have reported mixed findings (e.g., Schloss, Schloss, & Harris, 1984; Spence & Marzillier, 1979, 1981). The number of types of interventions that are grouped under the rubric of *social skills training* is large, and additional research is needed to explore their relative effectiveness. Additionally, generalization of treatment gains to natural settings is a major issue, and opportunities to practice treated behaviors in the natural environment should be provided (Hops et al., 1985). Training of personnel would also provide continuity of expectations across settings and might facilitate generalization (Kiburz et al., 1984). Some researchers have also used self-management techniques to promote generalization (e.g., Kelly et al., 1983; Warrenfeltz et al., 1981), and this suggests that different approaches may be required for different stages of learning (e.g., acquisition, maintenance). Smith (1989) has discussed these various stages of learning, and she hypothesizes that equivocal results of research might be due to the fact that subjects are at different stages of learning. Finally, the appropriateness of targeted skills is perhaps the most fundamental issue, as there is little experimental validation of the specific skills that are related directly to social competence (Hops et al., 1985).

F. Other Studies

In addition to the categories of treatments already presented, several researchers have explored the effectiveness of other types of interventions with respect to improving the social behaviors of behaviorally disordered adolescents. For example, Polirstok and Greer (1977) and Rosenberg and Graubard (1975) taught students to modify the social behaviors of teachers and/or peers and to become more reinforcing to others in their social contacts. These studies, of course, overlap with some of the goals of the research already presented in the areas of self-management and social skills (e.g., Brigham et al., 1985). Another interesting study was conducted by Evans, Evans, Schmid, and Pennypacker (1985), who explored the effects of vigorous exercise on classroom behaviors of six emotionally disturbed adolescents. These students, who were 12 and 13 years old, received special services in a resource room for the behaviorally disordered and in a noncategorical special education class. Talk-outs were a serious and consistent problem reported on by teachers, and teacher ratings and the number of completed math problems were also recorded daily. The experimenters compared the effectiveness of jogging, football, and outdoor reading in improving classroom behavior. Although there was variability in the data both within and across subjects, the results suggested that vigorous exercise may be a valuable therapeutic technique. Exercise conditions were associated with a higher percentage of math problems completed, higher teacher ratings, and a lower number of talk-outs per class period. The authors concluded that an exercise program may be helpful to use in conjunction with other behavior change procedures. Certainly, additional research in this area would be desirable, as it shows creativity in programming, promotes physical fitness, and may also serve the purpose of teaching adolescents outdoor recreational skills that may allow them to better compete and socialize with their peers.

G. Summary

Considerable progress has been made in the development and validation of behavioral interventions that target the social behaviors of behaviorally disordered adolescents. Although many questions and issues remain, such as the selection of the most critical social skills to modify, a growing body of literature exists that can serve to guide those who work with these adolescents. Future research will require attention to the various issues raised to refine the treatments and determine the types of individuals who benefit the most from the various interventions.

V. FUTURE RESEARCH ISSUES

In a relatively short period of time, the behavioral model has shown its value for understanding and treating adolescents with behavior disorders. Social and token reinforcement, contracting, punishment and reinforcement, self-management, social skills training, and other treatments have all been found to be effective in various situations. The repeated demonstrations that these techniques are capable of producing significant changes in functioning underscore that the behavioral model is a major treatment approach with behaviorally disordered adolescents. The

TABLE 6
Studies with Social Dependent Variables: Other Studies

Author	Label	N	Setting	Treatment	Implementor	Dependent Variable(s)	Results
Barbrack & Maher (1984)	Conduct problem (regular class)	72	High school	Degree of pupil involvement in setting counseling goals	Counselors	Degree of pupil goal attainment, pupil perception of goal attainment, pupil satisfaction with counseling	Greater levels of pupil involvement more effective in goal attainment
Evans, Evans, Schmid, & Pennypacker (1985)	Emotionally disturbed	6	Resource room for the behaviorally disordered and noncategorical special education class	Vigorous exercise	Experimenter	Talk-outs, number of completed math problems, Teacher ratings	Decrease in talk-outs and increase in teacher ratings and problems completed
Polirstock & Greer (1977)	Behavior problem	1	Regular classes	Training student in reinforcement techniques and use of taped cues in conjunction with a token economy	Student	Teacher approval and/or disapproval behaviors	Student and teacher approval and disapproval highly correlated
Rosenberg & Graubard (1975; Exp. 1)	Special education pupils	7	Special and regular class	Students trained to modify teacher behavior	Special class teacher and students	Positive and negative teacher-student contacts	Positive teacher comments increased, negative comments decreased
Rosenberg & Graubard (1975; Exp. 2)	Emotionally handicapped	6	Special and regular class	Students trained to modify regular class peers	Resource class, teachers and students	Positive and negative contacts between subjects and target peers	Special students were able to modify behavior of peers

findings of this review are compatible with those reported in previous papers (e.g., Cullinan et al., 1982; Schloss et al., 1986; Skiba & Casey, 1985). Additional research in this area will no doubt further refine and extend the value of these procedures and lead to more complete technologies and interventions with behaviorally disordered adolescents. To this end, a number of issues need research attention: (a) the settings in which interventions are studied, (b) descriptions of subjects, (c) use of social validation data, (d) qualitative research issues, (e) comparative and component analysis research, and (f) choice of target behaviors. In the following sections, these research issues are elaborated upon and suggestions are given to redress some of the limitations with the available research.

A. Settings

Federal mandate (PL 94-142) now requires that handicapped students be provided with a free, appropriate education in the least restrictive environment (LRE). The LRE mandate states that, to the maximum extent possible, handicapped students are to be educated close to their nonhandicapped peers. Recent figures published by the Office of Special Education and Rehabilitation Services address this feature of the law with respect to the education of students handicapped by their behavior (U. S. Department of Education, 1986). While 93% of handicapped students overall were educated in integrated public schools, only 80% of students with behavior disorders were educated in these settings. Additionally, while 68% of all handicapped students received part of their education in regular classrooms, only 44% of students identified as behaviorally disordered were educated in these environments. As Lerner (1989) noted, PL 94-142 does require schools to provide a continuum of placements, and *LRE* and *mainstreaming* are *not* synonymous terms. However, these data suggest that we need to continually monitor the degree to which the educational opportunities for behaviorally disordered students are consonant with federal mandates and that we need to be sure that clear justification exists for more restrictive placements. These data also raise the possibility that students with severe behavior disorders who require intensive intervention are more likely to be identified and, once identified, are served in more restrictive settings. More study of how to effect a successful transition to less restrictive school and community settings as progress is made in more restrictive settings is certainly needed.

Applied behavior analysis may be interpreted as the application and scientific evaluation of procedures for modifying important behaviors in practical situations (Baer, Wolf, & Risley, 1968; Kazdin, 1977). Clearly, it is the behavioral excesses and deficits of behaviorally disordered adolescents in regular (mainstream) classes that result in their initial referral and placement in alternative settings such as self-contained classes, day schools, and residential facilities. If important changes are to occur with this population in mainstream settings, either as a result of an intervention or as a generalized effect, research needs to be conducted in these settings. In the research reviewed, only 14 studies were conducted in regular class settings, whereas 16 were in special classes, 14 in residential or institutional programs, 7 in psychiatric inpatient or outpatient clinics, 8 in group or community homes, and 3 in other settings. The overwhelming majority of behavioral strategies have been studied in settings far removed from regular classrooms. If these procedures are going to assist in improving the functioning of adolescents with behavior disorders, and, perhaps, lead to the increased mainstreaming of these students, behavioral researchers will need to experimentally test their procedures in regular class settings.

B. Subject Description

Adequate descriptions of subjects are necessary in all empirical efforts to reasonably evaluate, apply, and generalize the findings of research. Unfortunately, in the education of students with behavior disorders, issues of definition, classification, and diagnosis remain unresolved (Cullinan et al., 1983). The ambiguity in these areas has resulted in research populations not being well defined (Lakin, 1983), and the diagnostic criteria or identification procedures have not been carefully described either (Kavale et al., 1986). Previous research reviews (e.g., Epstein, Detwiler, & Reitz, 1985) have indicated that a clear need exists to more effectively communicate the results of research and interventions for individuals who work with children and adolescents with behavior disorders.

The findings of this chapter are in complete agreement with previous reviews in that the populations were not adequately described in terms of diagnostic or classification criteria (see Olinger et al., 1988). In most cases, subjects were included in these studies on the basis of teacher or researcher judgment or by meeting the guidelines provided in the federal definition of serious emotional disturbances. Additionally, many of the studies lacked information on demographic characteristics, family background, primary behavioral disorder, educational history, and overall behavioral adjustment. Also, the subjects in these studies were labeled as *seriously emotionally disturbed, behaviorally disordered,* or *delinquent,* yet very few of the studies offered specific information on the patterns or dimensions on which the subjects were disturbed or the actual behaviors the subjects displayed. The lack of specificity in the areas of subject description, identification procedures, and diagnostic criteria limits the generalizability and usability of the results of this research to other researchers and to individuals who work with this population.

A major goal in conducting research with behaviorally disordered adolescents is to better understand the development of the disorder and to be able to initiate viable treatment programs. For meaningful research to be conducted in this field, a number of changes need to occur. First, researchers need to provide as much detail as possible on the subjects who were included in the investigation. Greater use of marker variable information (Keogh, Major-Kingsley, Omori-Gordon, & Reid, 1982), which are the variables that are helpful in describing the distinctive aspects of the population, would enhance the value of the research. Second, rather than merely relying on the federal guidelines to define the population, researchers need to state how they operationally defined the term *behavioral disorders* or *serious emotional disturbances*. Third, the actual identification criteria and procedures leading to classification, whether they were clinically or statistically derived, need to be articulated.

C. Social Validation

Historically, applied behavior analysis has been concerned with bringing about behavior changes of enough magnitude to have practical value to the treated individual. To the degree that a treatment regimen can influence a significant change in functioning, the intervention has been judged to be successful. Therefore, the concept of social validation has been included as another criterion by which to judge the importance of an intervention. Social validation thus refers to the extent to which obtained changes in behavior actually bring the treated individual's behavior in line with the prevailing standards or expectations of acceptable functioning (Wolf, 1978). These changes, then, should result in more options in life for a person.

Social comparison and subjective evaluation have been suggested as two ways to gauge the social validity of a study (Kazdin, 1977). The social comparison method involves the direct assessment of the target student and a nonidentified individual to whom the targeted student can be reasonably compared. The value of normative peer data is quite obvious, particularly with respect to determining the competency levels required in mainstream settings prior to the reintegration of behaviorally disordered adolescents. Although some social comparison data were used in a few studies (Jones & Van Houten, 1985; Meichenbaum et al., 1968; Minkin et al., 1976; Reynolds & Coats, 1986; Schloss, Harriman & Pfefier, 1985), overall, such data were included in only five (9%) of the studies. The subjective evaluation approach asks individuals who normally are in contact with the targeted student (e.g., parents, teachers), or who are otherwise qualified to assess the student (e.g., expert opinion), to judge the social significance of any treatment effects. Subjective evaluation can also be used to select target behaviors and to assess consumer satisfaction with respect to the nature of the procedures and their cost in terms of available resources. For example, in this review, subjective evaluation was used to assess treatment acceptability (Paniagua, 1985), to select target behaviors (Kiburz et al., 1984), and to evaluate the results of treatment (Brigham et al., 1985; Christoff et al., 1985; Welch, 1985). Altogether, however, subjective evaluation was applied in only 15 (28%) of the cases.

This review indicates that social validation approaches represent a relatively untapped resource for individuals conducting applied research with behaviorally disordered adolescents. Because the education of these students occurs in a social context with their handicapped and nonhandicapped peers and their teachers, it would be an error to continue this omission. Social validation can be useful in determining the degree to which a behaviorally disordered student's performance is discrepant from that of comparison peers, identifying objective criteria for changing or terminating interventions, suggesting the degree to which behavioral improvement approaches the level needed for competence in natural settings, and evaluating the social effectiveness of treatments. Additionally, these data need not be difficult to obtain. For example, school grades are one source of social comparison data (Jones & Van Houten, 1985; Schloss et al., 1985). Given the value of social validation approaches, future researchers need to incorporate these procedures into their research designs.

D. Quality of Research

The quality of the research in this area can be gauged by looking at several methodological and design components. Each of the studies was evaluated on their assessment of the dependent and independent variables and the inclusion of generalization and follow-up measures.

1. DEPENDENT VARIABLES

Dependent variables were evaluated in terms of the clarity of operational definitions and the reporting of reliability data. Of the 53 studies, 43 presented operational definitions of the dependent variables in a clear and concise manner. This is an important criterion because, if definitions are not written clearly, it is difficult if not impossible to replicate the study. Researchers reported reliability data for the measurement of the dependent variable(s) in 45 studies. The evaluation of these data is a complex issue, for there is a relationship between the rate of behavior and the formula used to calculate reliability (Repp, Nieminen, Olinger, & Brusca, 1988). This review thus did not apply an arbitrary standard to all studies. As Repp et al. (1988) recommended, reliability scores and the methods used to calculate them should be provided so that consumers of research can make their own evaluations.

2. INDEPENDENT VARIABLES

The importance of reliability in behavioral research is well established (Baer et al., 1968), yet the collection of reliability data appears to be restricted to the dependent variable. The importance of gathering data on the independent variable has been discussed elsewhere (Peterson, Homer, & Wonderlich, 1982); however, such data are rarely collected. In this review, information regarding the correct and consistent implementation of the treatment was reported in 6 (11%) of the 53 studies. For example, Barbrack and Maher (1984) interviewed the counselors who implemented their treatment and reviewed documentation at the end of the study and thus determined that the counselors adhered to the design. As another example, Reynolds and Coats (1986) monitored a therapist's adherence to the treatment via audiotape. Obviously, if researchers are to attribute improved behavioral functioning to the programmed intervention, data will need to be collected on the fidelity of the treatment. Also, failure to provide such information will very likely lead to problems for other researchers and practitioners in replicating treatment procedures.

3. GENERALIZATION

Skill generalization to other settings was assessed in 11 (21%) of the studies. For example, Kiburz et al. (1984) incorporated techniques to facilitate maintenance and generalization of social skills across different settings within a residential state mental health facility. In another study (Lebsock & Salzberg, 1981), generalization of results from a small therapy room to a special class was monitored. In this case, both settings were in a public school. Overall, however, skill generalization is not assessed nearly enough. Additionally, because many of the studies took place in restrictive (e.g., residential, institutional) settings, 21% is an unacceptably low level and provides little information about how these subjects functioned in natural settings.

4. FOLLOW-UP

Follow-up data were reported in 21 (40%) of the studies. Of those that included follow-up data, the time at which these measures were taken ranged from less than two weeks (24%) to one month (19%) to more than one month (57%). To truly evaluate the effectiveness of treatments, more information about the maintenance of effects over time must be provided.

5. SUMMARY

These findings on the quality of research in relation to the four dimensions described appear to be compatible with previous reviews. Lack of attention to fidelity of treatment, generalization, and follow-up in research with behaviorally disordered children and adolescents has been reported elsewhere (Schloss et al., 1985; Skiba & Casey, 1985). If this area of study is to continue to contribute to the education of adolescents with behavior disorders, researchers will need to include measures in these often neglected areas.

E. Research Designs

For the most part, appropriate single-subject research strategies were used. These designs have allowed researchers to show that a functional relationship existed between the intervention and the target behavior. While these designs have shown various behavioral interventions to be effective with this population, other questions regarding treatment efficacy exist and will require the use of other research designs. Comparisons among different behavioral treatments and component analyses of treatment packages are two issues that will require alternative approaches. For example, Barlow and Hersen (1984) have suggested that either an alternating-treatment design or a traditional between-group comparison design with careful attention to individual change could be used to study the relative effectiveness of treatments. Ongoing innovation in the area of design is also needed. As Baer, Wolf, and Risley (1987) expressed, the codification of research designs may have unfortunately resulted in applied researchers transforming questions to fit known designs, whereas, instead, the design should fit and answer the original question. Van Houten (1987) also cautioned that it is pointless to compare interventions in many cases unless we know how to make each treatment optimally effective. Furthermore, valid comparisons between techniques cannot be made unless both are applied optimally and equally well (Van Houten, 1987).

As stated, another major design issue involves component analyses. Treatment procedures rarely consist of a single procedure; instead, they involve several basic components, each of which contributes to its effectiveness. For example, a social skills intervention usually consists of several components, including demonstration, role-playing, guided practice, verbal rehearsal, corrective feedback, and reinforcement. Yet, experimental demonstrations that such a social skills program is effective leave an unanswered question concerning whether some aspect may be removed without loss of effectiveness. If a component is very expensive, time-consuming, or difficult to use, component analyses research is suggested to streamline the intervention program.

F. Choice of Target Behaviors

Adolescence is a period of life when an individual needs to make progress on several developmental-educational goals. Four areas have been identified as being particularly important for adolescents (Epstein, 1982; Epstein & Cullinan, 1979). First, *social participation* is important because proficiency in this area is critical to successful peer relations and adult adjustment. A second goal is *academic* competence because adolescents must build upon and consolidate their basic "tool" skills in reading, writing, and arithmetic and elaborate on their developing learning strategies to become independent learners. A third goal is *community participation*, as adolescents need to learn about cooperating with community officials, taking care of communal property, promoting action on important societal issues, and participating in community activities. Finally, adolescents need competence in *career and vocational preparation* through awareness of various career possibilities, learning skills essential to gaining and maintaining employment, and generally developing independent adult living skills. While the extent to which adolescents achieve these four developmental-educational goals varies, failure to achieve one or more of these goals to an appropriate degree within a reasonable time increases the probability that an individual will experience some adjustment problems in adulthood (Epstein, 1982).

This review was restricted to studies with social dependent variables; however, the behaviors must be viewed within the context of the broader behavioral repertoire that is represented by the four developmental-educational goals. Adolescents with behavior disorders are known by their failure to develop competence in these domains, and, unfortunately, except for social deportment, behavioral researchers have not adequately addressed the needs of the population in the areas of academic, vocational, and community competence. Future reviews should evaluate our progress, for example, in the important area of academic competence. Also, it is recommended that behavioral researchers develop, implement, and evaluate interventions to orchestrate improved functioning in these areas.

G.   Other Issues

Behavioral researchers interested in improving education for adolescents with behavioral disorders must address several other important questions. They will be only briefly discussed here. First, much of the research can be characterized as single short studies with little, if any, systematic investigations being conducted. Very few researchers are actively engaged in pursuing a line of investigation with adolescents with behavior disorders. For example, in the study of self-management procedures, it is the rare research group (e.g., Feindler, Marriott, Iwata, 1984; Feindler et al., 1986) that has reported more than one study; thus several cogent treatment issues remain that no researcher or research group has systematically investigated. For example, questions concerning the optimum conditions that account for the effects of self-management strategies, whether self-management techniques are more effective in maintaining than in acquiring behavior, or how to use self-management as a tool to have behavioral gains generalize to other settings, have not undergone sufficient empirical study. Until this situation changes, important strides in understanding how these complex behaviors are developed and maintained, and how they can be successfully treated, will not occur.

To date, researchers have investigated the effects of consequent events, contingency management strategies, and basic self-management and social skills programs. These interventions have added significantly to our understanding of the effects of consequent events but have provided minimal knowledge on our understanding of other variables that control behavior in classroom settings. In this regard, we need more research on how setting events, teacher instructional behavior, peer interactions, and teacher expectations influence the behavior of this population and how these factors can be used as a part of a treatment regimen. In other words, we need a more comprehensive empirical view of the contexts within which the treatments discussed here have been applied.

Another area for future research is that of prevention of childhood and adolescent mental health problems. A necessary condition for prevention is the ability to predict the onset of problem behavior (Gelfand, Ficula, & Zarbatany, 1986). Without such predictive ability, it is difficult, if not impossible, to evaluate and scrutinize prevention efforts. Myriad high-risk factors, including child abuse, dysfunctional families, television violence, and inadequate instruction, to name a few, have been identified as environmental factors that are related to behavior disorders (Cullinan et al., 1983). Unfortunately, for the vast majority of problems experienced by adolescents, and for those that were reviewed in this chapter, it is not possible to anticipate outcomes (Gelfand et al., 1986). Nonetheless, preventive research efforts need to commence, as this population could very likely benefit from such programs. To be effective, prevention actions should include early identification of problem behaviors, the use of school-based programs that are applied early and are comprehensive in nature, and the inclusion of the family and community members and peers as part of the program.

VI. CONCLUSION

In sum, during the past 25 years, there has been a great deal of impressive program development and research in the use of applied behavior analysis strategies to improve the social functioning of adolescents with behavior disorders. The behavioral techniques reviewed in this chapter have all been found to be effective to varying degrees with different individuals with social behavioral needs in various situations. The challenges of developing more effective interventions that are generalizable and durable and address more complex target behaviors in naturalistic settings are exciting. Given the positive changes that have taken place, we are optimistic that future efforts will continue to lead to research and programmatic activities that will help these adolescents.

NOTE

1. PL 94-142 uses the term *serious emotional disturbance* to label students with behavior disorders. We prefer the term *behavior disorders* because it more accurately reflects the types of students and the problems that schools are serving in special education programs.

REFERENCES

Alberto, P. A., & Troutman, A. C. (1986). *Applied behavior analysis for teachers.* Columbus, OH: Charles E. Merrill.

Alley, G., & Deshler, D. (1979). *Teaching the learning disabled adolescent: Strategies and methods.* Denver: Love.

Baer, D. M., Wolf, M. M., & Risley, T. R. (1968). Some current dimensions of applied behavior analysis. *Journal of Applied Behavior Analysis, 1,* 91-97.

Baer, D. M., Wolf, M. M., & Risley, T. R. (1987). Some still-current dimensions of applied behavior analysis. *Journal of Applied Behavior Analysis, 20,* 313-327.

Barbrack, C. R., & Maher, C. A. (1984). Effects of involving conduct problem adolescents in the setting of counseling goals. *Child and Behavior Therapy, 6,* 33-43.

Barlow, D., & Hersen, M. (1984). *Single case experimental designs: Strategies for studying behavior change.* New York: Pergamon.

Bizzis, J., & Bradley-Johnson, S. (1981). Increasing the school attendance of a truant adolescent. *Education and Treatment of Children, 4,* 149-155.

Braaten, S. A. (1985). Adolescent needs and behaviors in the schools: Current and historical perspectives. In S. Braaten, R. B. Rutherford, & W. Evans (Eds.), *Programming for adolescents with behavioral disorders* (Vol. 2, pp. 1-10). Reston, VA: Council for Children with Behavioral Disorders.

Brigham, T. A. (1982). *Managing everyday problems: A manual of applied psychology for young people.* Pullman, WA: Self-Control Research and Training Unit, Washington State University.

Brigham, T. A., Hopper, C., Hill, B., deArmas, A. D., & Newsom, P. (1985). Case studies and clinical replication series: A self-management program for disruptive adolescents in the school: A clinical replication analysis. *Behavior Therapy, 16,* 99-115.

Christoff, K. A., Owen, W., Scott, N., Kelley, M. L., Schlunt, D., Baer, G., & Kelly, J. A. (1985). Social skills and social problem solving training for shy young adolescents. *Behavior Therapy, 16,* 468-477.

Clarizio, H. F. (1979). Adolescent development and deviance. In D. Cullinan & M. H. Epstein (Eds.), *Special education for adolescents* (pp. 29-62). Columbus, OH :Merrill.

Cullinan, D., & Epstein, M. H. (1989). The behavior disordered. In N. G. Haring & L. McCormick (Eds). *Behavior of exceptional children* (5th ed., pp. 153-194). Columbus, OH: Charles E. Merrill.

Cullinan, D., Epstein, M. H., & Kauffman, J. M. (1982). The behavioral model and children's behavior disorders: Foundations and evaluation. In R. L. McDowell, F. Wood, & G. Adamson (Eds.), *Educating disturbed children.* Boston: Little, Brown.

Cullinan, D., Epstein, M. H., & Lloyd, J. (1983). *Behavior disorders of children and adolescents.* Englewood Cliffs, NJ: Prentice-Hall.

Drabman, R. S. (1973). Child versus teachers: Administered token programs in a psychiatric hospital school. *Journal of Abnormal Child Psychology, 1,* 68-87.

8th annual report to Congress on the implementation of the Education of Handicapped Children's Act. (1986). Washington, DC: Department of Education.

Elder, J. P., Edelstein, B. A., & Narick, M. M. (1979). Adolescent psychiatric patients: Modifying aggressive behavior with social skills training. *Behavior Modification, 3,* 161-178.

Elliott, S. N., Gresham, F. M., & Heffer, R. W. (1987). Social-skills interventions: Research findings and training techniques. In C. A. Maher & J. E. Zins (Eds.), *Psychoeducational interventions in the schools* (pp. 141-159). New York: Pergamon.

Emshoff, J. G., Redd, W. H., & Davidson, W. S. (1976). Generalization training and the transfer of prosocial behavior in delinquent adolescents. *Journal of Behavior Therapy and Experimental Psychiatry, 7,* 141-144.

Epstein, M. H. (1982). Special education programs for the handicapped adolescent. *School Psychology Review, 11,* 384-390.

Epstein, M. H., & Cullinan, D. (1979). Education of handicapped adolescents: An overview. In D. Cullinan & M. H. Epstein (Eds.), *Special education for adolescents: Issues and perspectives.* Columbus, OH: Charles E. Merrill.

Epstein, M. H., Cullinan, D., & Rose, T. L. (1980). Applied behavior analysis and behaviorally disordered pupils: Selected issues. In L. Mann & D. A. Sabatino (Eds.), *Fourth review of special education.* New York: Grune & Stratton.

Epstein, M. H., Kinder, D., & Bursuck, B. (1989). The academic status of adolescents with behavioral disorders. *Behavioral Disorders, 14,* 157-166.

Epstein, P. B., Detwiler, C. L., & Reitz, A. L. (1985). Describing the clients in programs for behavior disordered children and youth. *Education and Treatment of Children, 8,* 265-274.

Evans, W. H., Evans, S. S., Schmid, R. E., & Pennypacker, H. S. (1985) The effects of exercise on selected classroom behaviors of behaviorally disordered adolescents. *Behavioral Disorders, 11,* 42-51.

Feindler, E. L., Ecton, R. B., Kingsley, D., & Dubey, D. R. (1986). Group anger control training for institutionalized psychiatric male adolescents. *Behavior Therapy, 17,* 109-123.

Feindler, E. L., Marriott, S. A., & Iwata, M. (1984). Group anger control for junior high school delinquents. *Cognitive Therapy and Research, 8,* 299-311.

Fixsen, D. S., Phillips, E. L., & Wolf, M. M. (1973). Achievement place: Experiments in self-government with pre-delinquents. *Journal of Applied Behavior Analysis, 6,* 31-47.

Gelfand, D. M., Ficula, T., & Zarbatany, L. (1986). Prevention of childhood behavior disorders. In B. Edelstein & L. Michelson (Eds.), *Handbook of prevention.* New York: Plenum.

Greenleaf, D. O. (1982). The use of structured learning therapy and transfer programming with disruptive adolescents in a school setting. *Journal of School Psychology, 20,* 122-130.

Guetzloe, E. (1980). The least restrictive environment for adolescents with severe behaviors: Putting the pieces together. In R. B. Rutherford, A. G. Prieto, & J. E. McGlothlin (Eds.), *Monograph in behavioral disorders* (pp. 106-116). Reston, VA: Council for Children with Behavioral Disorders Publications.

Hall, R. V., Fox, R., Willard, D., Goldsmith, L., Emerson, M., Owen, M., Davis, F., & Porica, E. (1971). The teacher as observer and experimenter in the modification of disrupting and talking out behaviors. *Journal of Applied Behavior Analysis, 4,* 141-149.

Hargreaves, M. E., & McLaughlin, T. F. (1981). Reducing absences and tardiness in a junior high secondary special education classroom: The SCOPE program. *B. C. Journal of Special Education, 5*, 23-31.

Hogan, W. A., & Johnson, P. D. (1985). Brief report: Elimination of response cost in a token economy program and improvement in behavior of emotionally disturbed youth. *Behavior Therapy, 16,* 87-98.

Hops, H., Finch, M., & McConnell, S. (1985). Social skills deficits. In P. H. Bornstein & A. E. Kazdin (Eds.), *Handbook of clinical behavior therapy with children* (pp. 543-598). Homewood, IL: Dorsey.

Hunsaker, A. C. (1984). Contingency management with Chicano adolescents in a federal manpower program. *Corrective and Social Psychiatry,* 10-13.

Jamison, R. N., Lambert, W. E., & McCloud, D. J. (1986). Social skills training with hospitalized adolescents: An evaluative experiment. *Adolescence, 21,* 54-65.

Jones, D. B., & Van Houten, R. (1985). The use of daily quizzes and public posting to decrease the disruptive behavior of secondary school students. *Education and Treatment of Children, 8,* 91-106.

Kavale, K. A., Forness, S. R., & Alper, A. E. (1986). Research in behavioral disorders/emotional disturbance: A survey of subject criteria. *Behavioral Disorders, 11,* 159-167.

Kazdin, A. E. (1977). Assessing the clinical or applied significance of behavior change through social validation. *Behavior Modification, 1,* 427-452.

Kazdin, A. E. (1982). *Single-case research designs.* New York: Oxford University Press.

Kelly, W. J., Salzberg, C. L., Levy, S. M., Warrenfeltz, R. B., Adams, T. W., Crouse, T. R., & Beegle, G. P. (1983). The effects of role-playing and self-monitoring on the generalization of vocational social skills by behaviorally disordered adolescents. *Behavioral Disorders, 9,* 27-35.

Keogh, B. K., Major-Kingsley, S., Omori-Gordon, H., & Reid, H. P. (1982). *A system of marker variables for the field of behavioral disorders.* Syracuse, NY: Syracuse University Press.

Kiburz, C. S., Miller, S. R., & Morrow, L. W. (1984). Structured learning using self-monitoring to promote maintenance and generalization of social skills across settings for a behaviorally disordered adolescent. *Behavioral Disorders, 10,* 47-55.

Lakin, K. C. (1983). Research-based knowledge and professional practices in special education for emotionally disturbed students. *Behavioral Disorders, 82,* 128-137.

Lebsock, M. S., & Salzberg, C. L. (1981). The use of role play and reinforcement procedures in the development of generalized interpersonal behavior with emotionally disturbed-behavior disordered adolescents in a special education classroom. *Behavioral Disorders, 6,* 150-163.

Leger, H. J., Groff, D., Harris, V. W., Finfrock, L. R., Weaver, F. H., & Kratochwill, T. R. (1979). An instructional package to teach communication behaviors in a classroom setting. *Journal of School Psychology, 17,* 339-346.

Lerner, J. (1989). *Learning disabilities* (5th ed.). Boston: Houghton Mifflin.

Lipsitz, J. (1985). Programs for adolescents: What works and why. In S. Braaten, R. B. Rutherford, & W. Evans (Eds.), *Programming for adolescents with behavioral disorders* (Vol. 2, pp. 11-19). Reston, VA: Council for Children with Behavioral Disorders.

MacDonald, W. S., Gallimore, R., & MacDonald, G. (1970). Contingency counseling by school personnel: An economical model of intervention. *Journal of Applied Behavior Analysis, 3,* 175-182.

Mace, F. C., Brown, D. K., & West, B. J. (1987). Behavioral self-management in education. In C. A. Maher & J. E. Zins (Eds.), *Psychoeducational interventions in the schools* (pp. 160-176). New York: Pergamon.

Mastropieri, M. A., Jenkins, V., & Scruggs, T. E. (1985). Academic and intellectual characteristics of behaviorally disordered children and youth. In R. B. Rutherford (Ed.), *Severe behavior disorders monograph* (Vol. 8, pp. 86-104). Boston: College-Hill.

Mastropieri, M. A., Jenne, P., & Scruggs, T. E. (1988). A level system for managing problem behaviors in a high school resource program. *Behavioral Disorders, 3,* 202-208.

Mastropieri, M. A., & Scruggs, T. E. (1987). *Effective instruction for special education.* Boston: College-Hill.

Matson, J. L., & Olinger, E. (1985). Mental retardation. In P. H. Bornstein & A. E. Kazdin (Eds.), *Handbook of clinical behavior therapy with children* (pp. 125-157). Homewood, IL: Dorsey.

McNamara, J. R. (1971). Teacher and students as sources for behavior modification in the classroom. *Behavior Therapy, 2,* 205-213.

McNeil, J. K., & Hart, D. S. (1986). The effect of self-government on the aggressive behavior of institutionalized delinquent adolescents. *Criminal Justice and Behavior, 13,* 430-445.

Meichenbaum, D. H., Bowers, K. S., & Ross, R. R. (1968). Modification of classroom behavior of institutionalized female adolescent offenders. *Behavior Research and Therapy, 6,* 343-353.

Mercer, C. D. (1987). *Students with learning disabilities* (3rd ed.). Columbus, OH: Charles E. Merrill.

Minkin, N., Braukmann, C. J., Minkin, B. L., Timbers, G. D., Timbers, B. J., Fixsen, D. L., Phillips, E. L., & Wolf, M. M. (1976). The social validation and training of conversational skills. *Journal of Applied Behavior Analysis, 9,* 127-139.

Olinger, E., Epstein, M. H., Karsh, K., Ormsby, D., & Pray, V. (1988). Applied behavior analysis and behavioral disorders: A report on the use of marker variables in treatment studies. *Education and Treatment of Children, 11,* 63-69.

Ollendick, T. H., & Hersen, M. (1979). Social skills training for juvenile delinquents. *Behavior Research and Therapy, 17,* 547-554.

Osborne, S. S., Kiburz, C. S., & Miller, S. R. (1986). Treatment of self-injurious behavior using self-control techniques with a severe behaviorally disordered adolescent. *Behavioral Disorders, 11,* 60-67.

Paniagua, F. A. (1985). Development of self-care skills and helping behaviors of adolescents in a group home through correspondence training. *Journal of Behavior Therapy and Experimental Psychiatry, 16,* 237-244.

Peterson, L., Homer, A. L., & Wonderlich, S. A. (1982). The integrity of independent variables in behavior analysis. *Journal of Applied Behavior Analysis, 15,* 477-492.

Phillips, E. L. (1968). Achievement place: Token reinforcement procedures in a home-style rehabilitation setting for "pre-delinquent" boys. *Journal of Applied Behavior Analysis, 1,* 213-223.

Polirstok, S. R., & Greer, R. D. (1977). Remediation of mutually aversive interactions between a problem student and four teachers by training the student in reinforcement techniques. *Journal of Applied Behavior Analysis, 10,* 707-716.

Pomeroy, J., & Gadow, K. D. (1986). Adolescent psychiatric disorders. In K. D. Gadow (Ed.), *Children on medication* (Vol. 2, pp. 137-172). Boston: College-Hill.

Repp, A. C. (1983) *Teaching the mentally retarded.* Englewood Cliffs, NJ: Prentice-Hall.

Repp, A. C., Nieminen, G. S., Olinger, E., & Brusca, R. (1988). Direct observation: Factors affecting the accuracy of observers. *Exceptional Children, 55,* 29-36.

Reynolds, W. M., & Coats, K. I. (1986). A comparison of cognitive-behavioral therapy and relaxation training for the treatment of depression in adolescents. *Journal of Consulting and Clinical Psychology, 54,* 653-660.

Rosenberg, H. E., & Graubard, P. (1975). Peer use of behavior modification. *Focus on Exceptional Children, 1*(6), 1-10.

Rutherford, R. B., & Polsgrove, L. J. (1981). Behavioral contracting with behaviorally disordered and delinquent children and youth: An analysis of the clinical and experimental literature. In R. B. Rutherford, A. G. Prieto, & J. E. McGlothlin (Eds.), *Monograph in behavioral disorders* (pp. 49-69). Reston, VA: Council for Children with Behavioral Disorders.

Sanson-Fisher, R. W., Seymour, F. W., & Baer, D. M. (1976). Training institutional staff to alter delinquents' conversation. *Journal of Behavior Therapy and Experimental Psychiatry, 7,* 243-247.

Sanson-Fisher, B., Seymour, F., Montgomery, W., & Stokes, T. (1978). Modifying delinquents' conversation using token reinforcement of self-recorded behavior. *Journal of Behavior Therapy and Experimental Psychiatry, 9,* 163-168.

Santogrossi, D. A., O'Leary, K. D., Romanczyk, R. G., & Kaufman, K. F. (1973). Self-evaluation by adolescents in a psychiatric hospital school token program. *Journal of Applied Behavior Analysis, 6,* 277-287.

Schloss, P. J., Harriman, N. E., & Pfefier, K. (1985). Application of a sequential prompt reduction technique to the independent composition performance of behaviorally disordered youth. *Behavioral Disorders, 11,* 17-23.

Schloss, P. J., Kane, M. S., & Miller, S. (1981). Truancy intervention with behavior disordered adolescents. *Behavioral Disorders, 6,* 175-179.

Schloss, P. J., Schloss, C. N., & Harris, L. (1984). A multiple baseline analysis of an interpersonal skills training program for depressed youth. *Behavioral Disorders, 9,* 182-214.

Schloss, P. J., Schloss, C. N., Wood, C. E., & Kiehl, W. S. (1986). A critical review of social skills research with behaviorally disordered students. *Behavior Disorders, 12,* 1-14.

Schultz, R. M. (1987). Truancy: Issues and interventions. *Behavioral Disorders, 12,* 117-130.

Skiba, R., & Casey, A. (1985). Interventions for behavior disordered students: A quantitative review and methodological critique. *Behavioral Disorders, 10,* 105-112.

Smith, D. D. (1989). *Teaching students with learning and behavior problems* (2nd ed.). Englewood Cliffs, NJ: Prentice-Hall.

Smith, D. J., Young, K. R., West, R. P., Morgan, D. P., & Rhode, G. (1988). Reducing the disruptive behavior of junior high school students: A classroom self-management procedure. *Behavioral Disorders, 13,* 231-239.

Snyder, J. J., & White, M. J. (1979). The use of cognitive self-instruction in the treatment of behaviorally disturbed adolescents. *Behavior Therapy, 10,* 227-235.

Spence, S. H., & Marzillier, J. S. (1979). Social skills training with adolescent male offenders: I. Short-term effects. *Behavior Research and Therapy, 17,* 7-16.

Spence, S. H., & Marzillier, J. S. (1981). Social skills training with adolescent male offenders: II. Short-term, long-term and generalized effects. *Behavior Research and Therapy, 19,* 349-368.

Sulzer-Azaroff, B., & Mayer, G. R. (1977). *Applying behavior analysis procedures with children and Youth.* New York: Holt, Rinehart, & Winston.

Swanson, L. H. (1985). Improved same sex and heterosocial interactions of emotionally disturbed adolescents. *Journal of School Psychology, 23,* 365-374.

U.S. Department of Education. (1986). *Tenth annual report to Congress on the implementation of the education of the handicapped act.* Washington, DC: Government Printing Office.

Vaal, J. J. (1973). Applied contingency contracting to a school phobic: A case study. *Journal of Behavior Therapy and Experimental Psychiatry, 4,* 371-373.

Van Houten, R. (1987). Comparing treatment techniques: A cautionary note. *Journal of Applied Behavior Analysis, 20,* 109-110.

Warrenfeltz, R. B., Kelly, W. J., Salzberg, C. L., Beegle, C. P., Levy, S. M., Adams, T. A., & Crouse, T. R. (1981). Social skills training of behavior disordered adolescents with self-monitoring to promote generalization to a vocational setting. *Behavioral Disorders, 6,* 18-27.

Wasserman, T. H. (1977). Negative reinforcement to alter disruptive behavior of an adolescent in a day treatment setting. *Journal of Behavior Therapy and Experimental Psychiatry, 8,* 315-317.

Welch, G. J. (1985). Contingency contracting with a delinquent and his family. *Journal of Behavior Therapy and Experimental Psychiatry, 16,* 253-259.

Wolf, M. M. (1978). Social validity: The case for subjective measurement or how applied behavior analysis is finding its heart. *Journal of Applied Behavior Analysis, 11,* 203-214.

Wood, F. H. (1987). Issues in the education of behaviorally disordered students. In R. B. Rutherford, Jr., C. M. Nelson, & S. R. Forness (Eds.), *Severe behavior disorders of children and youth* (pp. 15-26). Boston: College-Hill.

AUTHOR INDEX

A

Agran, M., 7-8, 9, 13, 14, 15, 18, 19, 23, 24, 26, 30, 36-53
Alberto, P. A., 127, 133
Albion, F. M., 43, 49
Alpert, D., 89, 92
deArmas, A. D., 136, 143, 147
Azrin, N. H., 76, 77

B

Baer, D., 9, 13, 15, 22, 23, 26, 31, 32
Baer, D. M., 107, 116, 145, 148, 149
Baer, G., 137, 147
Barlow, D., 136, 149
Berven, N. L., 87, 88
Billings, M., 86-99
Bires, J. A., 113, 114
Bleiberg, J., 62, 63
Bootzin, R. R., 87, 88
Bowers, K. S., 133, 147
Braaten, S. A., 124, 125
Braukmann, C. J., 127, 147
Brigham, T. A., 37, 38, 136, 143, 147
Buenning, W., 72-73
Burgio, L. D., 40, 49
Burke, W. H., 63, 71

C

Carnine, D., 24, 30, 31, 32
Carroll, J. L., 44-45
Casey, A., 124, 145, 149
Cataldo, M. F., 106-107, 109
Catania, A. C., 51, 53
Chadsey-Rusch, J., 9, 14, 15, 18, 19, 29, 30, 46
Cho, D. W., 91, 92, 93
Christoff, K. A., 137, 147
Christophersen, E. R., 104-118

Christophersen, M. R., 114
Cornick, J., 74, 78
Crosson, B., 72-73
Cullinan, D., 123, 124, 125, 126, 131, 137, 145, 146, 150, 151

D

Davies, K., 43, 50, 51
Deer, M., 39, 45
Dershewitz, R. A., 106-107, 109, 110, 113

E

Ellis, L. L., 9, 13, 15, 18, 19, 26, 30, 47
Engelmann, S., 24, 30, 32
Epstein, M. H., 122-152

F

Fawcett, S. B., 106-107, 109
Feindler, E. L., 137, 151
Finch, M., 137, 142
Finney, J. W., 106-107, 109
Fixsen, D. L., 127, 147
Fodor-Davis, J., 7-8, 9, 15, 18, 19, 26, 30, 37, 39, 40, 45, 47
Foxx, R. M., 76, 77
Franzen, M. D., 56-80
Freedman, P. E., 62, 63

G

Gallagher, S. S., 105, 106, 110, 115, 117
Ghosh, A., 95, 96
Gianutsos, J., 61, 71
Gianutsos, R., 61, 71
Giles, G. M., 70, 76
Glisky, E. L., 70-71
Goldstein, G., 60, 61, 70, 73

SUBJECT INDEX

A

Ability, defined, 59

Academic competence, adolescent behavior disorders and, 150

Academic instruction, self-instructional training and, 41-44

Accident proneness, 106

Activities of daily living, brain-impaired and, 76

Adaptive behavior, brain-impaired and, 62

Adjustment behavior, brain-impaired and, 62

Adolescent behavior disorders, behavioral treatment of, 122-152; behavioral contracting and, 131-133; exercise and, 143; punishment and, 133-136; reinforcement and, 133-136; selection of studies, 126; self-management and, 136-137; social reinforcement and, 127-131; social skills training and, 137-142; token reinforcement and, 127-131

Adolescent behavior disorders research, future issues in, 143-151; choice of target behaviors, 150; dependent variables, 148; design of, 149-150; follow-up and, 149; generalization and, 149; independent variables, 148; quality of, 148-149; settings for, 143-151; social validation and, 147-148; subject description and, 146-147

Adolescent development, theories of, 124

Aggression: brain-impaired and, 73-75; injured children and, 106; self-management and, 137

American Academy of Pediatrics, 113, 114

Anger control, self-management and, 137

Anticipation training, 41

Aphasic deficits, 59, 63, 68-69

Arithmetic computation, self-instructional training and, 43

Assessment: computer-based, 93-95; computer simulations and, 89-90; measurement theory and, 60; neuropsychology and, 58-59; of attention, 64

Assistance requests, self-instructional training and, 14, 46

Attending behavior, attention assessment and, 65

Attention, assessment of, 64

Attention problems, brain-impaired and, 64-66

Auditory discrimination deficits, 60

Avoidance paradigm, brain-impaired subjects and, 63

B

Behavior: language controlling, 31, 37-38; rule-governed, 38; self-managed, 38; speech internally controlling, 37-38

Behavioral analysis, internal events and, 38

Behavioral clinical neuropsychology, 57-59

Behavioral coding systems, computers and, 94

Behavioral Consultant System, 91-92

Behavioral contracting: adolescent behavior disorders and, 131-133; brain-impaired treatment and, 63

Behavioral decision-making, computer simulations and, 89

Behavioral interventions, injury control in children and, 114-117

Behavioral model, adolescents with behavior disorders and, 122-152

Behavioral neuropsychology, 59-62; conceptual considerations in, 60-61; pragmatic considerations in, 61-62; traditional neuropsychology versus, 59-60; treatment goals of, 60

Behavioral prosthetic, 58, 60; sensory and behavioral deficits and, 66, 67-68

Behavioral therapy, brain-impaired individuals and, 56-80; activities of daily living and, 76; aggression and, 73-75; attention problems and, 64-66; combined treatments and, 77; future research and, 79; inappropriate behaviors and, 75-76; memory deficits and, 70-73; perceptual deficits and, 66-68; planning and organization deficits, 76-77; sensory deficits and, 66-67; social and adaptive behavior and, 73-76; speech and language deficits, 68-70; treatment studies, 62-64